D1457439

The Art of Americanization at the Carlisle Indian School

John Choate, "Group of Dakota Sioux girls from the Rosebud and Pine Ridge Sioux Agencies as they arrived in native dress at the Carlisle Indian School, October 5, 1879," 1879. Albumen. Photo courtesy of Cumberland County Historical Society.

The Art of Americanization at the Carlisle Indian School

Hayes Peter Mauro

University of New Mexico Press
Albuquerque

© 2011 by the University of New Mexico Press
All rights reserved. Published 2011
Printed in the United States of America
16 15 14 13 12 11   1 2 3 4 5 6

Library of Congress Cataloging-in-Publication Data

Mauro, Hayes Peter, 1970–
    The art of Americanization at the Carlisle Indian School / Hayes Peter Mauro.
        p. cm.
    Includes bibliographical references and index.
    ISBN 978-0-8263-4920-0 (cloth : alk. paper)
    1. United States Indian School (Carlisle, Pa.)—History. 2. Indians of North America—
Education—Pennsylvania—Carlisle—History. 3. Indians of North America—Cultural
assimilation—Pennsylvania—Carlisle—History. 4. Indians of North America—
Pennsylvania—Carlisle—Ethnic identity—History. 5. Indians of North America—
Pennsylvania—Carlisle—History—Pictorial works. 6. Americanization—History.
7. Art—Political aspects—Pennsylvania—Carlisle—History. 8. Photography—Political
aspects—Pennsylvania—Carlisle—History. 9. Propaganda—Pennsylvania—Carlisle—
History. 10. Racism in education—Pennsylvania—Carlisle—History. I. Title.
    E97.6.C2M28 2011
    973'.0497—dc22
                            2010043207

Contents

Introduction

In the turbulent post–Civil War era known as the Gilded Age, a time of rapid industrialization due in large part to migration from rural areas and foreign lands, creating culturally acceptable identities for immigrants, the poor, Native Americans, and African Americans was part of the federal government's mission. By means of aesthetic transformation, these groups were to be converted from an assumed state of degenerate Otherness into model "American" citizens.[1]

A major part of this conversion was visual. One common trope was the "before-and-after" portrait, which displayed the Other in his or her allegedly degenerate state before Americanization, and again following its conclusion (see figs. I.1 and I.2.).

Art historians have insightfully explored representations of race in various visual media. Albert Boime argues persuasively that representations of race in American cultural history, especially those made during the nineteenth century, were ideologically as well as aesthetically coded. The definitions of race and its attendant racial hierarchies were dependent on such visual models. In this sense, these models played a major part in various Americanizing projects. Boime has written:

> Black is a pigment indispensable to artistic practice . . . There are no gray areas in the content of stereotypes . . . Throughout the nineteenth century it was the idea of opposition of black and white (and red and white in North America as well) that fired the energies of painters and sculptors . . . The confusion of formalistic categories with ideological biases is a singular phenomenon in the history of art that has been sorely neglected. The racial opposition of black and white . . . is intimately associated with the religious dualism of Good and Evil.[2]

Although his book *The Art of Exclusion* focuses on representations of African Americans in the nineteenth century, as the quotation above suggests, Boime's logic can be applied to images of Native Americans. His work, as well as that of other historians, suggests that the mingling of ideological predetermination with aesthetic convention has parallels in other media, such as photography and illustration.[3]

As historian David Wallace Adams has pointed out, late nineteenth-century Anglo-America required all non-Anglo-Saxon ethnic groups to assimilate. Adams sees this as a totalizing concept, referring equally to aesthetic, social, linguistic, religious, and economic assimilation.[4] The logic of such assimilation could be visually established for a broad public by means of photography and illustration.

This text will critically analyze visual imagery produced at the Carlisle Indian Industrial School as a specific instance of the aesthetics of Americanization at work. Located in Carlisle, Pennsylvania, the school was established by an act of Congress in 1879. Carlisle founder Richard Henry Pratt (1840–1924) conceived of the school as a military-style boarding school. Pratt and his successors succeeded in maintaining congressional funding for nearly forty years. Once taken from their reservation homes, Native American youths would be transformed from their supposed state of savagery into civilized American citizens.

The ideal of American citizenship assumed by the school's Anglo-American founders valued Christianity over spiritualism, competition over tribalism, and physical hygiene and mental discipline over the supposed dirt and sloth of reservation life.[5] These values legitimized the federal government's near annihilation of the continent's indigenous inhabitants.

The near-constant uprooting and moving about inherent in the process of cultural transformation suggests the nature of the power differential in this kind of boarding school. Traditionally, boarding schools had educated the offspring of the elites of Europe and the United States. Unlike students at elite boarding schools, Carlisle's indigenous students were forced into the boarding school experience. Bringing them to a boarding school hundreds or even thousands of miles away from their ancestral homelands and reservations was a practice designed to sever them from their culture and history and to transform their minds and bodies. The experience could be likened to that of a soldier in basic training. As sociologist Erving Goffman has put it:

> The recruit comes into the establishment with a conception of himself made possible by certain stable social arrangements in his home world. Upon entrance, he is immediately stripped of the support

provided by these arrangements. In the accurate language of some of our oldest total institutions, he begins a series of abasements, degradations, humiliations, and profanations of self . . . He begins some radical shifts in his *moral career*, a career composed of the progressive changes that occur in the beliefs that he has concerning himself and significant others.[6]

Goffman's chilling analysis of the boarding school and other "total institutions" such as mental hospitals, prisons, and concentration camps offers an incisive critique of the Carlisle program of assimilation. It was precisely the "moral career" that Pratt and others sought to target in the school's allegedly savage students, forcibly transforming generations of subaltern youths with the aim of upholding the dominant Protestant middle-class culture.

The government's valuing Christianity over indigenous traditions reflects a Weberian equation of religiosity and economic success that was an overriding assumption at Carlisle.[7] The socioeconomic elevation of the student was seen in direct proportion to his or her spiritual elevation out of the doldrums of "primitive superstition."[8]

The school's efforts to instill in the students a competitive work ethic over the perceived communalism of Native American tribes was a necessary cornerstone of the ethos of industrial capitalism then gaining dominance over almost all Americans, irrespective of race or class. In observing the changing social relations of the early industrialized United States, Italian philosopher Antonio Gramsci has commented on what he terms the "rationalization of production and work." According to him, the promotion of efficiency in industrial economies requires that government and industry work in concert to mechanize the body and mind of the worker by means of the minute structuring of workers' lives both at work and at home.[9]

The worker's movements, thoughts, and aspirations have to be brought into equilibrium with his or her new place in the industrial order. The intent of the Carlisle photographs was to show this process of rationalizing the body and mind of the worker. Besides attaining citizenship, Christian spirituality, and sobriety, the students were also converted over time into disciplined workers.[10] The rigid, formulaic aesthetics of many of the images reflects this purpose, as figure I.3 shows.

The notion that physical hygiene and mental discipline were better than the supposedly unhygienic living conditions on the reservations was emblematic for Pratt and other social reformers of the indigenous population's status in relation to Anglo America. Cultural historian Anne McClintock has graphically characterized this notion with reference to soap. She argues that the commodity of soap epitomized for modern Europeans the difference between European hygiene and indigenous dirtiness.[11] In this sense, bodily hygiene became an aesthetic yardstick of civilization. Indeed, Western physical hygiene was always the first transformative principle imposed on the newly arriving students.

The values assigned to Native Americans—often irrespective of tribal culture and identity—can be correlated with the problems thought to be the principal cultural and political stumbling blocks to the new industrial order. Repressing these perceived characteristics, then, would foster industrial capitalism. The idea that degenerate tendencies demanded institutional repression was a cornerstone in the founding philosophy of Carlisle. Using typically positivistic rhetoric, Pratt characterized assimilation years later in his autobiographical *Battlefield and Classroom*:

> Participation in the best things of our civilization through being environed by them was the essential factor for transforming the Indian. The small number of Indians in the U.S., then given as 260,000, rendered their problem a short one. It was surely only necessary to prove that Indians were like other people and could be as easily educated and developed industrially to secure the general adoption of my views. All immigrants were accepted and naturalized into our citizenship by that route and thus had a full fair chance to become assimilated with our people and our industries. Why not the Indian?[12]

As Pratt's views suggest, the journey from "Indian" to "civilization" was one often thought of in ritualistic terms by advocates of cultural assimilation, whether that assimilation occurred at Carlisle, the Hampton Institute in Virginia, or Hull House in Chicago.

It is helpful to think of forced assimilation in the context of the dominant cultural narratives of the day, especially the narrative of personal and national identity that the ruling classes used to explain their own affluence, power, and success. Stories of self-improvement over time by means of overcoming external and internal obstacles, the model for anyone striving for status and respectability, were exemplified in Theodore Roosevelt's autobiographies *The Strenuous Life* (1910) and *The Autobiography of Theodore Roosevelt* (1913). As president, Roosevelt had supreme administrative authority over not only Carlisle, but all federal Indian policy. In his *Autobiography*, in a chapter aptly titled "The Vigor of Life," Roosevelt recounted the key transformative experience of his early life:

> Having been a sickly boy, with no natural bodily prowess . . . I was at first quite unable to hold my own when thrown into contact with other boys of rougher antecedents . . . Yet from reading of the people

I admired–ranging from the soldiers of Valley Forge, and Morgan's riflemen, to the heroes of my favorite stories . . . I felt a great admiration for men who were fearless and who could hold their own in the world . . . Then an incident happened that did me real good. Having an attack of asthma, I was sent off by myself to Moosehead Lake. On the stage-coach ride thither I encountered a couple of other boys . . . they found that I was a foreordained and predestined victim, and industriously proceeded to make life miserable for me . . . The experience taught me what probably no amount of advice could have taught me . . . I decided that I would try to supply its place by [athletic] training.[13]

Roosevelt's story is both uniquely personal and culturally relevant to the Gilded Age. Rife with time-honored American cultural tropes such as the stagecoach and the soldiers at Valley Forge, the story rehearses a commonly repeated theme of the day. To arrive at true American adulthood, especially manhood, one had to confront one's fears and weakness and overcome them by strengthening oneself physically, in the manner of Anglo-American forefathers who were "fearless and could hold their own" in the colonial wilderness. Such a narrative was embodied in Roosevelt's own lifestyle and biography, but more important, served as a metaphor for survival in the emergent system of industrial competition. Roosevelt's story is both modern in its advocacy of conquering material obstacles through personal responsibility and yet oddly atavistic in its invocation of the gritty physiological strength supposedly needed for reaching American manhood.

This conception of manhood was fundamental to transforming the male students at the school. They were to be reshaped from their perceived ill-formed, chaotic, and primitive original state into a virtual replication of the virile, self-reliant, and yet law-abiding model embodied by Roosevelt. Under the watchful guidance of Pratt, Roosevelt, and other Euro-American leaders, generations of young male students at Carlisle were required to adopt such values and undergo strenuous physical and mental tests to advance themselves from savage to citizen.

The school's founders and subsequent administrators deployed visual imagery in the forms of life masks, photographs, and pseudoscientific illustrations to show the efficacy of the institution's assimilationist mission. The centrality of the visual in this process represents a uniquely American fixation: a naïve correlation between appearance and reality. Art historian Wayne Craven makes use of this assumed correlation in his book *Colonial American Portraiture*. In speaking about what he terms the Calvinist Protestant underpinnings motivating patrons of colonial American portrait painters, Craven argues that "when they had their portraits painted they wanted their material success shown therein, for aside from exhibiting social standing it was emblematic of their being in God's favor."......[14] The descendents of those same Puritans applied this idea when trying to prove the uplifting effects of their reeducational policies on the indigenous youths at Carlisle two centuries later. This study will examine the busts, photographs, and illustrations produced at and in association with the school with this strain of thought in mind.

Victorian pseudoscience also informed the production of imagery at the school. Antebellum pseudoscientific notions of racial superiority had perhaps been discredited with the abolition of slavery and Reconstruction, but such pernicious thinking was reconfigured rather than abolished during the Gilded Age. Underlying assumptions of Anglo-American cultural superiority justified the assimilationist and expansionist government policies that shaped the paternalistic discourse surrounding the school's founding. In place of phrenology and physiognomy, Gilded Age reformers pointed to newly emergent "sciences" such as criminology, anthropometrics, the American School of Anthropology, and social Darwinism in arguing for Indian reeducation. The "scientific" anthropological discourse that arose from the work of Lewis Henry Morgan (1818–1881) and others was a key legitimizing force in the cultural politics of assimilation.[15]

Pratt publicly claimed to despise essentializing racial sciences,[16] but such ideas did influence the artists, illustrators, and photographers he hired. The seemingly straightforward images of transformation that came out of Carlisle were informed by a complex matrix of political, sociological, scientific, and theological ideas.

The first two chapters of this book will consider historic visual representations of the Native body by white artists and the relation of these representations to a group of life-mask bust portraits executed in 1877 by the self-taught Southern sculptor Clark Mills (1810–1883), best known for his heroic equestrian bronze sculpture of Andrew Jackson in Lafayette Square in Washington, D.C. Pratt and the Smithsonian Institution commissioned Mills to complete a series of plaster life masks of a group of Native Americans captured during frontier warfare whom Pratt had detained at a military prison in Florida. Joseph Palmer of the Smithsonian later created ethnographic busts from the orignal life masks done by Mills at Fort Marion, an example of which is seen in figure I.4. Pratt's ambition went far beyond detaining Indians in prison. He wished to start a boarding school that would civilize even the most hardened frontier-era insurgents. Pratt hired Mills to "prove" through visual means the criminal nature of these prisoners, and their resulting need for Pratt's brand of education. Pratt would deploy the busts as pseudoscientific evidence that the indigenous peoples left on the frontier could and should be transformed into "Americans."

Pratt noted in his autobiography, *Battlefield and Classroom*, that both the Congress and the Smithsonian Institution, the leading political and scientific institutions in the country, enthusiastically endorsed the project.[17] The Smithsonian's second secretary, appointed in 1878, was Spencer F. Baird (1823–1887), a longtime resident of Carlisle, Pennsylvania, who was eager to expand the Smithsonian's holdings into the area of ethnography. Perceived by these powerful institutions as legitimate scientific documents of the continent's earliest inhabitants, the busts eventually made their way into the Smithsonian's collections.

This acquisition was significant, for the federal government's interest in ethnographic classification of the nation's indigenous populations was linked to its need to close the frontier and thus cast the Native population into the annals of "natural history." In short, the Indian was to be "museified."

Mills was a staunch advocate of phrenology, which posited direct correlations between one's interior psychic state and exterior physical attributes such as the shape and proportions of the skull. Although phrenology's influence peaked before the Civil War, many in the country steadfastly maintained belief in its principles even after Emancipation. This study will argue that phrenology's emphasis on dividing the brain into sections for minute craniological measurement was influential on postwar anthropometric measurement, as seen in the more legitimate postbellum sciences of criminology and physical anthropology.

A significant antecedent of the busts, and a source of their "scientific" credibility, was the Philadelphia doctor Samuel Morton's book *Crania Americana* (1839).[18] The lithographic illustrations in this book, the first scientific attempt to classify Native Americans, lent legitimacy to later endeavors, such as that of Mills.

I will consider these objects in relation to Victorian pseudoscientific thought on the nature of criminality, to previous and concurrent representations of indigenous Americans, and to the practice of life- and death-mask portraiture in the nineteenth century. This latter medium often recorded what were assumed to be phrenological attributes. Artistic and scientific impulses converged in these busts, with the final purpose of ethnographic documentation. The body of the prisoner was a metaphoric tabula rasa onto which the values of civilization could be inscribed.

Chapters 3 and 4 examine the school administration's consistent use of photography as another medium intended to legitimize its project. The school's administration intended the photographs produced there, which span its entire history of forty years, to control public perception of the institution. Two professional photographers, John N. Choate and Frances B. Johnston, were instrumental in this effort. John N. Choate (1840–1902) was a professional photographer who owned a studio in Carlisle. He served as the school's quasi-official photographer from 1879 until his death in 1902. Choate's well-known before-and-after portraits (seen in figs. I.1 and I.2) served as Pratt's primary evidence in convincing Congress to fund the institution during the school's early years.

By a deft manipulation of background, props, cropping, clothing, posing, exposures, and lighting, Choate intended his audiences to read these images as comparative portraits. His most critical audiences, of course, were the government leaders and bureaucrats in Congress and the Department of the Interior to whom Pratt was responsible. Choate's underlying assumption, which we should not take for granted, was the notion that educated bourgeois Anglo-American men *would* indeed read the paired images in such a causal narrative manner. Choate made the first photograph in the pair as the student entered the school and made a second several months or years later. He intended the altered external appearance of the individual in each picture to be a convenient signifier of the efficacy of Carlisle's civilizing process.

This study will examine possible reasons for the assumed legitimacy of such images. As suggested above, I will focus on the notion of aesthetic correspondence, which assumed exact parallels between appearance and character, an idea that dates back to the seventeenth century. I will chart the history of this notion in depth, paying special attention to the imaging of the Native body on film and in art, a necessary context for a correct reading of Choate's imagery.

Chapter 5 examines the work of Frances Benjamin Johnston (1864–1952), the best-known photographer Pratt hired. Johnston initially came to Carlisle in March 1901 and made photographs for a sequential album that Pratt intended to document the school's educational methods and vocational training. The resulting images, one of which figure I.5 shows, like much of Johnston's work are technically polished. The prints, still available for viewing at the Library of Congress, display students rigidly posed in the school's classrooms and workshops, seemingly absorbed in learning their new job skills, language, domesticity, and religion. Perhaps more clearly than any other images produced at the school, Johnston's provocative album highlighted what French philosopher Michel Foucault has termed the "disciplining" of the body. In other words, one senses an industrial ethos at play, as the images purport to display the manufacture of this "new and improved" set of indigenous bodies.

Context, again, is crucial for understanding these images and others like them (such as Johnston's Hampton Institute series).[19] Johnston's photographs should be seen as part of the history of labor during the Gilded Age. Captains of industry, wishing to squelch industrial competition, began imposing the "scientific management" principles of industrial psychologists such as Frederick W. Taylor.[20] The Carlisle experiment may be seen as a forerunner to Taylorism, as the photographs produced at the school stress industrial efficiency, bodily discipline, and an extreme visual conformity. The school's photographic representations of the indigenous body are both atavistic and visionary: intended to show some miraculous change from the feral raw material of the students' original state of being to neat conformity with the newer industrial order.

Yet these iconographically dense and compositionally rigid images betray subtle inconsistencies, especially when one considers them in context. Both at the school and shortly following graduation, students experienced alarming rates of illness, delinquency, decline, and death. Clearly, the rigidly posed masklike photographs told only the official side of the story. I will consider them not only in relation to their production but also in relation to the histories of the students themselves. Previous scholarship about Carlisle has largely overlooked this topic.

Chapter 5 will also consider a rare sanctioning of student photographic practice. In 1895, Pratt allowed John Leslie, a student and apprentice to Choate, to photograph the school grounds (see, for example, fig. I.6). The school's print shop published the resulting series of images. This album, which has received no previous scholarly attention, is significant for representing the work of a photographer of indigenous descent. Leslie's work displays a surprising technical proficiency. The images are diverse. Some are noticeably less rigid and seemingly avoid the compulsion to prove specific assumptions that one sees in the professional work. Others, emulating the formulaic approach of Choate's and Johnston's images, unwittingly participate in a matrix of representations as Leslie's own voice as a photographer blended with the school's institutional voice. The reasons for this album's production and the ramifications of its appearance are significant. Pratt seems to have allowed Leslie's images to appear in an effort to "prove" the degree to which the students had internalized the mandates of life at the school. Leslie was in certain respects a model student, as he would go on to open his own photography studio following his graduation. Pratt and others interpreted Leslie's acquisition of a trade as an affirmation of the school's pedagogical aims.

The final chapter will conclude by considering another instance of student "empowerment" at Carlisle, the school's storied football program. Pratt agreed only reluctantly to initiate the program. His fears of student injury and bad publicity were outweighed by both student enthusiasm for the sport and his own need to prove the "fitness" of the male students when in direct athletic competition with youths from legendary Anglo-American schools like Harvard. This section will examine images of Carlisle players and how such images were representationally ambivalent. While ostensibly empowering the male students, they also played into racialized theories of eugenic fitness and irrational fears of the "treacherous" and "warlike" nature of indigenous men.

In addition to considering cultural contexts and themes specific to the United States of the Gilded Age, I use critical theory here to flesh out innovative historical readings of much of the photographic materials.[21] This study considers all such photographic images, both the "official" (the work of Choate and Johnston) and the "unofficial" (the work of Leslie) in a framework indebted to French philosopher Michel Foucault and French linguist Roland Barthes. The photographs exist at a crossroads. On one side, an institutionally hegemonic practice is overtly at play. The stage of representation is set in advance to convey the effects of positivistic reformist improvements vis-à-vis the assumed unhygienic Native body.

The totalizing appearance of such representations is akin to what Foucault termed *panopticism*, a constant surveillance facilitated by modern architectural and technological innovations with the purpose of disciplining and controlling the human body. Specifically, Foucault uses the terms *examination* and *docility* to describe the notions of institutionally enforced display and an institutional channeling and emasculating of human physiological functions.[22] With this in mind, it is significant that the students were "examined" constantly, not only by photographers, but by the school's administration, teachers, and other students. These photographs are only one documentary expression of this ethos, which pervaded every aspect of life at the school.

Nevertheless, the mainly ideological role of the images is ever present, exposed by the fact that the intent of many of these images clearly did not coincide with the social realities at the school. I will therefore read these images closely, considering the overt representational format, or what

Barthes has termed the *studium*, and search for visual ruptures and inconsistencies in student voices, akin to what Barthes termed the *punctum*.[23] In all cases, the institutional *production* of these images will be considered. With this study, I hope to offer innovative interpretations of nineteenth-century American visual representations of race by fleshing out interconnections between visual practices often thought discrete: the didactic, artistic, and scientific.

In more relevant art historical terms, Carol Armstrong has clearly elucidated the Foucault-Barthes dilemma. In her book *Scenes in a Library*, Armstrong concisely sums up this theoretical debate. She sees the followers of Foucault, such as John Tagg, as highlighting the institutional or structural contexts in which photographs travel. From this perspective, their meaning is determined *externally* by the institutional agenda for which they are used as representation. Conversely, Armstrong characterizes the Barthesian view, represented by her own methodology, as one in which the medium itself takes inevitable precedence over any institutional agenda of framed meaning. In other words, for Barthes and his theoretical followers, the photograph is an autonomous, irrepressible, and indexical form of representation, the meaning of which is determined *internally* by its own innate traits as medium rather than by external mandates. In this text, I wish to accommodate both views, which I feel offer significant interpretive tools. Therefore, I want to analyze both institutional contexts *and* the "specialness" of the photograph. In much boarding-school imagery, one can detect both agendas at play—institutional hegemony and the irrepressible qualities of photography as medium.[24]

Scholars of American art history must of course be aware of the risks inherent in using twentieth-century French critical theory in the analysis of uniquely American cultural imagery from an earlier period. One may question the cultural relevance and appropriateness of such applications as well as the usefulness of retrofitting a critical paradigm. Yet past scholarship in the fields of American art history, American studies, and American literary criticism has proven that one can use clarifying theoretical models while simultaneously preserving the cultural integrity of the subject. Scholars of art, photography, literature, and cultural history in the U.S. Gilded Age have already made headway in merging the once-disparate concerns of Americanist scholarship and French critical theory. Jackson Lears, Sarah Burns, Kathleen Pyne, Alan Trachtenberg, and others have deftly applied Marxist, Freudian, and French poststructural thinking to American cultural problems.[25] Further, recent scholarly debates have raised questions about the relevance of "visual culture" material for art historical investigation. Such questions do need reckoning, and reflect an understandable concern for disciplinary integrity in lieu of the recent onslaught of scholarly studies of such topics as snapshot photography, popular illustration, television programming, advertisements, and even web design. Nevertheless, scholars continue to draw relevant parallels between seemingly more commonplace or banal media representations and the critically defined canons of American art.[26]

I

The "Savage" and Antebellum Science

The Indian Body as Tabula Rasa

Francis E. Leupp, who served as the commissioner of the Bureau of Indian Affairs of the United States under President Theodore Roosevelt from 1904 to 1909, was the federal government's leading official advocate for the education and "civilization" of the continent's indigenous populations during that time. Leupp thought of the problem of educating the Indian in conspicuous terms, as he was fond of using aesthetic or industrial-sounding metaphors in arguing for the need for Indian education. Referring to the winning over of the indigenous peoples living within the nation's expanding territory, he once stated, "but our main hope lies with the youthful generations who are still *measurably plastic*."[1]

On reflection, however, Leupp's metaphor of measurable plasticity was neither new nor unique in the context of American culture at the turn of the twentieth century. Leupp made the comment about the Roosevelt administration's support of a "transformative" boarding school education for indigenous youths on the latter's assumption of the presidency in 1901. Nevertheless, before the first such boarding school in Carlisle, Pennsylvania, in 1879, one may find decades of similar verbal, visual, and political discourse used to characterize Anglo America's variable perceptions of the nation's indigenous inhabitants. In fact, the notion of the Native body and mind as being a Lockean tabula rasa for the inscribing of the fears, values, and desires of white civilization informed much federal policy toward the Native American.[2] In this sense, the aesthetic perceptions of the Native body was no mere peripheral issue to Euro-American leaders, but rather was a central aspect of the history of the relations between these two groups.

The resulting manner in which white artists and photographers represented the figure of the Native American therefore tells us of these shifting, shadowy, and ill-conceived views of the so-called Red Man. As I stated in the Introduction, such aesthetic metaphors are hardly incidental. Rather, they implicitly reveal both overt and covert ideologies and assumed relations of power between groups. In the culture of the United States in the nineteenth century, the stakes were high: Such renderings alternately gauged, reinforced, or determined the definition of the term "American." The history of such representation would later play a significant role in the perceived "legitimacy" of many boarding-school images. Therefore, this chapter will endeavor to sketch the history of such imagery during the decades leading up to the era of reservations and boarding schools.

The Birth of "Scientific" Knowledge and the "Purity" of the Native Body

The examination of the Native American body as an aesthetic object was a central concern for American artists charged with painting, drawing, and illustrating this "exotic" frontier figure. This examination was concurrent with early social scientific investigation, as many intellectuals and leaders needed to establish a coherent national identity. Such an identity was crucial to the nation's leaders because it would offer an alternative to the fatalism of the Old World order of aristocratic privilege and establish a genealogical tradition seemingly missing from the new society's character.

In this vein, Thomas Jefferson published his famous *Notes on Virginia* in 1784, a document he intended to forge a systematic understanding of the once-wild territory of the newly formed state. One of his primary concerns in this document was presenting a history and physical survey of the state and its native inhabitants. Jefferson's intellectual ambition made the state an object of knowledge for newly emergent modern disciplines: archaeology, political science, geography, and economics.[3] Jefferson's document is central to this discussion because it represents an important forerunner to later nineteenth-century government attitudes toward Native Americans.

Jefferson wrote that his extensive dealings with the state's indigenous populations gave him knowledge of their histories, languages, and cultures. He stated that he gained one primary source of this knowledge during archaeological digs in the state. For Jefferson, the most intriguing finds were the many skeletal remains of the state's ancient inhabitants. Of these remains, he wrote that he found human skulls in the most abundance but that, regrettably, most had degenerated to the point of being useless for scientific investigation. Nevertheless, he argued that from the remains found, he was able to date the arrival of the area's tribes and their various routes of migration.[4] Jefferson's use of the skulls from burial grounds as his primary source of ethnographic knowledge is significant. The indigenous skull would become the centerpiece of scientific investigation and knowledge of the Indian throughout much of the next century (see fig. 1.1).

As president, Jefferson continued in his concern with issues of Anglo-American and Native American relations: His views would prove important for these relations well into the nineteenth century. In an 1802 address to the leaders of various tribes, he characterized what he saw as a viable program for a future friendship between the groups. Central to his plan was to

> endeavor in all things to be just and generous toward you, and to aid you in meeting those difficulties which a change of circumstance is bringing on. We shall . . . see your people become disposed to cultivate the earth, to raise herds of useful animals, and to spin and to weave, for their food and clothing . . . We will with pleasure furnish you with implements for the most necessary arts, and with persons who may instruct you how to make use of them.[5]

As early as 1802, decades before the government set up massive programs of Indian removal and transformation, Jefferson put forward a benign-sounding plan to integrate and educate the country's Native population, given the "change of circumstance" on the horizon. The changing circumstance to which he refers is most likely the continued westward expansion and industrialization of the country. This was something that was already underway by 1802, and something that he correctly understood as a threat to the continued existence of Native American culture in its pre-Colonial form.

Jefferson's views on Indian education were both deterministic and radically democratic. Although he was undoubtedly sincere in his sympathy with the emerging plight of the Indian, one should remember that in *Notes on Virginia* he established scientifically based distinctions between the variously defined races in Virginia—the African American, the Native, and the Euro-American.[6]

Jefferson acquired most of his knowledge of indigenous groups from archaeological digs, and thus in his mind the Indian was chiefly a figure of the then-emergent discipline of natural history. It was precisely this notion of the Native American as a figure of natural history, rather than one of *human* history, that would serve as the main pretext for later government policies of Indian removal and transformation. Although the president wished to endow the tribes with some of the tools and implements of civilization, he remained ambivalent on the question of whether different racial groups could or should live on equal terms in white society.[7]

The distinction between "nature" and "civilization" emerges clearly when one considers not only the scientific but the artistic view of the Native American that many prominent Euro-American artists of the nineteenth century held. In a sense, Jefferson's discovery of indigenous remains and his resulting theorizing of their history and culture were significant for the history of artistic reckoning with the Native American. His friend Benjamin Latrobe best illustrated the Jeffersonian view of Native American culture in a series of watercolors. Although Latrobe's representations of the Indian lack the violence, overt condescension, and pseudoscientific pretense of images completed later in the century, his perceptions of them were anything but positive.

Latrobe completed the watercolor that figure 1.2 shows shortly after arriving on a trip to New Orleans in January 1819. He represents the Native American in two figures here—the figure on the top register with long, flowing dark hair, and the larger-scale seated woman below. Given their format, Latrobe intended these images as little more than quick, impressionistic sketches of his perceptions on arriving in the city. Nevertheless, his written account of his arrival reveals a more uncomfortable view, one that contradicts the seemingly neutral appearance of the sketch. In his journal, he wrote of feeling unpleasantly surprised by the degree of racial mingling in the city's riverside market. He described the indigenous merchants and traders as "filthy savages half naked."[8] Such perceptual ambivalence toward the Native American was common in the Jeffersonian era, as Jefferson himself was caught between sympathy and the sobering knowledge that conflict lay on the historic horizon.

As the political tenor in the capital changed over time from a Jeffersonian discourse of ambivalent accommodation to the Jacksonian policies of confrontation, artists began to more systematically and "scientifically" make images of Native American subjects. Painter George Catlin (1796–1872) was among the first Euro-American artists to seek out and visually represent the indigenous inhabitants of the frontier in the 1830s (see fig. 1.3). Catlin wrote voluminously about his early experiences traveling into the frontier along the Missouri River in 1832. He often evoked the emergent dualism between the "polite world" of the East and the realm of "nature" in the "Western World" of the frontier. In one poignant letter, Catlin wrote that he preferred nature because it affords him "living models of such elegance and beauty" and an "enthusiastic admiration of man in the honest and elegant simplicity of nature." Further, Catlin wrote that the Natives he met led lives of "truth" and "chivalry" unfound in the "civilized" world.[9]

It would become a commonplace for artists and explorers to see the open lands of the frontier and its inhabitants in contradistinction to the urbane culture of the Northeast. Art historian Frances Pohl has argued that many artists of the Jacksonian Era (1828–circa 1850) who wished to render picturesque or even sublime views of the nation's land went one step further and collapsed the distinction between the Native American inhabitants and the land altogether. Thus, artists such as Thomas Cole (1801–1848) would paint the two subjects as if they were *necessarily* linked in some essential, quasi-religious sense. Pohl argues that Cole does this in works such as *Distant View of Niagara Falls* (1830).[10] In his work, Cole would often encourage the viewer to see the Native as just another part of the sublime whole by the viewer—something inextricably linked to the savagery and purity of the land.

Pohl goes on to argue that associating the Native body with the untamed, forbidding, and yet alluring land of the frontier is by no means merely poetic license. She proposes the idea that artists and their patrons were often financially and politically invested in exploring and seizing these lands. She states that views such as Cole's, which afford the viewer a distanced, hieratic survey of the sublimity of the scene and its "pure" indigenous inhabitants, suggest what she terms a "magisterial gaze."[11] She concludes that this gaze was instituted into visual representations of such scenery and may therefore be seen as a visual analog to the ambitions of possessive capitalism in relation to the frontier.[12]

One must therefore consider visual representations of Native Americans during the early nineteenth century in relation to larger political, social, and economic ambitions held by the artists, photographers, and patrons involved. Although Catlin was sincere in his view of the Native American as "chivalrous" and "pure," one needs to consider the cultural implications of such a perception. Often, the perceived "purity" of the frontier and its inhabitants was an implicit acknowledgment not only of the supposed corruption of the East, but also of the fear of an imminent destruction of that purity. As art historian Charles Colbert has stated in reference to this Romantically inflected discourse: "[A]s long as the Indians were considered a dying race, the rhetoric of those who descried the adoption of European ways could be tolerated, even savored, as the crepuscular effulgence of a waning people."[13]

Science, Art, and Democracy: Phrenology Gains a Foothold in America

It then becomes clear that the figure of the Native American in fine art representations such as Cole's was weighed down with the needs of white civilization. Even when intended to be flattering or ennobling in a Romantic sense, these representations nevertheless contained the dialectical specter of an imminent material cultural demise. The Indian would become a controversial figure in the white imagination, assigned the best and worst qualities of both "Man" and "Nature."

When considering the dualism of Man and Nature and its relation to questions of race, it is important to recall that this duality was central to American philosophy of the day, specifically that of Ralph Waldo Emerson (1803–1882). Emerson and his philosophical followers, the transcendentalists, saw Nature as that which is

> all that is separate from us, all which Philosophy distinguishes as the NOT ME, that is, both nature and art, all other men and my own body, must be ranked under this name, NATURE . . . *Nature*, in the common sense, refers to essences unchanged by man; space, the air, the river, the leaf.[14]

From Emerson's perspective, the distinction between "Me" and that which is "Not Me" was important in preserving the sanctity of Nature in relation to the human will. In this view, Nature took on an autonomous quality, existing eternally irrespective of the ebbs and flows of human history. In his conception of the self and external Nature, Emerson clearly distinguished between "Man" and that which belongs to the realm of an "essence" unchanged by Man. He defined this essential quality as the various features of Nature, especially open space. In artistic representations of the Native American at this time, one gets a complex sense of the varying perceptions of the indigenous population. There is an overriding sense that the Indian is cast as the "Not Me" role in the Emersonian scheme, as seen in Cole's images.

In Catlin's work, there is a surprising sense of individuality conferred on the subjects. When the subject was a high-ranking chief, Catlin represented him in a manner becoming a bourgeois portrait. These subjects are grave, serious, and often depicted in bust-length format, all in keeping with Catlin's claim that many of his models therefore maintained the dignity of ancient Greco-Roman athletes (see fig. 1.3).[15] Therefore, some might wish to infer that Catlin was more likely to view the Native American as a sympathetic figure with a sense of humanity and dignity. Although some of Catlin's writings confirm such a conclusion, Charles Colbert has recently fleshed out the artist's intellectual dependence on pseudoscientific knowledge in perceiving his Native subjects.[16]

Alternatively, in Cole's images, the Native becomes unified with the landscape he inhabits. In short, he becomes an aspect of Nature in the Emersonian sense. Even in some of Catlin's images (see, for example, fig. 1.4), viewers get the sense from his treatment of the figure in landscape that he too saw the Indian in terms "Natural" rather than "human." Even when seeing them as more human, he was filtering their reality through his own academic artistic training by assigning classical qualities and significances to their existence. His practice is disturbing, because its logical conclusion is to depict the Indian as a distanced, static figure, one unchanged by history and thus something other than human in either the individualist Emersonian sense or even the evolutionist Darwinian sense.[17] Such ambiguities often plagued white perception of the Native American during this period, opening the door for establishing a more repressive, systematic body of knowledge.

Although representations of the indigenous American varied and multiplied in the fine arts, parallel interrelated forms of visual representation were used in the scientific world to classify the Indian biologically. It is in the notion of the Native as linked to the land he inhabited that we can detect the emergence of a systematic "scientific" body of knowledge surrounding the Native collective identity.

Charles Colbert has made great headway in considering the parallels between the ostensibly "fine art" rendering of the Native American by Catlin and others and the pseudoscientific visual representations that would appear in the 1830s. Specifically, Colbert argues that we may also read Catlin's portraits in terms of that artist's interest in the contemporaneous pseudoscience of phrenology. By perceiving the Native in such terms, Catlin and other artists effectively participated in setting Indians into a category of existence that white culture would ultimately consider less than human and less than civilized.[18] The government would use this classification to justify its policies of Indian removal and transformation. To understand this complex process, it is necessary to consider the history of phrenological knowledge in the United States. Artists and illustrators concretized such a knowledge, which was subsequently applied to racial politics during the Jacksonian era and beyond. A discussion of phrenology in relation to representations of Native Americans is critical to understanding postbellum boarding-school imagery.

In simple terms, phrenology was a pre-Freudian science of the human mind. The word derives from the Greek terms *phren* and *logy*, "mind" and "discourse."[19] Its practitioners used its principles to judge another person's character, capabilities, and attributes simply by looking at the size, shape, and proportions of that person's skull and face. Colbert has put it concisely: "[I]ts primary concern was to identify the moral code inscribed in the human form."[20] The central tenet of phrenology was that systematic and predictable aesthetic correspondences existed between one's interior self and one's external appearance.

Historians of phrenology date the origin of the pseudoscience to the writings of the Swiss theologian and physiognomist Johann Caspar Lavater (1741–1801). Lavater began outlining the science he termed "physiognomy" in his famous book *Physiognomical Fragments to Promote the Knowledge and Love of Mankind* (1775).

The text laid out a system by which one could decipher another human being's moral character simply by viewing that person's facial features. He illustrated such correspondences with his famous silhouette portraits (see, for example, fig. 1.5). Lavater wished to merge his joint concerns of metaphysics and science, appealing to modern empiricism in the service of what he saw as spiritual knowledge. From this perspective it becomes clear that physiognomy had its origins not only in empirical science but also in Protestant spirituality.[21]

Lavater claimed that specific facial features and proportions corresponded neatly to internal spiritual and moral traits. One could thus read the face of another and thereby judge the person's intentions, capabilities, and overall character. In short, one could gain knowledge of the invisible by viewing the visible. Many historians have attributed this wish to see the invisible to the newly emergent democratic and industrializing social landscapes of the eighteenth and early nineteenth centuries. In a new world in which the once sacrosanct order of aristocracy and clergy had partially given way to a newer secularized world of urbanization, anonymity, and mechanization, many felt ill at ease and lost. To gain a sense of perceptual balance and control in this potentially chaotic "Modern" world, sciences such as physiognomy and, later, phrenology allowed people to navigate an unfamiliar social landscape with greater ease. Also, these sciences granted people the opportunity to "read" potential rivals in social, political, and professional life in a more democratic fashion, because the older hierarchies implied by noble birthright no longer held sway in many situations. Therefore, physiognomy is best seen as a specifically Modern and middle-class worldview.[22]

Lavater originally intended physiognomy to be a synthesis between religious and scientific bodies of knowledge. Others picked up on his ideas and tried to gain greater academic acceptance by lending them a more scientific quality. Primary among this next generation of pseudoscientific practitioners was Austrian doctor Franz Joseph Gall (1758–1828).

Gall first proposed a physiognomic body of knowledge in the 1790s under the term "craniology." In explaining human behavioral patterns, Gall went beyond Lavater by insisting that particular "faculties," or character traits, were visible in the human skull. These faculties were visible because they found correspondence in a particular "organ," or area of the brain underneath the skull. The theories advanced in Gall's internationally renowned study of the mind *Recherches sur le Système Nerveux en Général* (1809) would become the foundation for phrenological thought into the early twentieth century. Gall illustrated the craniological correspondences in a format that would become iconic in phrenological texts.[23]

As figure 1.6 shows, Gall delineated a person's faculties on the surface of the skull and upper face. Each numeric section in the drawing matched a specific organ within the brain. If a person was endowed with a certain faculty, the corresponding organ was enlarged in that person's brain, thus producing a related formation on the surface of the skull. It was by positing a correspondence between inner quality and outward appearance that the craniologist could set up a strictly empirical basis for the theorized correspondence.

According to Gall's system, if a person was intelligent, a bulge at the top of the forehead would be the dominant feature of the head. Similarly, if a person had exceptional moral qualities, according to contemporaneous Protestant definitions of the term, that person would inevitably have a heightened skull crown. Although Lavater would credit God with the existence of enhanced physiognomic traits, Gall wished to give craniology a greater empirical sense, and thus avoided affixing direct metaphysical causes. According to Gall, all such functions were anatomical in nature. The mind functioned much as other organs, such as the heart and the stomach, and therefore created corresponding effects on the body's physiological makeup.[24]

Despite his ambition to systematize craniology and lend it the veneer of a legitimate science, Gall was first a physician and did not capitalize on the entrepreneurial implications of this newly credible form of scientific knowledge. It was left to Johann Gaspar Spurzheim (1776–1832) and George Combe (1788–1858) to popularize what would become phrenology in the English-speaking world.

Spurzheim, a German doctor, met Gall in 1800 during the latter's lecture tour around Europe. Gall had presented his new science of craniology to elite intellectual audiences. On their meeting, Spurzheim impressed the older Gall with his intelligence and ambition, and the two became collaborators in promoting craniology, eventually coauthoring the *Recherches* in 1809. Despite their collaborations, within a few years their respective professional ambitions and doctrinal differences caused a rift. Because of this rift, Spurzheim spent several years in England and Scotland, lecturing independently and publishing works on craniology in English, thus becoming the progenitor of the pseudoscience in the English-speaking world.[25]

In contrast to his mentor, Spurzheim believed that craniology could be a popular undertaking, practicable by anyone with discipline. He viewed it not as an academically elite science but in a more positivistic sense. Gall believed that human beings were mentally static and thus could not change their "good" or "bad" craniological faculties. In contrast, Spurzheim felt that his version of the science (which he renamed "phrenology" in 1815) could in fact be a life practice, akin to other healthy practices. Therefore, it was Spurzheim who gave phrenology a liberal middle-class connotation, one in stark contrast to the deterministic science proposed by his mentor.[26]

Because of this liberalism, and because of his facility with English, Spurzheim attracted massive audiences in the United Kingdom and the United States. It was during his estrangement from Gall that he attracted his most devout adherents, and consequently during the opening years of the century the "science" gained a cultural foothold in the United States. Among his followers in Scotland was a young lawyer named George Combe, who was responsible for applying the principles of phrenology to Native American skulls during his own tour in the United States in the late 1830s.

Although he did not set foot in America until August 1832, Spurzheim enjoyed wide cultural influence there much earlier. What was eventually to become popularized as phrenology made its way into the country through a Philadelphia banker named Nicholas Biddle around 1806. Biddle heard Gall lecture in Germany on the topic and enthusiastically promoted the new science on returning to the United States. Other medical professionals from the Northeast, including John Bell and Charles Caldwell of Philadelphia, effectively institutionalized and passionately defended the science after hearing Gall and Spurzheim in Europe.[27]

It was now that phrenology's influence began to spread well beyond the medical establishment of Philadelphia. Charles Colbert notes that phrenology was transmitted to generations of fine artists in New York, Boston, and Philadelphia not only through the establishment of various phrenological societies in those cities but also, and more importantly, through direct institutional links.[28] Colbert states that John Bell, the doctor who promoted phrenology early on, was appointed professor of anatomy at the Pennsylvania Academy in 1822, a position he would hold until 1839. Further, New York doctor John Francis, also an enthusiast of the pseudoscience, introduced Spurzheim's writings to John Wesley Jarvis (1780–1840) in 1816. Jarvis was one of New York's leading portraitists (see fig. 1.7) during the period, and the city commissioned him to do official portraits of leading veterans from the War of 1812. It is therefore relevant to postulate that phrenology would appeal to an artist so used to representing the physiognomies of the nation's early military exemplars. Finally, Francis was a colleague of William Dunlap and assisted Dunlap as the latter wrote the first history of art in the United States.[29] All of these connections point to the centrality of phrenological thought in artistic practice in the United States during the first half of the nineteenth century. Especially important in the intersection of phrenology and the visual arts was the visual representation of the human form, most commonly seen in phrenological illustration (see, for example, fig. 1.8).

Spurzheim's tour in 1832 only confirmed his preestablished celebrity. The notion that one could improve oneself through exercising particular faculties came as a welcome and seductive idea to the American bourgeoisie, unaccustomed to the stark determinism of European aristocratic culture. It was Spurzheim who altered Gall's assignment of phrenological value to particular parts of the mind. Spurzheim believed the mind comprised not only the organ of the brain but was itself an organ that could be exercised. His doctrine went far beyond the strict anatomical approach of Gall. He was the first well-known practitioner of phrenology to apply it to the myriad social topics of concern to middle-class American audiences. These topics included religion, education, and socially pathological behavior.[30] Nevertheless, Spurzheim followed Gall in making use of the iconic phrenological illustration of the head as the frontispiece to his English-language text *Outlines of Phrenology* (1829). This image rapidly became a staple in American phrenological publications later in the century because of his influence (see fig. 1.8).

Spurzheim argued that by exercising particular phrenological organs, one could emphasize or de-emphasize particular faculties. For example, if one systematically avoided violence, one's organ of "Destructiveness" would decrease both in size and influence in relation to the rest of the brain. Gall had called this faculty "Murder," but Spurzheim wished to downplay Gall's deterministic lexicon and substituted a more scientific-sounding word based on more open-sounding faculties.[31]

Phrenological illustrations supposedly proved all of this because they divided the brain into phrenological organs. The display of disembodied skulls and plaster casts was important as another primary form of empirical evidence. The phrenological society of Boston started this practice by purchasing hundreds of "racial skulls" as well as Spurzheim's entire cast collection from the Harvard Medical School in 1835.[32] It was this type of illustration, based on firsthand phrenological examinations, that would come to inform the racial perceptions of various groups within American society.

Following Spurzheim's unexpected death in Boston in November 1832, phrenology remained at the forefront of academic training in the United States, both in art and medicine. Spurzheim's pupil George Combe picked up where his teacher left off. It was Combe who would do the most to apply phrenological knowledge to the study of race in American art and culture.

Following Spurzheim's death, phrenology found many prominent Anglo-American apologists in the United States. During the 1830s, the influence of the pseudoscience increased exponentially. Although certain intellectuals such as Charles Caldwell supported it, entrepreneurs such as Combe and the brothers Orson and Lorenzo Fowler of New York exploited Spurzheim's teachings commercially. During the ensuing decades it would become a widely disseminated body of knowledge, and thus gain a populist following. This mass following, coupled with an aura of medical credibility, allowed phrenological knowledge to infiltrate the touchy area of race relations in the United States for decades to come.

By 1838, Combe's fame had surpassed that of the deceased Spurzheim as the leading intellectual proponent of pseudoscience in the English-speaking world. Beginning in 1829, Combe published editions of a collection of his essays on phrenology, morality, and social life entitled *The Constitution of Man*. This compilation was essentially a regurgitation of Spurzheim's applications of phrenology to daily life. In it, Combe proposed several key ideas in the application of phrenology to race relations. As the title suggests, he intended the book to serve as a "constitution" for social life. He argued this point by proposing various "normative" social parameters intended to foster equanimity in society. His studies in phrenology were to serve as the empirical raw data for these philosophical arguments. By imposing the ideas of phrenology onto social questions, Combe hoped to fix healthy standards for the English-speaking civilizations. He thus harped on themes ranging from temperance and hygiene to filial piety, individualism, and property ownership.

A likely source of the text's popularity and perceived legitimacy by Anglo-American audiences was its deft grounding in both modern Anglo-Saxon philosophical discourse and its subtle use of Old Testament biblical overtones. In these respects, Combe's opening paragraph is telling:

> A statement of the evidence of a great intelligent First Cause is given
> in the "Phrenological Journal," and in the "System of Phrenology."
> I hold this existence as capable of demonstration. By NATURE, I
> mean the workmanship of this great Being, such as it is revealed to
> our minds by our senses and faculties.[33]

In this excerpt, Combe displays an intellect well versed in Enlightenment philosophy and its implications for metaphysical belief. While upholding the notion of a pantheistic "design" of nature, he clearly sought to modernize his arguments by appealing to the basic precepts of Enlightenment thought, specifically that of German philosopher Immanuel Kant (1724–1804). This is clear in Combe's breakdown of reality into that designed by the "First Cause . . . great Being" and that which is knowable to the mere mortal through his or her senses and phrenological faculties. In this way, Combe asserts phrenology as a prime means of grasping the Real by using the basic senses. This distinction, between the senses and some external, absolute reality, is a popularized echo of Kant's distinction between the "phenomenal" and "noumenal" worlds. Essentially, Kant saw reality as consisting of the sensual (i.e., phenomenal) and the unknowable, or what he commonly termed "things-in-themselves" (i.e., noumenal).[34] The basic dichotomy of our internal perceptual mechanisms and the external objective reality of nature was fundamental to phrenology as well as to a host of other Enlightenment-era European sciences and disciplines.

Finally, Combe's text was no doubt comforting to his bourgeois readership, given its emphasis on the creationist aspect of positive phrenological faculties. For Combe all of nature, including one's phrenological faculties, was the product of a "natural law" determined by the "Creator." Therefore, one's ancestors were created with innate faculties, and these were transmitted genetically down through the generations to the present. All "moral law" was thus derivative of this natural order, and a violation of these natural laws led one down the path to destruction. One's relative moral standing was, in turn, visible in the size and proportion of one's phrenological organs.[35]

The moralizing text seemingly hit a chord with Anglo-American audiences. Combe's book was successful in the United States, selling more than 300,000 copies in the United Kingdom and the United States from the time of its appearance in 1829 until 1860. Historian Roger Cooter has stated that the book outsold Darwin's *Origin of Species* in 1859–1860 and was the fourth-highest-selling book in the two countries over these decades.[36]

Combe consolidated his leading role in the field during a tour of the country in 1838–1840. He gained celebrity status, with hundreds attending his lectures. Luminaries who attended his lectures included not only artistic elites such as Rembrandt Peale but also political leaders, including John Quincy Adams, William Henry Harrison, Martin Van Buren, and Horace Mann. His audiences considered Combe's ideas both philosophically and scientifically valid. His election to the nation's premier scholarly societies, including the American Philosophical Society and the National Academy of Sciences, bears this out.[37]

Combe's friendship with Peale suggests his ideas were considered applicable to artistic matters. Combe even analyzed Peale's posthumous equestrian portrait of George Washington while visiting the painter's studio. After viewing Peale's work, Combe concluded that in phrenological terms, Washington's cranium had reached a stunning balance of faculties.[38] Obviously, the teleological nature of Combe's pronouncement did little to dampen the enthusiasm he met.

Peale's enthusiasm for phrenology as an aesthetic system is unsurprising when we consider his own background in the arts. Peale's father, Charles Willson Peale (1741–1827), was a scientist and painter well known for merging the genres of scientific documentation and portraiture in his own work. Not only was the elder Peale a self-fashioned gentleman of art and science, but he also came of age during the late colonial and revolutionary eras. One is reminded of art historian Wayne Craven's famous arguments about the functions of colonial portraiture and the artistic rules governing its commission and production.

Specifically, Craven writes that patrons during the colonial period sought portraits that presented them in a favorable metaphysical and material light. Colonial patrons wished to show the Calvinist piety of their newly carved out lives before the eyes of God. By cautiously displaying their mercantile affluence within a portrait, they could accomplish two tasks at once: affirm their social status and spiritually define themselves as a beneficiary of God's goodness. This representational form could metaphorically suggest the alignment of their spiritual existence with their material existence. Craven and others have argued that this was the key component of identity for bourgeois colonial America.[39]

Artists such as Charles Willson Peale and Rembrandt Peale, sharing this puritanical heritage with their fellow artists and their patrons, were undoubtedly influenced by the Calvinist worldview. Also, in embracing Enlightenment science, knowledge such as that seen in phrenology would only complement these metaphysical assumptions about the relationship between one's interior and exterior being. Because many perceived it as complementing Puritan metaphysics and aesthetics, phrenology was able to gain a foothold in the United States.

The Scientific Savage: Samuel Morton, Measurement, and Proving Savagery

It was during Combe's stay in the country that he met and collaborated with another luminary of the Philadelphia intelligentsia, the doctor Samuel G. Morton (1799–1851). With Morton, Combe would propose a new and more controversial application of phrenological knowledge and aesthetics. Rather than use phrenology to glorify Anglo-American cultural exemplars, Combe and Morton used it as a tool to flesh out innate faculties of and to prove qualitative differences between variously defined racial groups.

Morton was a prominent doctor and the nation's leading craniologist. He is remembered in the history of science as the leading American advocate of the pre-Darwinian evolutionary theory of polygenesis. The legitimacy of polygenesis as a scientific doctrine was a high-stakes proposition in the United States: The idea that members of separately defined racial groups had distinct biological origins and unchanging characteristics was used to justify slavery.

Morton began learning the theories of natural history and other emergent Enlightenment sciences at a young age. Encouraged by his stepfather, who was a mineralogist, he went on to earn two medical degrees, from the Universities of Pennsylvania and Edinburgh.[40] Immersed in the intellectual atmosphere of 1820s Scotland, Morton inevitably absorbed Spurzheim's ideas, which the latter had spread in the United Kingdom through lectures and writing. In this sense, he and Combe came of age together intellectually under the spell of early phrenology.

Following his return to Philadelphia from Scotland, Morton gradually established himself as a leading practitioner in the competitive medical atmosphere of the city. He was elected to the American Philosophical Society in 1828, the same institution that would enthusiastically welcome Combe a decade later. Morton later held the post of instructor of anatomy at Pennsylvania College and served as a doctor at the Philadelphia Almshouse, a charitable hospital founded in 1729 to relieve the city's poor.[41] Like others of his generation who maintained an unshakable interest in phrenology, Morton had significant influence over the broadcasting of official knowledge about the human body. Further, his experience at the almshouse likely stirred his interest in perceived physiological differences between members of differing racial and socioeconomic groups. This was an interest shared by many of his class, including the reform-minded Charles Caldwell. For such thinkers, the lower standards of hygiene and health evident in many of the city's impoverished inhabitants were physical evidence of a class-based moral deficiency. This was an idea that mainstream medical opinion would maintain in the country well into the twentieth century.[42] It is also significant for both the history of phrenology and its visual representations, because phrenologists would insist on a craniometric basis for the pathologies of the poor and subaltern.

Through the 1830s, Morton's increasing interest in proving a craniological and thus a scientific basis for racial differences led him to acquire a massive collection of human skulls.[43] The skull was the primary source of knowledge and evidence for early natural historians and phrenologists interested in establishing definitions for the intertwined concepts of race and nationhood.[44] It is important to recall that the central principle of phrenology is the supposed correlation between skull shape and proportion and specific faculties of character. This principle was also Morton's main motivation, because he categorized and hierarchized humanity under the twin rubrics of "race" and "nation." It was in this context that Morton met Combe during the latter's American tour. Together, they would collaborate on what would become the authoritative text on the topic of scientific knowledge of Native Americans, Morton's *Crania Americana, or a Comparative View of the Skulls of Various Aboriginal Nations of North and South America*.

The book is a tour de force of linking imagery and text in the service of scientific proof. Morton hired Philadelphia lithographer John Collins to make the final illustrations that were to serve as the visual proof for the phrenological arguments Morton and Combe made (see fig. 1.9). In a section of the text titled, "Explanation of Plates," Morton offered an aesthetic explanation and analysis of the book's frontispiece, a reproduction of a portrait originally made by Philadelphia painter John Neagle (see fig. 1.10). That Morton "proves" his theories of phrenology with his interpretation of an image is obvious in this section, because Morton praises Neagle for his realistic rendering of the "Omahaw" [*sic*] chief Big Elk as painted "from life." He then explains that the draftsman M. S. Weaver copied Neagle's portrait. He praises Weaver as "a young artist of great promise in both accuracy and beauty of delineation." T. Sinclair later reproduced Weaver's drawing after Neagle in lithographic format. Further on in his commentary, Morton managed the leap from artistic beauty to phrenological exactitude when praising the various artists for capturing the chief's "retreating forehead," "low brow," "dull and seemingly unobservant eye," "large aquiline nose," "high cheek bones," "full mouth and chin," and "angular face."[45] Through setting up a credible artistic chain of representation, Morton tried to further viewer perception of the scientific legitimacy of the illustrations.

The correlation Morton intended was that the credibility of the illustrations as artistic product should reinforce their acceptance as legitimate scientific evidence. Indeed, the lithographs carried out by Collins and Sinclair are compelling. Their detail and sense of weight and dimensionality do strike one when paging through the text. In this sense, they may be placed historically in the tradition of serious medical and scientific illustration, a modern tradition dating to the Renaissance and first seen in the anatomical drawings of Leonardo da Vinci and Andreas Vesalius. Significantly, Leonardo and Vesalius both sought to acquire and pass on knowledge of the body's inner workings through its anatomical makeup. For Leonardo, these internal workings were the new basis of explanation of a person's external, manifest behaviors. During the Renaissance in Europe, such ideas were subversive and revolutionary, because they substituted anatomical motion for divine predetermination when trying to explain human behavior.

Further, the use of facial and cranial illustration was important in establishing artistic knowledge of human emotion and expression in early modern European culture. This is most clearly seen in the use of such imagery by Charles Le Brun (1619–1690), Petrus Camper (1722–1789), and others, leading to Lavater's silhouette portraits in the late eighteenth century (see figs. 1.11–1.13).[46] It is important to bear in mind the long artistic tradition on which Morton and Combe depended to have their characterizations read as both artistically pleasing and scientifically valid.

That Morton felt compelled to explain his use of particular artists would indicate a tacit awareness of the importance and precariousness of using such imagery for scientific proof. Throughout the text, the two took great pains to argue for not only the artistic legitimacy of their illustrations but also the resultant scientific legitimacy, because all phrenological knowledge is chiefly visual.

For instance, Morton would go on to explain that the most important phrenological measurement is the angle or slope of the forehead, commonly called the "facial angle." Morton measured this angle with a device known as the "facial goniometer," which he illustrated in the book (see fig. 1.14). The measurement from this device was compiled, with other data, in a table of facial measurements. This table was the primary source of data that allowed Morton and Combe to assert the various cranial capacities of an array of Indian tribes in comparison to other races. In his explanatory essay, Combe asserted that this data disproved the age-old assumption by philosophers that all races and individuals have equal capacities to learn. He argued that differences in skull volume and capacity disproved philosophical errors and showed that phrenology was the only valid science for determining intelligence, character, and other cranial functions.[47]

Perhaps most disturbing in all of this is Morton's and Combe's claim that Native Americans, together with what they called "Ethiopians," had the lowest *cultural* attainment when compared with Morton's three other racial groups: Caucasians, Mongolians, and Malay. Both claimed that this was not because of topography, climate, or other external circumstance, but rather to unchanging "racial" characteristics, as seen in the skulls in Morton's collection.[48] Morton would credit this difference to polygenesis, the doctrine that racial groups with differing physiological characteristics therefore had differing biological origins. The authors took the difference in biological origin to prove that change and thus evolution could not take place in various cultures or "nations." In fact, Morton went so far as to use Egyptian hieroglyphs as proof of his startling claim. He argued that racial characteristics remain constant throughout history because one may *see* these differences graphically illustrated in ancient art forms of all kinds.[49]

The assertion that images uncovered during contemporaneous archaeological explorations could serve as proof of the eternal nature of race reveals perhaps the most anachronistic and stunning aspect of Morton's system. He contended that humanity was descended from Adam and Eve, as in the story in the Old Testament.[50] Therefore, his conception of time and history as subjects of study was clearly restricted by the orthodox Christian belief that the world is only several thousand years old. According to this logic, it might therefore sound plausible that Egyptian hieroglyphs display age-old depictions of unchanging racial features.

It was under the influence of this logic that Morton was able to show a final comparison in his illustrations. He presented the reader with a series of skulls he collected from various sources, including military expeditions. Most of the skulls in his book were representative of particular indigenous tribes from both North and South America (see fig. 1.1). Through his use of the facial goniometer, he stated that he was able to uncover phrenological and thus cultural distinctions between the tribes, claiming that certain of them had reached higher degrees of civilization than others.[51] More important for his agenda, however, was his use of an illustration of a skull supposedly belonging to a Swiss national who had recently died (see fig. 1.15). Morton argued that the steeper facial angle in the Swiss skull suggested both a higher degree of civilization and a biologically discrete origin for the Caucasian.[52]

This view might strike us as wildly out of step with modern science. Nonetheless, it is important to consider that around this time, polygenesis, based on a creationist logic of separate origins for races, still had credibility among many in the nation's scientific establishment. Specifically, Louis Agassiz (1807–1873), a Swiss naturalist and Harvard professor, supported polygenesis as late as the 1870s. Agassiz even made an effort to accommodate the newer doctrine of Darwinism within this system.[53]

Polygenesis, creationism, and phrenology survived in this country well into the late nineteenth century in credible scientific and artistic contexts. This offers provocative material for reinterpreting depictions of race executed not only before but *after* the Civil War and Emancipation. Historians of American art and culture often see the war as a stark chronological line, after which antebellum racial theories died away. As we will see, many people did indeed renounce such theories. Nevertheless, the logic of racial purity and supremacy would covertly inform institutionalized representational practices in this country well beyond the end of the war. The competing ideologies of assimilation, segregation, and eugenics[54] would not dispel but rather accommodate and reconfigure pseudoscientific thought in the wake of Darwinian evolution.

2

Producing the Indian
Indexing and Pathologizing the Native American

Clark Mills, Phrenology, and a National Ideal

Given this convergence of ideas about race, anatomy, and aesthetics in the United States, it is not surprising that, eventually, phrenological measurements would be used in the graphic comparison and hierarchizing of various forms of organic life. Illustrations such as figure 2.1 are the most unnerving exhibition of all that Morton and Combe imply with their arguments about facial angles. This image, which historian John Davies used as the frontispiece to his 1955 book *Phrenology: Fad and Science*, would become a commonplace in phrenological illustration because of its convenient superimposition of species. The representational logic of such an image is based on Morton's notion that the degree of the facial angle corresponds to the proportional size of various phrenological organs, which in turn correspond to intelligence and capacity.[1]

In what may strike the modern reader as a wildly illogical set of aesthetic comparisons, the illustration proposes an organic hierarchy from the lowest animal species, the serpent, to the highest of "species," the Caucasian human. The measurement of the facial angle served to prove this hierarchy. Therefore, the creature with the most severe facial angle, the snake, was placed at the bottom of the scale, a position that implied a phrenologically defined degraded intellectual state. From the nonhuman species of snake, dog, elephant, and ape, such illustrations would eventually work up to the human realm. Starting with the "human idiot," the illustrator moved forward phrenologically to the "Bushman" (what Morton called the "Ethiopian"), to the "uncultivated," the "improved," the "civilized," the "enlightened," and finally, the "Caucasian-highest type."

Here the racial hierarchies of phrenology are made plain. As I stated earlier, Morton and Combe ranked Native Americans only slightly higher than the "Ethiopian," thus giving a sense of their place in the phrenological world. For the artistic rendering of racial types, these ideas would be far from inconsequential in the United States of the nineteenth century. Specifically, Combe published another widely read text titled *Phrenology Applied to Painting and Sculpture* in 1855.

Combe's stated intention in this tract was to give the artist and the critic a scientific basis for the production and evaluation of the highest-quality fine art, and therefore to prevent them from slipping into the realm of "mere opinion." Continuing in this vein, Combe asserts phrenological principles of bodily shape and proportion as the artist's best alternative for presenting the most faithful recording of the human form and character in a work of art, based as they are on anatomical precision.[2]

As we've seen, many artists welcomed Combe's application of phrenology to the fine arts, because they were struggling to find comprehensive artistic guidelines with which to represent the nation's various groups. Among the most prominent sculptors to adopt Combe's Americanized version of phrenology was Clark Mills (1815–1883). In fact, it is in various institutions' assumptions about the artistic and scientific legitimacy of Mills's work that we may notice a bridge between antebellum pseudoscience and postbellum reformist agendas.

Recent art historical scholarship has revealed Mills's indebtedness to pseudoscience. Less known is his centrality in government debates about the education and reform of allegedly uncivilized groups such as Native Americans. Although Mills did come of age as an artist in the antebellum South, his influence over official opinions of race would be much more far-reaching than his provincial background might suggest.

While working as a young plasterer in Charleston, South Carolina, in the mid-1830s, Mills consulted a local phrenologist, hoping to gain insights into his own capacities.[3] By so doing, Mills wished to use the pseudoscience for help as he aimed for a more prestigious career. As we saw in the previous chapter, one of the main selling points in Combe's more practical version of phrenology was its supposed applicability to questions of middle-class American life, including career choice. As Colbert has noted, many Americans of the time consulted phrenologists about sensitive topics such as career choice and marriage. Trust in phrenology led to the establishment of a vast pseudoscientific industry that would persist into the early twentieth century.[4]

The phrenologist told Mills that he was indeed suited for a more prestigious career, that of fine artist. The phrenologist arrived at this professional evaluation based on his assertion that Mills's skull was heavily pronounced around the cranial organ, signaling a talent for sculpture. Mills later stated that he was skeptical of the science and at first did not believe the diagnosis. However, in an 1853 interview with the *American Phrenological Journal*, Mills stated that a few days after the evaluation, he was drawn to an Italian sculptor living in Charleston when he saw the man carrying a bust of Napoleon Bonaparte. Mills claimed that he went to the man and gained instruction in plaster cast making. He caught on quickly and learned the art, fulfilling the phrenologist's odd prediction.[5]

From this early experience, Mills embarked on his career. He quickly progressed from doing casts of his in-laws to making a marble bust of John Calhoun, the famed Southern legislator. As his fame grew, the federal government commissioned Mills to sculpt the famous equestrian portrait of Andrew Jackson in Lafayette Square in Washington (see fig. 2.2). *American Phrenological Journal*'s interview with Mills ended by claiming that phrenology was no mere "humbug," but a legitimate science that in his case redeemed his professional life.[6]

A consideration of contemporary response to Mills's memorial portrait shows how his work was perceived from the time of the federal commission of 1853. Writing at the artist's death in 1883, at least one anonymous critic lambasted the statue as "proof of the bad taste and extravagance of our national legislature," insisting that its appearance failed to justify the $70,000 federal layout for its fabrication. Additionally, the obituary offered a stinging summation of Mills's body of work by stating, "He was an estimable man in private life, but it cannot truthfully be said that art suffers from his departure."[7]

Although Mills's work received mixed critical reaction, undoubtedly reflecting a regional aversion to his Confederate roots among many in the Northern states, his federal patrons nevertheless admired his work. Specifically, at the Jackson statue's inauguration in Washington on 8 January 1853, Mills and his work received high praise from proslavery Senator Stephen Douglas (1813–1861), who would be narrowly defeated in his presidential bid by Abraham Lincoln several years later. Douglas's address is valuable for providing insight into official artistic taste at the time. It also lends a sense of the views of some among the nation's leadership on the broader and more abstract questions of history, heroism, and progress. Referring to Mills, Douglas passionately stated:

> The statue before you is the work of a man exalted by his enthusiasm for the glorious deeds and wise acts of a hero and statesman. It is

the work of a young, untaught American. I cannot call him an artist. He never studied or copied. He never saw an Equestrian Statue, nor even a model. It is the work of inborn genius, aroused to energy by the triumphant spirit of liberty which throbs in the great heart of our continent—which creates the power of great conceptions, the aspiration of the will, the *mental faculty* and the manual skill, to eternalize the actors who ennoble the country, by giving their forms and expressions to imperishable materials.[8]

In his impassioned approval of Mills's work, Douglas clearly appealed to the individualistic, "self-made man" ethos of antebellum American culture. For Douglas, Mills's self-taught background was apparently far from a handicap, and in fact worked in the sculptor's favor. Because of this background, the artist was able to maintain his aura of fierce independence in relation to the northeastern academic establishment. Douglas here assumed that Mills's competence as an artist was therefore the work of "inborn genius" and a "triumphant spirit of liberty," two qualities germane to success in the country's republican democratic order. Interestingly, Douglas went further by citing Mills's "mental faculty." Considering antebellum American culture, it is tempting to read this praise as a phrenological reference. Douglas's choice of the term "faculty" necessarily evoked the pseudoscience in this historical context, because the term most often appeared when phrenologists evaluated a person's cranium to decipher that person's capacities. Also, the notion of an innate "mental faculty" being responsible for artistic "genius" found a welcome parallel in Combe's 1855 text *Phrenology Applied to Painting and Sculpture.* Combe contended that both appreciating and creating fine art are byproducts of favorable phrenological dispositions. For Combe, phrenology was the only way to set up objective standards of beauty for art. Specifically, he said that the capacity to appreciate the "three attributes" that determine beauty in art—"Form," "Proportion," and "Color"—are directly related to one's phrenological faculties of "Form," "Size," and "Color," respectively.[9] In this sense it is significant that Mills's origins as a sculptor—as opposed to his training as a mere plasterer—were the direct result of a phrenological examination.

Visualizing Indianness: The Smithsonian and Ethnographic Collecting

It was in his commission to sculpt the Jackson portrait that Mills would gain artistic credibility in the eyes of officialdom. Not only was the statue a popular artistic success at the time, but Mills's grounding in phrenology was seen as a "scientific" asset in the accurate representation of human types. It was thus that the Smithsonian Institution hired Mills in 1878 to cast his little-known but important plaster life masks of Indian prisoners held at the military prison at Fort Marion, Florida.

Although much of Mills's earlier work was in the service of heroizing cultural exemplars such as Calhoun and Jackson, his work at Fort Marion was intended to prove a different order of aesthetic truth. He was given the enormous commission of completing dozens of plaster life-mask portraits of sixty-four of the young indigenous frontier resisters imprisoned at Fort Marion. This weighty commission, which was to serve as one of the cornerstones of the Smithsonian's ethnographic collection, is a testament to the government's faith in Mills not only as an artistic genius but also as a scientific illustrator. To understand the masks in context, it is necessary to consider the Smithsonian's history as a credible institution of science. Further, it is necessary to analyze the complex collaboration between Mills, Richard Henry Pratt, and the Smithsonian's second secretary, Spencer F. Baird.

Pratt, who would eventually found the Carlisle Indian School in October 1879, spent his early career in the U.S. Army as a young recruiter during the Civil War. Like many of his generation, Pratt would come of age during this conflict, and his resulting views on a host of questions ranging from race to education to science to national identity were shaped by this rupture of national unity. Following his experience in the war, he has written that on receiving his officer's commission in 1867, he was given the uncommon and difficult task of commanding a regiment of African American troops on the frontier.[10]

He and his new command were charged with the unenviable and controversial task of clearing the nation of its indigenous population to make way for white settlement in the West. During this command, Pratt employed several Indian scouts to gain insights into the languages, cultures, and migration patterns of tribes in the Indian Territory (present-day Oklahoma), the area he was to cover. It was in interacting with these scouts that Pratt would later write, "They had manly bearing and fine physiques. Their intelligence, civilization, and common sense were a revelation, because I had concluded that as an army officer I was there to deal with atrocious aborigines."[11]

Pratt's view of the Native tribes was ambivalent and in a sense contradictory. Although he argued that even the so-called Five Civilized Tribes[12] of the Indian Territory lacked a viable history, culture, or past when compared with white civilization, he laid a good portion of the blame for their seemingly degenerate living conditions on the shoulders of the federal government.[13] Pratt felt that the indigenous populations had never received a fair opportunity to prove themselves in the civilized world but had instead been neglected, lied to, and bullied onto reservations by the government. At first glance, Pratt's thinking seems surprisingly progressive and liberal for a man in his position at the time. In fairness to him, it must be noted that he did not favor the then-popular notion that the indigenous population should either be quarantined or physically liquidated. He insisted that the Indian could and should receive education with the aim of cultural integration. This belief would lead to his political activism for the cause of establishing a school for Indians.

While regulating Indian movement on the frontier, it was Pratt's job to enforce treaties such as that signed at Fort Laramie in 1868, which provided for establishing tribal and intertribal reservations on which the Indians were to remain. Pratt and his command were responsible for arresting offenders who rejected these geopolitical boundaries. Pratt sent the fiercest resisters, those who committed what he called "the most outrageous crimes," such as rape, plundering, or murder, to Fort Sill, Indian Territory, the army's most secure frontier prison.[14] According to Pratt, the War Department eventually decided to take these habitual offenders away from the frontier entirely and send them to the East Coast to prevent the spread of their disruptive ways.[15]

To preserve the sanctity of emergent frontier property relations as defined by treaties and legislation such as the Fort Laramie Treaty and the Dawes Act of 1887,[16] young warriors who refused to surrender were deemed "hostile" and isolated from the rest of their tribe. Pratt transported seventy-four of the most notorious frontier resisters from Fort Sill to the Spanish-era military prison of San Marcos (renamed Fort Marion) on the east coast of Florida, hundreds of miles from the front lines of potential conflict.[17]

It was at Fort Marion that Pratt began to consider seriously a new role for the young leaders of the native tribes, and a concurrent role for visual imagery in propagating his ideas. Early photographs of the prisoners, who arrived following an exhausting and fatal[18] journey in the spring of 1875, are often anonymous and qualitatively amateur (see fig. 2.3). They purport to show the unhygienic and seemingly uncivilized condition of the prisoners on arrival. Although these early images were not clever, professional, or systematic in their showing of life at the fort, they nonetheless are forerunners to Pratt's later, more systematic efforts with photography at Carlisle. In the Fort Marion images, one can sense the emergent before-and-after logic that would become the centerpiece of Pratt's propaganda at the school. Compare, for example, figures 2.3 and 2.4. In the latter image, Pratt, his wife, and their infant daughter posed at the far left of the image with the

Indians, presumably to prove the "tameness" of the newly uniformed prisoners. Some early images from Fort Marion were even reproduced as prints in periodicals such as *Harper's Weekly*, and thus reached substantial audiences in the Northeast (see fig. 2.5).

The significant appearance of these images in such a publication reveals what was at stake for the nation. The attempt to govern the seemingly ungovernable resisters was, from the first, high on Washington's political agenda. With this in mind, it logically follows that the viewer was encouraged to infer that in the former image the prisoners were sullen, unkempt, and still largely savage, whereas in the latter image they seem socialized, groomed, and orderly. Pratt claimed that his vocational training program, which he introduced at the prison, was responsible for these seemingly miraculous comparative changes.

In what would later become a centerpiece of his disciplinary school program, Pratt instituted what he termed "industrial" training for the prisoners at Fort Marion. This program was reflective of his belief that the Indian was better served by receiving occupational training while incarcerated. Therefore, to instill a sense of independence and to raise money, Pratt had the prisoners sew clothing, polish seashells, collect fossil specimens, and even give archery lessons to visitors.[19] He designed these menial tasks to force them to interact with the surrounding communities of whites. In this sense, one may see penal, militaristic, and educational discourses converging in his reformist agenda for the prisoners.

This is perhaps unsurprising from a historical perspective, as French philosopher Michel Foucault has noted. In his book *Discipline and Punish*, Foucault argued that one of the central mechanisms of penal control in the modern world is the "reform" of the prisoner, to reabsorb the prisoner's newly disciplined body into the larger social body. Much of this reform is to be carried out in reeducation and regimentation: That is, in retraining the mind and body to force its movements and rhythms to conform to those of mainstream bourgeois culture outside the prison's walls. Further, Foucault has cited the implementation of constant surveillance as another key component of this ethos. Pratt imposed both, as, in addition to his industrial training, he insisted the prisoners guard themselves constantly, even outfitting some with uniforms and weaponry, as figure 2.6 shows. This practice graphically illustrates how he was initially successful in converting his charges into what Foucault termed "objects and instruments of the exercise of power."[20]

Pratt's apparent success with his prisoners, who were thought savage or barbaric by most white Americans, soon brought attention from Washington.

To get a sense of how the public saw these newly civilized charges, one need only consider how the incoming prisoners were initially perceived by even the most astute observers. For instance, on seeing the train on which the prisoners traveled pass by as it approached the fort, even the liberal abolitionist Harriet Beecher Stowe reacted to their exotic appearance:

> Between two and three years ago there passed by us on the St. Johns River a party of captured Indians from our Western Frontiers. They were the men who had been the terror of our settlers, who had done many a deed of savage cruelty and blood . . . being the wildest, the most dangerous, the most untamable of the tribes . . . They were looked upon in their transit with the mingled fear and curiosity with which one regards dangerous wild beasts. Gloomy, scowling, dressed in wild and savage habiliments, painted in weird colors, their hair adorned, they seemed more like grim goblins than human beings . . . one of the number on the transit threw himself from the cars into the palmettos, and was shot as would be a tiger escaped from a managerie.[21]

Stowe's commentary is rife with suggestion and metaphor. Clearly, she shared the perception of many white Americans of the Native. As well as sensing their "wildness" and "savagery," Stowe also expressed ambivalence about their status as human (i.e., by likening them to "wild beasts," "grim goblins," "tiger"). This sense of astonishment at the sight of the famous resisters was one that apparently rendered problematic their social and even biological classification. The spectacle of the Indians traveling from Fort Sill to Fort Marion was one that at first Pratt resented. But as time wore on, the shrewd army officer would learn that such initial impressions might be artificially heightened and subsequently defeated by his deft use of visual imagery. For if Indians were at first seen as only marginally human, Pratt could do little worse by trying to civilize them according to the definitions of the Anglo-American scientific and political establishment.

Besides Stowe, other intellectuals in the country reacted sharply to the prisoners at Fort Marion. Importantly for Pratt and his reformist agenda, Spencer F. Baird of the Smithsonian displayed the most interest in his charges. Baird's interest suggested the perceptual ambivalence many Anglo-American intellectuals experienced when trying to understand these men. On hearing of the prisoners at Fort Marion and Pratt's relative success in bringing the Indians closer to civilization, Baird was enthusiastic and from the start supported Pratt's agenda. The two would correspond on the topic repeatedly from 1877 to 1880, and Baird initially proposed including the prisoners in the Smithsonian's new ethnographic halls:

My mention of the Variety of Indians under your care at St. Augustine, has excited in the minds of several gentlemen who are especially interested in the subject of Indian ethnology, a desire that I should ask from you a list of the tribes represented in your detachment; also whether if some suitable person were sent to St. Augustine, he could have facilities for obtaining from them . . . to a limited number of words, of their tribes respectively. I would also ask, on my own account, whether you think you could induce these Indians to allow a plaster cast to be taken of their faces, to be used in making representations of heads for survey by figures that we have at the Institution. We possess something like 100 full sets of clothing which we desire to make up into life-size figures, but for which we lack a sufficient number of Indian faces. We have had some casts taken here, & other figures made from photographs, but the latter are not very satisfactory, & as we do not wish to duplicate any face, it would be very agreeable to us if we could have good likenesses. The operation is not at all painful, nor even especially uncomfortable, & requires but a short space of time for its accomplishment. I presume that fifty could be taken in one or two days. Perhaps the inducement of being represented in full war panoply at Washington might be a sufficient inducement to accede to the proposition.

Possibly we might also send a photographer to take photographic portraits of the command . . . [22]

This letter is revealing of Baird's early motivation for wanting casts of the Indian heads. Baird was trying to model a "Hall of Native Peoples," one that would become a cornerstone of many natural history museums in the United States in coming decades. Through constructing complex dioramas, Baird wished to have a three-dimensional visual analog that would most accurately represent the ethnographic conditions of life among the nation's indigenous inhabitants—a life defined by ethnologists as pure and untouched by white settlement. The busts made from the casts of the heads were to top off the mannequins that were to be placed in the museum's dioramas, and the indexical[23] quality of the portraits would reinforce the scientific legitimacy of the scenes.

Baird's conception of scientific authenticity and truth was one deeply rooted in his training as a natural historian and scientific generalist. Baird followed his well-rounded education at Dickinson College in Carlisle, Pennsylvania, by extensive field research of indigenous bird and fish species in the Pennsylvania countryside. Like Jefferson, Baird was interested in tracing ancient migratory patterns through examining skeletal remains. His investigations led him to compose detailed encyclopedic classifications of the region's species, something considered a prime task of the naturalist at the time. This work established the young scholar as a leading American authority in the fields of ornithology and ichthyology, and led to his close friendship and collaboration with his fellow ornithologist and painter John J. Audubon (1785–1851). It was this specialty that he brought to the Smithsonian when hired as an assistant secretary in 1850. By the early 1850s, Baird's scientific ambitions, and his ambitions for the Smithsonian, transcended the study of birds and marine life, and he began to move into the area of human life by applying his encyclopedic skills to human subjects. Baird was taking after his mentor Agassiz by developing a keen interest in the biological relationships between different races of human beings.[24]

Baird's interest in the Fort Marion prisoners is unsurprising given the tenor of his early publications. In 1851, he translated, edited, and contributed to German naturalist Johann Heck's *Iconographic Encyclopedia of Science, Literature, and Art*. The multivolume work was a nod to the Enlightenment ethos of museologically classifying all imaginable life-forms, as the title suggests. Baird and Heck used complex illustrations in the support of Heck's classifications of human racial groups, which figures 2.7–2.9 show, basing his conceived racial differences on similar evidence used by phrenology— the human skeletal structure.

Specifically in figure 2.7, which groups bustlike representations from various ethnic groups in a "family of man" arrangement around a racialized global map, various skull types are compared at the bottom. The authors intended the skull illustrations to read from left to right in descending order, as the intersecting lines fixed the various facial angles of different races. In keeping with the principles of natural history, ethnology, anthropology, and phrenology, Baird credited the Caucasian race with the largest average facial angle, and thus that race occupied the premier aesthetic and textual position in that section of the book. Baird considered non-Caucasian races "varieties of mankind," thus eschewing the dehumanizing aspects of Morton's polygenesis. However, he insisted that the question of human ancestry was still "far from solved," and that differences in facial structure may be taken as a valid explanation for differing "character . . . manners . . . and customs."[25] Baird and Heck stopped short of overtly assigning value judgments to the differences in culture between various racial groups, and thus their examination of race may be seen as more properly scientific than that of Morton and Combe. Nevertheless, the positioning of the various groups in the illustrations and text taken together with the contemporary context of discussions about facial angle suggest a bias toward Caucasian superiority.

It is in this intellectual context that Baird wanted busts of the prisoners for the museum's ethnographic collection. Baird was eager to send the Smithsonian's best modelers. He initially selected William Palmer, a sculptor in the museum's employ. In two important letters dated 12 and 14 June 1877, Baird told Pratt of Palmer's initial selection and his subsequent replacement by Mills:

> I have taken advantage of your kind encouragement in regard to the matter of the face masks of the Indians, and one of our most expert modelers (Mr. Wm. Palmer) . . . We send with him four barrels of casting plaster, which will, we hope, be sufficient for his needs. The suggestion to some of our American ethnologists, that through your kindness we were to obtain face masks of these Indians, has been received with extreme interest; & we feel satisfied that no more acceptable addition can be made to our ethnological museum than what will be the first series of such objects, prepared in the United States.
>
> We should be glad to have a good mask of *every* Indian, to be numbered and accompanied by a memorandum of the name, age, tribe, size, and, if possible, the weight. We should also like to have, in a few cases, arms and hands of the Indians, in such attitudes at Mr. Palmer may designate. These will enable us to study the anatomy of those portions of the body, and to use the molds for completing lay figures of the Indians. We will also be glad to have a cast of the entire body in one or more instances, & are willing to pay to any one—say five dollars—for the privilege of obtaining it. Might it not be well, in order to encourage the Indians and show them that the operation is entirely painless and not particularly uncomfortable, to permit yourself to be modeled first? It is an operation that is continually practiced, without more than a slight temporary inconvenience.[26]

Significantly, on agreeing with Mills shortly after writing the letter on June 12, Baird immediately withdrew Palmer and replaced him, seemingly because he perceived Mills to be a superior artist. The work of a simple "modeler" apparently would not do for Baird, which highlights Baird's concern for aesthetics. This faith in Mills testifies to his status in the eyes of many in Washington; he had his studio there and was thus well placed to gain federal commissions. Two days later, Baird would write:

> I wrote you yesterday that we had resolved to send Wm. Palmer, one of our assistants, to St. Augustine to take casts of the Indians. Since then, however, we have been able to make a satisfactory arrangement with Mr. Clark Mills, the eminent sculptor, who will proceed in his stead, & will be able to do the work much better. He has a patent process, by which the whole head & face can be taken without inconvenience, the composition not adhering to the hair, & not being

productive to the slightest annoyance, while the operation takes but three minutes. I will ask him to do you first, so as to encourage the Indians![27]

Baird's shift to Mills as a superior alternative was sparked by the former's wish to strengthen the museum's new collection as much as possible. As the museum's new secretary, and as one who wished to introduce an ethnographic bent to the collection, Baird clearly had a large professional stake in the new ethnographic halls and wished them to reach the highest possible aesthetic similitude. For instance, Baird wrote that he wanted to enhance the realism of the finished busts by having the faces painted "Indian Red,"[28] supporting the aesthetic notion that redness stood as a scientific and artistic metaphor for Indian identity. The aesthetics of the display would seemingly have played the deciding role in the public's reception of the dioramas. This would have been becoming for an institution whose stated mission was to serve as a national museum of science per the mandates of its congressional founding in 1846.[29]

Further, it is also important to consider the perceived status of the life mask as a medium of representation for both artistic production and scientific opinion in the United States at this time. That Baird insisted to Pratt that busts made from mere photographs were not sufficient in arriving at the degree of similitude he needed for his figures betokens the first-order indexicality of the life mask. Many saw the life mask as the superior means by which to get a facsimile of the character of the subject, for good or ill. Because of a life mask's direct imprint from the living subject, scientists and artists saw the busts resulting from this process as more animate and thus credible as representation. Mills was only the latest in a strong and officially approved tradition in life-mask portraiture in the United States.

Dating to 1785, this tradition began in the United States when the French sculptor Jean-Antoine Houdon (1741–1828) made a life mask of George Washington (1732–1799) in preparation for the latter's famous sculptural portrait now in the rotunda of the Virginia state capitol (see fig. 2.10). Thomas Jefferson initiated the idea of preserving the character of cultural exemplars for posterity while he was serving as the government's minister to France. Houdon had previously completed a bust of Benjamin Franklin (1706–1790), Jefferson's predecessor in Paris, and Franklin suggested Houdon for the task of a portrait of Washington.[30] Jefferson recognized the historic import of this potential commission, as he stated in a letter to Virginia Governor William Henry Harrison:

... Of course no statue of Gnl. Washington which might be a true evidence of his figure to posterity could be made from his picture. Statues are made every day from portraits; but if the person be living they are always condemned by those who know him for want of resemblance, and this furnishes a conclusive presumption that similar representatives of the dead are equally unfaithful. Mons. Houdon, whose reputation is such as to make it a principle object, was so anxious to be the person who should hand down the figure of the General to future ages, that without hesitating a moment he offered to abandon his business here, to leave the statues of Kings unfinished, and to go to America to take the true figure by actual inspection and measurement . . . [31]

Jefferson's letter pointed out the benefits of the life mask. Both he and Houdon wished for the sculptor to come to America to do a cast of Washington in person, to give a vital imprint of the subject. Their reluctance to settle for a second-order reproduction, a distaste later echoed by Baird, was clear. Also, Houdon was a meticulous worker and insisted on from-life measurements of Washington's entire body, to secure the most truthful portrayal of his character for posterity. Further, Charles Colbert has suggested that the sculptor Hiram Powers (1805–1873) used Houdon's measurements and one of his finished busts to attain exacting proportions for his own phrenologically inspired busts of Washington in the 1840s and 1850s (see fig. 2.11).[32] The notion that exacting anthropometric measurements had a direct correspondence with the character of the sitter in bust portraiture was seen as a guiding aesthetic principle that underwrote artistic practice from the heights of Enlightenment portraiture through antebellum phrenology to the later mandates of the Smithsonian in securing the life masks of the Fort Marion prisoners.

Baird saw Mills as a viable practitioner in this vein, due largely to his well-known life mask of Abraham Lincoln, executed in February 1865 (see fig. 2.12). Today, this bust is in the collection of the National Portrait Gallery in Washington. Mills produced the mask by first applying a layer of oil to the president's face. This was followed by a thin coat of wet plaster, which took fifteen minutes to dry. After the plaster dried, Mills instructed Lincoln to twitch the muscles of his face, loosening the plaster and allowing Mills to break it off. Mills completed the process by rebuilding the pieces and forming the final mask.[33] This method was similar to the one he would employ in Fort Marion twelve years later.

Because of Mills's place in this lineage of lifelike portraiture, Baird sent him to Florida, and according to Pratt he arrived at Saint Augustine around July 1. From all accounts, Mills worked quickly and efficiently, completing

sixty-four casts that arrived back in Washington by July 28.[34] What remains
in the Smithsonian's collection today are painted plaster busts made from
the original Mills casts, of which figure 2.13 is a sample. Facial molds also
were made from the original masks, of which figure 2.14 is a sample. These
items are unfortunately all that remains of the original Mills casts in the
Smithsonian's collection. These facts, coupled with Baird's original statements about his intent for the casts, as facial complements to the museum's
ethnographic diorama figures, have led to some confusion among anthropologists and art historians who have considered these items.

What is known is that Mills did indeed complete the original casts at
Fort Marion. In fact, in his autobiography, Pratt describes Mills's working
method in detail. Although he and Baird were originally apprehensive that
the prisoners would need to be subjected to the process through force or
bribery, Pratt wrote of his surprise at Mills's ability to complete the task
efficiently:

> The subject was seated in a chair, and a large muslin sheet tucked in
> about his neck to protect his clothing. A flexible cap, fitting close,
> protected the hair. A preparation of plaster which hardened quickly
> was built over the head, the neck, then the ears and face. Breath-
> ing was accomplished through apertures in the nostrils. When the
> material hardened, it was carefully broken, removed, and piece by
> piece built back into form. When this was completed it became the
> perfect mold; a material which prevented the plaster from sticking
> was put over the inside and then a plaster mixture poured within this
> and rolled around until it was made sufficiently thick for shipment.
> When this hardened the mold was broken off and an exact head of
> each subject produced.[35]

Pratt's account is crucial because it is the only one remaining that
details the on-site process of making the original casts and busts. The busts
currently in the institution's collection are not the originals made by Mills,
but exact replicas from the casts made by William Palmer's father, Joseph
Palmer, a modeler on staff at the museum. Joseph Palmer (1836–1913), born
in England, served as taxidermist, modeler, and restorer at the Smithsonian
for decades following his emigration to the United States in 1868. According
to the Natural History museum's website, Joseph Palmer served as the museum's chief preparator for some time, and besides being a skilled sculptor he
also painted colors onto his figures. He was seemingly skillful in modeling
lay figures for dioramas, and thus may have painted the heads as well.[36]
Interestingly, Palmer's dual expertise in taxidermy and anthropological lay
figures suggests how the fields of zoology and anthropology overlapped

conceptually at the time. Such an overlapping, coupled with the establishment of primitive dioramas representing the nation's indigenous cultures, shows how the museum assigned the Indian an evolutionary role existing in the realm of natural history more than in that of human history.

These replicas were executed before 1947, when the busts and face masks made their way into the museum's physical anthropology department.[37] Assuming they are the work of Palmer after Mills, they would obviously have to date from some time between 1877, the date they arrived back in Washington from Fort Marion, and 1913, when Palmer died. Therefore, questions remain about the intent and status of the original collection.

The museum's current curator, David Hunt, has stated that the originals are lost and the original intent of the casts was *not* pseudoscientific in the phrenological sense. Hunt bases his assertion on the correct information that Mills originally used flexible skullcaps when taking the molds, to protect the subjects' hair.[38] Pratt's description of the casting confirms that Mills used skullcaps, as does the smooth texture and drab, unpainted coloring on the crowns of the current busts, which Baird intended to bear wigs simulating an "Indian" hairstyle. However, these considerations do not dismiss the possibility of an underlying pseudoscientific motivation for the casts and resulting busts. The motivation for the original casts and busts is an important point. It was the nature of the prisoners that Pratt often pointed to when arguing for the subsequent need for boarding-school reeducation for the nation's indigenous population.

In fact, Baird's own discourse surrounding the making and later cataloging and display of the Mills busts would confirm the presence of at least some pseudoscientific preconception of the prisoners. The *Proceedings of the National Museum for 1878* and the correspondence between Baird and Mills shed further light on the question. As secretary of the Smithsonian, Baird was responsible for gathering and publishing the annual *Proceedings*, a multivolume publication that gave a yearly summation of the museum's significant acquisitions and discoveries. Baird discusses the Pratt-Mills collaboration in Volume 1 of the 1878 *Proceedings*:

> The attention of anthropologists in later years has been directed very closely to the *shape of the head, of the lineaments, and of the external form generally* of mankind during life, instead of being confined to the cranium and the skeleton, and every opportunity of securing accurate casts, in plaster, of the native races of a country is eagerly embraced . . . It has always been difficult to obtain face casts of the North American Indians. They manifest a deeply rooted aversion to the process required . . . a superstitious fear generally of being

imitated in any manner, even by the pencil or camera . . . no difficulty was experienced in securing these casts, as the Indians had
every confidence in the statements of Captain Pratt, who had them
in command, that there would be nothing detrimental to either soul
or body in the process, and indeed, he himself was first subjected to
it to reassure them.[39]

In this explanation, Baird invoked the rhetoric of then-current research
methods of physical anthropology, in which a comparative anthropometric
measurement was thought to be a valid external indicator of a culture's
social evolution. Thus, Baird did indeed wish to transcend the narrow confines of phrenological investigation, but in so doing, he favored the more
legitimate and therefore powerful discourse of physical anthropology. In
wanting to get beyond the exclusive study of the "cranium and the skeleton," Baird wished for a more comprehensive anthropometric and thus
cultural comparison between races, one that in the later nineteenth century
would supplant phrenology in scientific legitimacy.[40] To confirm this view
of Baird's scientific orientation, one need only consider the importance of
anthropometrics in the writings of Baird's contemporary Lewis Henry
Morgan (1818–1881), then the leading exponent of the emergent American
School of physical anthropology.

In his principal work, *Ancient Society* (1877), Morgan made an ambitious
attempt to track the cultural evolution of variously defined racial groups.
He focused chiefly on an extended anthropological comparison between
the Iroquois tribe of New York state and white civilization. Among the
criteria Morgan used in this comparative effort is the "geometric" trajectory
of various cultures, from the "primitive" stages of savagery and barbarism
to the advanced stage of civilization. Although he admitted that all people
ultimately belong to the "human family," Morgan's central concern was to
determine why particular groups have either failed or succeeded in evolving
out of the lower stages of existence, according to his definitions of these
stages. Morgan was therefore trying to establish an aesthetic outline of the
"shape" of time in evolutionary terms, with human physiology as the central
metaphor in the discussion.

Specifically, Morgan claimed that one may see the relative cultural
attainment in differing racial groups by referring to various environmental
and physiological conditions of human existence. The two key concepts for
him were "discoveries and inventions" made by various groups, and "external institutions," such as marriage, private property, and forms of government. Morgan argued that throughout history, as societies made discoveries
in the progressive mastery of nature, the brains of those groups best suited

to master the environment grew as a result. He therefore implicitly credits what he terms the "Aryan" race as having the most developed mental organ, something that presumably one may verify empirically.[41]

In this sense, we may understand the emphasis on the aesthetic proportion of the human head and skeleton as measures of the anthropological attainment of civilization, here defined as the progressive mental and physical mastery of the environment. Although the polygenic thesis of Morton was jettisoned by the next generation of scientists, who were trying to make sense of race, anthropometric differences as seen in skull size and proportion were reconceptualized to fit in with physical anthropological knowledge.

Further, Baird requested from Pratt a detailed list of the alleged atrocities and crimes committed by each prisoner.[42] This is curious, as one may question why or how such knowledge would be relevant to a display intended to show the "natural" conditions of various indigenous American tribes before Euro-American incursion. Baird went on to publish Pratt's list of atrocities in the 1878 *Proceedings*. Each corresponded to the bust of a particular prisoner. Also, he noted the physical dimensions, age, and tribe of each prisoner, as well as that person's "consanguity," or racial makeup. For instance, in the case of Zotom, Baird described the young man as follows:

> 30713 (38) Zo-tom (Biter)- *Warrior*
> Arrested at Salt Fork, Red River, Indian Territory, February 18, 1875.
> Was in party headed by Mah-mante, killing two colored men on Salt Creek Prairie, between Jackson and Belknap, Texas, 1870 or 1871. Participated in the attack on buffalo hunters at Adobe Walls, early in spring 1871.[43]

In addition to this rap sheet, as it were, Baird listed Zotom in a statistical chart with all the other prisoners. The chart outlined each prisoner's tribe, tribal rank, height, weight, age, indigenous name, English-language name, and the museum's accession number of his bust. Therefore, each subject was given a totalizing, minute, and in a sense dehumanizing statistical breakdown.

This treatment is perhaps unsurprising, however, when we also consider the newly credible and systematized ethos of criminology, which was arising as a twin science to physical anthropology in the 1870s in the United States and England. The lists of the *Proceedings*, when considered with the visual evidence of the busts and masks, are reminiscent of Alphonse Bertillon's (1853–1914) synoptic cards, an example of which figure 2.15 shows, then first being put into practice by metropolitan police forces in the Northeast.[44]

Alphonse Bertillon, prefecture of police in Paris during this era, developed an internationally renowned archival system by which to survey and identify arrestees. Bertillon's synoptic method went beyond individual identification and created a matrix of anthropometric measurements that he theorized all criminal types shared in common. From Bertillon, law enforcement in the United States absorbed the modern criminological notion that criminals have a particular look and share a recognizable set of physiological traits such as facial proportion. Bertillon's card represented perhaps the logical conclusion of this compulsive data gathering as a form of archival surveillance and power. Police could conveniently compile the information in one place, with photographic index and fragments of data lined up in a mutually supporting logic of surveillance. The cards served as a convenient device intended to provide law enforcement with a summation of the subject's existence in society.[45] In this sense, while the Fort Marion prisoners were ethnologically classified, they were simultaneously subjected to the new forms of criminological classification. The life mask portrait was the central link in the proof of their newly assigned sociobiological identities.

Finally, besides the phrenological grounding of Mills and the anthropometric concerns of Baird, the written correspondence between Mills and Baird sheds a more direct light on the pseudoscientific conception of the prisoners and the bust project. In a stunning slew of letters to Baird, Mills frankly offered his views of the Native American prisoners, and took their alleged phrenological predispositions and current condition of confinement as a prophetic sign of the fate of their race:

> We have completed all the Indian casts . . . they are undoubtedly the most important collection of Indian heads in the world, and when they have become extinct, as which fate is inevitable, posterity will see a facsimile of a race of men that once over ran this great country not only their physiognomies but phrenological development also.[46]

This letter clearly dispels any notion that phrenology and physiognomy were no longer underlying concerns in the aesthetic rendering, collecting, and resulting display of ethnographic subject matter following the Civil War. Significantly, Mills would present a sinister scientific basis for the emerging "Vanishing Race" discourse surrounding the existence of indigenous Americans around the fin de siècle.

In art historical terms, this notion would turn out to be a dominant one. It would be central to Euro-American representation of the Indian in projects ranging from Remington's famous frontier imagery to Edward S.

Curtis's mammoth photographic survey of the early twentieth century (see fig. 2.16). In all such cases, the "scientific" fact of extinction, based on anthropometric evidence and a social evolutionary rationale, was deployed under the guise of a neo-Romantic aesthetic trope to sooth memories of frontier atrocity and imprisonment.⁴⁷ In another startlingly frank letter, Mills would go on to confirm in technical phrenological terms his assessment of the heads he had just cast:

> When I began taking the casts of the Indians I found the size of the brain fully up to the average of the white race—I thought all that was necessary for them was education, but as I advanced I found that one set of [phrenological] organs were more fully developed than others . . . First, self-esteem was very large making them self-reliant—Distructiveness [*sic*] & Secretiveness large, the first having to kill their food, second having to obtain by stealth and strategy—Aliementiveness very large lives to eat—Locality large never gets lost—Eventuality—large, never forgets an event . . . Caution when developed is an exception to the race—It seems that those largely developed organs having been cultivated over so many generations have become permanent, they are transmitted to the posterity . . .⁴⁸

In his laundry list of phrenological faculties, Mills revealed to Baird how his early enthusiasm for the prospects of the indigenous tribes (Pratt claimed that Mills once referred to Zotom as, " . . . as perfect a specimen of physical manhood as he had ever met . . .") was gradually dashed. According to Mills, this was due to the "realities" of their relative organ development and the genetic inevitability of their respective behavioral pathologies. In Mills's pronouncements, one may see a summation of the plethora of racial stereotypes, both positive and negative, that phrenology and other sciences affixed to the Native American throughout the nineteenth century. Such stereotypes would subsequently inform both artistic practice and popular opinion. Mills's ambivalence was also reflective of the larger ambivalence of the political leadership toward the Indian Question, and the varying status of the Indian in the white mind. Most important in this letter is Mills's verdict on the prospect of Indian education and thus the overall capacity of a race to alter its destiny through proactive means.

This question was the central one involved in the founding of Carlisle, and one that sharply divided the nation's leadership. Given that Pratt would always publicly come down on the affirmative side of the issue, it raises the uncomfortable question of why he agreed to Baird's ethnographic project with such unqualified enthusiasm. If he believed that the Indian had no valid history or culture of his own, and the Indian therefore had to be uplifted from savagery to civilization, it is curious that he allowed the prisoners to be cataloged by the Smithsonian. Such treatment would imply a static cultural status suited only for exhibitory evidence of the trajectory of natural history. Such a gesture would surely have confirmed racial stereotypes held by many in the nation, and would further reinforce the notion of the Indian as a member of a "dying race." The troubling and complex relationships between visual representation, pseudoscience, legitimate sciences (such as anthropology and criminology), and boarding-school education would inform his founding of the school.

3

Producing Americans
Photography and Indoctrination at Carlisle

Photography, Race, and the Exigencies of Representation

In discussing the photographic production at Carlisle, it is first helpful to consider the school and its visual discourses against a more general backdrop. For although Pratt was trying to proffer specific notions of "race" and "Indianness" as categories through their visualization, his efforts are best understood when considering larger theoretical issues about race and photography in Victorian American culture.

This material's meaning is greatly illuminated when we consider it in relation to ideas promoted by the recent exhibition Only Skin Deep: Changing Visions of the American Self. This exhibition, curated by art historians Coco Fusco and Brian Wallis, was held at the International Center of Photography in New York in 2003–2004. It represents the most significant recent attempt to explain the complex relationship between race and photography in American cultural history.

In her introductory essay for the exhibition catalog, Fusco argues that as we try to uncover the ideological underpinnings of racial photography in the United States between circa 1840 and 1945, it is important to recognize that "race" was a culturally produced category subject to deployment, revision, and contestation. As a theoretical starting point, she sees this recognition as critical to understanding that race in photography is thus not a biological or naturally occurring category, as was often assumed during the period considered by the exhibition.[1]

It is important for this discussion that Fusco notes that the photographing of race, whether done for ostensibly "scientific" or "artistic" purposes, constituted a teleological form of representation. The seemingly straightforward appearance of these photographs, apparently offering a view into the cultural or biological reality of a given subject, disavows their intricately performed mise-en-scènes. In other words, white photographers would enter an already colonized space, such as the American West, and make photographs claiming to show indigenous subjects in their pure or primitive states, as if unfettered by the effects of Eurocentric industrial modernization. Photographers often turned such images into commodities by selling them to white audiences for purposes of ethnographic edification or vicarious pleasurable viewing, something done by Pratt to raise funds for the school. Fusco goes on to argue that such forms of representation and viewership reinforced colonial relations of racial and political domination.[2]

Finally, and perhaps most significant for Carlisle's brand of photography, Fusco points out that racial Otherness as a representational category in photography can exist only in tacit comparison to whiteness. That is, one is not Other in a cultural or racial sense unless one is posited as Other in relation to an assumed racial or cultural norm. In colonial photography, photographers assumed this norm to be white. In this context, she argues that whiteness is "the capacity to masquerade as a racial other without actually being one." Therefore, photographers sought to perform a racial transvestism in their images. Whites could vicariously consume the Other viewed in the photograph, and the Other could be made either more primitive or whiter, depending on the political exigencies of the moment. For Fusco, the upshot of this in the United States of circa 1840–circa 1945 was the notion that photography could therefore prove the civilizing and beneficial effects of what she terms "white Americanness."[3] It will now be helpful to consider photographic practice at Carlisle with Fusco's conception of white Americanness in mind, as these photographs graphically illustrate the critical ideas forwarded in this exhibition.

Pratt, Choate, and the Politics of Photographing Indians

As discussed in chapter 2, from the earliest phases in the planning for his school, Pratt recognized the efficacy of photography in promoting his efforts and bolstering the dual ideologies of Americanization and civilization. Pratt, like most other educated men of the time, was tacitly aware of the assumed realism photography proffered as a medium of representation. When he wrote of photography, he characteristically took two tacks when discussing the medium with others. In his correspondences, he would often assume a transparent, windowlike perception, in which the photograph functioned as an unquestioned and unproblematic copy of physical reality. For instance, when Pratt wrote to Rutherford B. Hayes on 25 January 1880, he opened his letter to the president by referring to photographs of the students, as if the images were unquestionable proof of the school's early success:

> A few days since I ventured to send you views of the buildings and groups of the Sioux youth here.
> I hope your interest in this feature of your administration will increase as it ought. It has grown up under your encouragement and will not fail in itself to demonstrate your wisdom. I believe it is destined to expand and urge forward all Indian education work to meet the needs of the Indians . . .
> . . . I am glad to report that we have the greatest encouragement to go ahead. Our students meet our highest hopes. The influence has reached to other tribes than those represented here; tribes like the Navajoes [*sic*] and Utes who have taken no interest in education heretofore.[4]

Similarly, in a letter to Representative Thaddeus Coleman Pound dated 14 January 1880, Pratt opened with an appeal to photographic truthfulness:

> I send you today a few stereo views of the Indian youth here. You will note that they came mostly as blanket Indians. A very large proportion of them had never been inside of a school room. I am gratified to report that they have yielded gracefully to discipline and that our school rooms, in good order, eagerness to learn, actual progress, etc., are, to our minds, quite up to the average of those of our own race. Isolated as these Indian youth are from the savage surroundings of their homes, they lose their tenacity to savage life, which is so much of an obstacle to Agency efforts, and give themselves up to learning all they can in the time they expect to remain here. [5]

In this letter, Pratt invoked the familiar reference to his new charges as "blanket Indians" on their arrival, in juxtaposition to the "actual progress" the students had made since being at the school. Pratt often invoked the term blanket Indian to deride those Native Americans still clinging to the savage ways of their preindustrial past. For him, the blanket Indian was a perversely atavistic figure, one at odds with positivist notions of progress and civilization. With the photographs, Pratt clearly wished to represent the "improvement" of his students over the brief time since they arrived at the school. Although many had *not* "yielded gracefully to discipline," he nevertheless intended the images to send the message that all had.[6]

Although Pound, a representative from Wisconsin, was an early supporter of congressional funding for Carlisle, Pratt desperately needed proof
of the school's early successes, because congressional opinion on his project
was sharply divided. The images to which Pratt is most likely referring in
these letters are three in particular made by John Nicholas Choate (1848–
1902), a professional photographer from the town of Carlisle whom Pratt
employed as the institution's official photographer from the school's opening in 1879 to Choate's death in 1902. (See figs. 3.1–3.3.)

By most historical accounts, Pratt's and Choate's collaboration was
largely successful in convincing the government elites that the school
deserved funding in its early years. Despite the political minefield Pratt had
to navigate in securing funds for the school, he was successful in attracting
substantial federal funding, and with Pratt's political savvy, Choate's photographs played the central role in this success.[7] According to historian David
Wallace Adams, following Carlisle's opening in October 1879, congressional funding for Indian education rose dramatically from $75,000 in 1880 to
nearly $3 million in 1900, just before Pratt's departure from the school.[8]

Further, Pratt made use of Choate's before-and-after portraits in several contexts (see figs. 3.4a and 3.4b).[9] One of the most important was to
convince indigenous leaders such as the Sioux chief Standing Bear to send
their own children to the schools. The historical record shows that Pratt
was also successful in this vein, as total boarding school attendance rose
from 4,651 in 1880 to 21,568 in 1900.[10] It is therefore important to consider
Choate's status and skill as a professional photographer as well as to conduct an analysis of some of his most well-known and effective imagery of
the school.

John Nicholas Choate was a successful regional photographer in central
Pennsylvania during the middle to late nineteenth century. And although
it is tempting to label Choate as simply a provincial photographer of little
importance, he was clearly instrumental in getting the Carlisle project off
the ground and securing credibility for Pratt's school. Further, he was not
a naïve photographer: He was careful and shrewd in self-promotion and
in marketing his images of the school and its students. Finally, his images
suggest a technical skill clearly beyond the scope of any amateur or week-
end photographer.

Despite Choate's central role in mediating public perception of the
school, Pratt rarely credited his photographer. As his personal letters reveal,
Pratt failed to mention Choate by name when writing to either President
Hayes or Representative Pound. What is known is that Choate was born
to a poor sharecropper in rural Maryland in 1848. Following the death of

his father in the Civil War, Choate worked as a farmhand for many years. From these inauspicious beginnings, he arrived in Carlisle in 1875, and had by then married a young woman whose brother was a professional portrait photographer in Altoona, Pennsylvania, named Edson McKillip. It is likely that Choate learned the trade from McKillip and was soon doing portraits and on-site landscapes in and around Carlisle professionally. In fact, Choate was so successful that he not only acquired a traveling studio that facilitated his landscape shots, as figure 3.5 shows, but he also opened a portrait studio in downtown Carlisle, only blocks from the site of the future Indian school.[11]

Like most serious photographers of his generation, Choate used the collodion/albumen glass-plate process popular at the time. Albumen was a positive/negative process initially developed by English sculptor Frederick Scott Archer in the early 1850s that combined the best of both the daguerreotype and calotype while overcoming the limitations of both. It combined large-format printing, detail, subtle tonal gradations, and reproducibility. By 1879, when the school opened, Choate had made hundreds of glass-plate negatives and stereographic cards of Carlisle, its inhabitants, and the surrounding countryside.[12]

Therefore, when Pratt employed him, Choate already had a large business and was the most respected photographer in the region. This reputation was largely a product of Choate's entrepreneurial self-fashioning. One of his primary techniques of self-promotion was producing cabinet cards and *cartes de visite* during his early years as a photographer. The card that figure 3.6 shows tells the prospective patron of Choate's dual professional ambitions: his studio is characterized as both "art store" and "photographic rooms." These words appear on a serpentine-styled ribbon, which encircles the recurrent motif in Choate's self-fashioning, a palette with brushes. The use of this symbol would signal that Choate had ambitions of being taken seriously as an artistic photographer, something that may seem surprising at first, considering the rather ethnographic content of much of his work. On the palette appears another recurrent symbol in Choate's advertising, a rising sun. The association of sunlight with photographic practice was a provocative and common symbol used by professional photographers in the United States at this time. One is reminded of the more famous use of a similar symbol by Eadweard Muybridge, who for a time went under the professional pseudonym Helios.[13]

In both cases, the association between the photographer and natural sunlight conveyed a sense of the photographer as an Apollonian all-seeing observer harnessing solar light in the faithful recording of nature. This was of course a key idea in nineteenth-century photography and was a cultural identity embraced by many ambitious professionals. Choate intended such symbolism to indicate that, far from being an insular provincial figure in photography, he was aware of larger conceptual and professional trends in the field. Like others in his field, Choate wanted to embody technical competence, documentary credibility, and artistic creativity in photography.

New Arrivals: To the Ends of the Earth

Choate executed the images that figures 3.1–3.3 show, the first made at the school, on 5 and 6 October 1879, the date when the original group of youths arrived via transcontinental rail from the Lakota Sioux reservation in what was then the Dakota Territory.[14] These important images therefore represent the initial photographic discourse at the institution and thus warrant closer consideration than they have traditionally received in scholarship on this topic.

With the first image, Choate opted for an iconic compositional formula in which he had the arriving male students sit and stand in the photograph's middle ground and stare out at the camera in a flat, rigid arrangement. Their appearance in the picture's middle ground, in front of the geometric, paramilitary barracks–style architecture of the school grounds while flanked by an authoritative-looking Pratt on the far left and an indigenous translator on the right was hardly coincidental. Such a stark composition would become the most favored by Pratt because it conveyed a sense of orderliness and submission on the parts of the new arrivals—crucial elements in his political propaganda.

The photographer made this image, like hundreds of others done at Carlisle by him and other white photographers under Pratt's instruction, with the expectations and preconceptions of Pratt's intended audience in mind. Most immediate and important in this vein were members of Congress and the presidential administration. Pratt viewed such photographic choices as necessary, because they effectively conveyed the appearances and bearing of these "blanket Indians" on their arrival at the school. Further, such a perception—of the indigenous American as savage and thus evolutionarily *retardataire*—was inherited from physical anthropology and earlier pseudoscience. It was one shared by most educated Euro-American men of the day, and thus fostered a teleological view in Pratt's audience. In other words, his main concern in the early photographs of the students was to reinforce the preexisting stereotypes of these students through deploying an appropriate photographic aesthetic.

Also significant in figure 3.1 is the direction of Pratt's own gaze. He stands on the far left of the image, slightly set off from the body of students. Pratt assumes a stiff and formal posture and is dressed in typically upper-middle-class Victorian masculine attire. His presence serves not only the necessary comparative visual function next to the savage bodies, but he also gazes intently to his left, paternalistically surveying his new charges. Not only does his civilized dress and bearing contrast sharply with the disheveled, exhausted, and sullen look of the students, but Pratt's intent gaze signifies an ethos of surveillance that would become a cornerstone of discipline at Carlisle. Pratt and other administrators constantly watched students on the campus grounds. More importantly perhaps, the students were continuously monitored by absentee, invisible off-site authorities via Choate's photographs. Further, the architectural layout of the school grounds, like that at Fort Marion, allowed Pratt to impose a panoptic ethos on the school's charges.[15]

Interestingly, however, this print contains one element perhaps unintended and even unwanted by Pratt. Along the bottom of the print, Choate's signature is still visible. Despite Choate's authorial gesture, Pratt rarely if ever mentioned Choate's name during the roughly quarter century that the latter served as the school's photographer. For instance, in the letters cited earlier, Pratt failed to credit Choate as author of the images. It was as if he was consciously trying to repress reference to an authorship for the images. This is not surprising. Pratt forwarded notions of photography in which authorship and execution were secondary to the ostensibly realistic content of the image itself.

Such a view of the medium's status was of course not specific to Pratt, but was a more widely held view of photographic representation in nineteenth-century Anglo-American culture. As concerning photographic portraiture, perhaps William Henry Fox Talbot put it best, writing in 1839 at the dawn of the medium's development:

> Another purpose for which I think my method will be found very convenient, is the making of outline portraits, or *silhouettes*. These are now often traced by the hand from shadows projected by a candle. But the hand is liable to err from the true outline, and a very small deviation causes a notable diminution in the resemblance. I believe this manual process cannot be compared with the truth and fidelity with which the portrait is given by means of solar light.[16]

The notion of portraits being exact recordings of the subject's "true outline" as produced by the "solar light" or "pencil of nature," as Fox Talbot alternately termed it, would be one attractive to Pratt. He was using a medium perceived in Anglo-American culture as being beyond convention, flawless, or, as Fox Talbot put it, beyond the "err" of the artist's hand.

The issue of photographic similitude would come up again in figure 3.3, the image this time of the female arrivals sexually segregated and photographed separately. This composition places the frazzled and tired young women in a parallel position opposite the camera. They are flanked by the same indigenous translator and Miss Sarah Mather, a professional teacher from the reservation who agreed to accompany Pratt and the children to Carlisle.[17] Mather, like Pratt, stands in a constrained, formal, Victorian-era pose while wearing the fashions of a middle-class Victorian Euro-American woman, down to the detail of the sun-blocking parasol in her right hand. She gazes intently to her left, surveying the girls, obviously echoing Pratt's gesture from the first photograph. The girls, like the boys, are compositionally boxed not only by the two harbingers of civilization (that is, Mather and the Indian translator in the suit), but by the severe military-style architecture of the school grounds, formerly a U.S. Army barracks.

Significantly, this image also engages the issue of gender. Although the boys in the previous image stand facing the camera rigidly, staring back in what may be perceived as defiance, the girls assume a much more timid posture. Many fold their hands and pull their blankets over themselves in a defensive gesture while assuming worried, frightened expressions. Others avert their gazes anxiously and don't even engage the camera. This gendered differentiation is unsurprising when one considers conventional gender roles in Lakota Sioux culture, the reservation from which most of the earliest Carlisle class arrived. Perhaps Plenty Kill, one of the initial male arrivals, best described the sharp difference in gender roles within the tribe.

Plenty Kill, later known by his Christianized name Luther Standing Bear, was the young son of the Sioux chief Standing Bear. Pratt sought such recruits, and even went to the Rosebud Agency on the Sioux reservation eagerly in search of the children of the most distinguished members of the Sioux nation. Plenty Kill is visible in the first male group photograph lying prostrate on the ground in front of the group. His head points toward where Pratt stands. In his famous autobiography, *My People, the Sioux*, Standing Bear wrote about how their elders prepped the young men of the nation for their long journey. He explained what he was thinking during his first meeting with Pratt in the early fall of 1879, in which the latter was pitching the idea of the new school to the children of the Sioux leadership:

My mind was working in an entirely different channel. I was thinking of my father, and how he had many times said to me, "Son, be
brave! Die on the battle-field [*sic*] if necessary away from home. It is
better to die young than to get old and sick and then die." When I
thought of my father, and how he had smoked the pipe of peace, and
was not fighting any more, it occurred to me that this chance to go
East would prove that I was brave if I were to accept it.[18]

Standing Bear suggests why the male students might appear more defi-
ant, direct, or confrontational in their group portrait. Not only had they
just endured an extended journey by train that none had ever experienced
before, but they had no idea what lay ahead. Later in his account, Standing
Bear would write that the young contingent felt that they were going to
the end of the earth and might fall off the edge.[19] Despite the terror of
the unknown and the extreme claustrophobia of the train ride, the boys
had thoroughly internalized their obligatory male Sioux subjectivity and
resigned themselves to their fate, a posture indicative of the brave men-
tality. In such a context, an overt display of fear in the face of the captors
would have been a sign of cowardice and dishonor. The dishonor would
have reflected not only on their own individual characters, but according to
the mandates of Sioux patriarchal culture, would also reflect on their male
ancestors. Significantly, Standing Bear chose to characterize the new venue
as a "battle-field." Perceiving assimilation as constituting a metaphoric battlefield was not only in keeping with the Sioux warrior ethos but ironically
paralleled Pratt's own characterization of the entire assimilationist effort,
as the title of his autobiography, *Battlefield and Classroom*, suggests.

Choate's signature is again just visible along the bottom of this positive
print of the female group. Choate sold this particular image commercially
in stereographic format.[20] It was therefore likely one of the images Pratt
had sent to Pound when he referred to the "stereo views" in his letter of
14 January 1880. Not only were the image and the people in it turned into a
commodity on the photographic marketplace, but the image was also produced and sold in the enhanced photographic format of the stereograph,
then wildly popular in the United States.

The stereoscope, a tool for viewing stereographic photographs, was
first developed by Scottish scientist David Brewster in 1849. The idea of
a stereographic photograph was known in the early 1830s, and was familiar to Fox Talbot. However, it was not popular in the United States until
Oliver Wendell Holmes invented an improved and cheaper stereoscopic
viewer in 1861. The stereograph was popular because of its perceived hyper-
realistic appearance. The photographer would set up one or more cameras

side by side and photograph the same scene from slightly different angles. Alternatively, an original single image could simply be printed twice. Then, the photographer would paste the two images side by side onto a cardboard mount. Viewers would look at the mounted images through the stereo-scope. The viewer placed mounted prints on a crosspiece in front of two lenses placed side by side.[21] When the viewer held the device up to the eyes, the stereographic images would appear to merge, producing a false three-dimensionality that appeared to jump off the prints and occupy the physical space in front of the viewer. The stereograph provided a more heightened simulation than the two-dimensional print, highlighting the perceived credibility of the representation.

With this device, the consumer of Choate's imagery could possess the Indian girls not only visually, but almost tactilely. Such an activity takes on a sinister note when one considers that stereoscopic images of ethnic and cultural Others were popular in the Western world at the time. They were often symbolic images which told of an imperialistic desire to occupy and control the spaces and bodies of such Others. Holmes, the American popularizer of the stereoscope, put it passionately:

> Oh, infinite volumes of poems that I treasure in this small library of glass and pasteboard! I creep over the features of Rameses, on the face of his rockhewn Nubian temples; I scale the huge mountain-crystal that calls itself the Pyramid of Cheops . . . I stroll through Rhenish vineyards, I sit under Roman arches, I walk the streets of once buried cities, I look into the chasms of Alpine glaciers, and on the rush of wasteful cataracts. I pass, in a moment, from the banks of the Charles to the ford of the Jordan, and leave my outward frame in the arm-chair at my table, while in spirit I am looking down upon Jerusalem from the mount of Olives.[22]

In typically poetic prose, Holmes outlined the vicarious experience of the stereograph. The Boston Brahmin found himself transported spiritu-ally from his "arm-chair" position on the Charles River to some of the most exotic tourist locales in the Western world, such as Egypt, the Middle East, and the Alps. Although the subject matter in the Choate stereograph is not nearly as far-flung, an exoticized perception was undoubtedly still present for his intended audience of upper-middle-class Euro-Americans. Further, although any people considered Other by Anglo-America were perceived as exotic, many assumed the stereograph granted the viewer some viable form of knowledge about the subject in the image, a quality of the medium often lauded by Holmes and others. Holmes's reference to the stereograph as a "small library of glass and pasteboard" bears out this view. Therefore, many consumers saw such images as didactic as well as entertaining. Thus, one could gain some knowledge about the dress and therefore the customs of the continent's indigenous population.[23]

The specific perceptual context for this image of the school's first female students may be read in an even more disturbing light, however. Images of Native American women were prolific in nineteenth-century American photography. Although many claimed to be mainly ethnographic, conveying visual data about subjects such as fashion, hairstyles, facial features, bodily proportion, environment, or tools and implements, others served as commodities intended to overtly eroticize the subject. Art historian Aleta Ringlero has written that the photographing of nude or seminude Native women became a profitable cottage industry at this time for many white photographers, such as Will Soule (1836–1908).[24] Soule and others working in this genre would take these young women to their studios and dress them in stereotyped, nonspecific clothing, pose them in a clichéd odalisque-like position, and surround them with artificial props intended to simulate a frontier landscape. Figure 3.7 shows an example of such a photograph. Photographers could then convert the images into cartes de visite and sell them to a mostly Euro-American public as curiosities. In her text, Ringlero argues that such imagery had a dual valence for its intended audience. On one hand, the young women were seen as enticing and eroticized; on the other hand, they were representative, in the white mind, of the danger and unhygienic living conditions of frontier life.[25]

It is in this dichotomy that we may realize a broader possible meaning of this image for Choate's contemporary audience. Although the dichotomized stereotype of the young Indian brave was that of the Noble Savage—Scalper, that of young Native women was balanced between the degenerate squaw and the sexually enticing seducer. Regardless of the content of a specific stereotype, photographs produced and mediated knowledge of young Indians. What Pratt wanted, then, was to rescue these girls from their culturally degenerate living conditions as he perceived them. In short, he eventually attempted to convert young indigenous women from unhygienic squaws into Victorian matrons by countering the former image with an improved image showing the effects of life at Carlisle. Figure 3.8 shows an example of this improved image. Pratt wanted domestication. This clash of cultures is never rendered in overtly sexual form in Carlisle imagery. Yet it is tacitly present not only in before-and-after images of the female students but also in the arrival image of figure 3.3, as viewers are invited to compare the proper Miss Mather with the comparatively uncivilized and thus unhygienic girls.[26]

In figure 3.2, Choate presents us with what would turn out to be a rarity in Carlisle photography. In this image, he arranged the male students in a surprisingly informal manner, with some sitting, some standing, and others leaning over the railing of the second floor of the nearby dormitory building. In an interesting change, Pratt is absent from this less-formal group portrait—the Indian interpreter, the intermediary between the Sioux language and English, is the only representative of authority. Choate also composed the picture differently than the other two. The first two are comparatively more iconic because they are straightforward, with the students neatly boxed in compositionally between the administrative supervisors, the interpreter, and the dormitory buildings and trees behind.

In contrast, Choate here chose to show the students arranged not only informally, but at a more oblique angle in relation to the building, which in turn juts out into the picture space more aggressively than in the first image of the boys. Although the image of the female arrivals displays a building at a similarly oblique angle, their facial expressions and postures differ significantly from those of the male arrivals. Their comparatively submissive postures in turn suggest a gendered narrative at play in which the appearance of the boys, with their direct gazes, suggests an air of hostility and confrontation. In this sense, the viewer must confront this array of young men, most of whom bear the typically sullen, confused, frightened, and resentful air of boarding-school students newly arrived following a harsh multiday train ride from the reservations. It is therefore tempting to see a sense of danger in this image, because the rigid order of the first has partially dissolved.

The students seen here, still clad in their ostensibly savage clothing and still bearing their trademark long flowing hair, likely would have offered a slightly more unsettling and even threatening appearance to the contemporary viewer. Such a suggestion is more believable when one considers the inherited knowledge about indigenous Americans. Not only were such people likely seen as exotic or as some ethnographic curiosity, but as I discussed in chapter 2, were also, more disturbingly, perceived in a criminal light. That male Native Americans were habitually rebellious, cruel, violent, and lascivious were crude stereotypes forwarded by many Euro-American thinkers of the day, ranging from reform-minded leaders like Pratt to postbellum pseudoscientific advocates like Orson Fowler.

Specifically, in Fowler's widely circulated phrenological publications, the Native American was phrenologically typecast as pathologically violent and inherently untrustworthy, characteristics allegedly visible in Fowler's crude illustration that figure 3.9 shows.[27] This illustration, taken from Fowler's famous text *The Practical Phrenologist*, intended to show the phrenological faculty of "Destructiveness," first proposed by Spurzheim in the 1820s. The acceptance of such a phrenological characterization of course rests on the cultural orientations of Fowler's white middle-class northeastern urbane readership.[28]

According to Fowler's definition of this category, it entailed "executiveness, serenity, sterness [*sic*], harshness, love of tearing down, destroying, causing, teasing."[29] The implication in Fowler's visual and textual narrative was both particular and more general. Not only was his generalized and stereotyped "Indian Chief"[30] an unsteady and unpredictable figure whose behavior could swing from "serenity" to "destructiveness" without reason, but the entirety of the indigenous population fell under this classification. Further, a larger implication was one based in the lingering white supremacist thought of Victorian pseudoscience. Specifically, when compared with the Anglo-American exemplars presented in his book, such as Washington and Franklin, Fowler saw the "Indian Chief" as falling well short of the standards of white civilization and thus comparable to a class of pathological urban criminal.[31]

In characteristic fashion, Fowler was trying to classify various racial and socioeconomic groups by phrenological characteristics such as skull shape and proportion. In his formula, the credibility of which largely rests on the pseudoscientific knowledge proffered by Morton's polygenic discourse in *Crania Americana*, the proportion of the head of his "Indian Chief" betrayed such sinister internal qualities. The nation's cultural, scientific, and political leadership seemingly discounted the thesis of polygenesis following the Civil War. Nevertheless, suspicion and resentment toward ethnically and culturally diverse groups was obvious in the intensifying postbellum debates surrounding frontier confrontation and mass immigration.

In the Choate photograph that figure 3.2 shows, it is clear that the seemingly random arrangement of bodies was at least partially sought by the photographer, because most of the boys are clearly aware of his presence. Therefore, it is tempting to conclude that Choate *wanted* a perceptual sense of an underlying disorder. This is suggested by Pratt's absence and by the irregular configuration of the figures *because of* his photographic absence. The image therefore suggests that militaristic discipline and constant surveillance are necessary to keep these potentially dangerous boys from sliding backward into their previous identity as "blanket Indians."

Compositionally, this image is also reminiscent of one roughly contemporaneous and much more well-known in the United States during this period. Specifically, Jacob Riis's *Bandit's Roost*, with its jutting, entrapping architecture and loosely arranged motley array of back-alley criminal types, offers a provocative comparison. In Riis's image, which figure 3.10 shows, the undesirables of the new urban underclass glare out at the photographer with an air of suspicion and sullen resentment that is not unlike that of the boys in Choate's photograph. Most of the men in his photo were likely Other to Riis's intended audience, the middle and upper classes of New York City during the Gilded Age.[32]

As Riis uncovered the underbelly of the new metropolis, Choate meant to show the atavistic underside of the expanding industrial nation. This was his equivalent to the "Other Half" needing rectification vis-à-vis the mainstream of American society. Such a linkage, between Judeo-Slavic and Mediterranean urban immigrants and the allegedly feral indigenous peoples of the western frontier may seem unlikely at first, yet it is a connection that historians have noted.

Specifically, American studies scholar Alan Trachtenberg has recently argued for such correlations in his study *Shades of Hiawatha: Staging Indians, Making Americans*. In this text, Trachtenberg persuasively argues that the Anglo-American establishment of the Gilded Age sought to Americanize the Jewish, Slavic, and Italianate immigrants from southern and eastern Europe, as well as the indigenous peoples of the continent. The methods for so doing were surprisingly similar in both cases and entailed closely related programs of bodily hygiene, vocational training, language acquisition, Christianization, social etiquette, and the enforced wearing of middle-class Anglicized dress.[33]

Even though his composition served to remind viewers of the need for Indian civilization given their potential "destructiveness," perhaps it is significant that Choate chose not to mass-produce and market this image as either a carte de visite or a stereograph. Marketable images of the Native Americans at the schools were those stressing the positive elements of the school's program: rigidity, conformity, learning, supervision, hygiene, and the like. Images of male new arrivals in their assumed unhygienic appearances in a seemingly random array without the presence of a school administrator or government official might have struck a different nerve.

In both early photographs of the arriving boys, the issue of a latent criminality needing surveillance, discipline, and order is suggested in compositional terms. This should not be surprising, however, when we consider the more immediate context of Pratt's treatment of the first group of captives both at Fort Marion and along the train routes from the reservations to the school. Taken in the larger context of an emergent aesthetics of

Anglo-American criminological discourse, and given the relative cultural identities of subjects, photographer, and audience, the rigid compositional formula of the first image suggests the police lineup. This was a newly emergent image in the visual culture of the United States after the Civil War.

Specifically, historian Sandra Phillips has offered a concise summary of this newly formed criminological idea and its attendant codes of bodily representation. Phillips argues that during the nineteenth century in the United States, a rapid refining in criminological techniques of identification took place. Citing a series of 1846 daguerreotype portraits of prison convicts carried out by Matthew Brady, she claims that beginning at that time, photography assumed the central role in defining the appearance of criminals. This fed into the larger context of a systematic emerging science of criminology, which sought to contain and predict criminal patterns of activity in the country's newly populous urban centers. In more specific terms, Phillips asserts that many Anglo-American reformers of the mid-nineteenth century, such as Eliza Farnham and Marmaduke Sampson, were vested in the notion of an aesthetic correspondence between a criminal's interior character and external appearance.[34] All of this assumed an aesthetic correspondence between the interior workings of the mind and the external facial and corporeal features taken to signify race and class. This idea was clearly at play both in Fowler's assessments of Native Americans more generally and in Pratt's and Mills's anthropometrically informed experiment at Fort Marion.

Also, art historian John Tagg has seen this pattern of representation continuing into the later nineteenth century, coming into full aesthetic maturity during the 1870s, just at the moment when Pratt founded Carlisle. Tagg makes a detailed and two-pronged argument for the centrality of this particular aesthetic used by photographers in the service of state power. Not only does he see standardized aesthetic arrangements in the mug shot, lineup, and rogue's gallery, but he also sees photography itself—how it functions beyond the frame—as critical in establishing the new industrial, social, and political order of the Victorian era. Tagg sees the full-facial focus, tight bodily spacing, aesthetic isolation and decontextualization, plain backdrops, sharp focus and calibration, and harsh frontal lighting as emblematic of this photography, which stood as an iconic metaphor for an emergent social order.[35]

Important for Tagg's argument, however, is the notion that such photography stood as valid metaphor for a new order because it was a technology of sight linked to large-scale institutions of the industrial world. Not only was it central to police work, but it also found uses in factories, hospitals, asylums, the military, and boarding schools (see fig. 3.11).³⁶

Whereas the photographic grouping of various subalterns created a cultural logic of guilt by association in many contexts, the familiar "round-up" image would become a staple in the iconography of the more specific context of Frontierist imagery. Frontier soldiers charged by the federal government with clearing the way for white settlement would often hire itinerant photographers to make images intended to display and therefore prove the capture of hardened resisters. Pratt's and Choate's arrival images closely relate to this trend. In one such image by photographer A. J. McDonald that figure 3.12 shows, the captors of the famed Apache leader Geronimo apparently felt it necessary to have such an image made and circulated. In a typical formula, they stand in the background, looking down at the photographer with rifles in hand, while the captives gaze out gloomily at eye level. Clearly, the weight of modern industrial technology compositionally oppresses the group: the transcontinental rail line and the high-powered rifles of the soldiers lend the sense of entrapment here. As in the Carlisle arrival images, the signs of civilization, whether they were architectural, technological, or human, served to set the representational mood in advance. Ironically, this band of Apaches was headed for Fort Marion in 1886, roughly a decade after Pratt's original arrivals.³⁷

Therefore, the ritualistic photographing of incoming students was no mere isolated or insular activity undertaken by Pratt for personal political gain. Personal ambition does partially explain the thousands of photographic negatives produced at the school. However, it fails to explain the relation of Pratt's own practice to those of the matrix of newly established institutions of the bourgeois state in Europe and the United States during the nineteenth century. As Tagg states, the simple "externals" or aesthetics of such images are inadequate for grasping the profundity of this photography. One needs to also consider the conditions that supply the groundwork for photography and its use more generally; specifically, those conditions that make it possible to make a photograph, to encode a photograph, to read a photograph, and to have a shared societal understanding of a photograph.³⁸

The linkage of boarding school imagery with representations in other subaltern contexts such as the prison and the ghetto promoted photographic consistency. Photographs of members of pathological groups, whether those people were in urban or frontier contexts, therefore took on discernible and consistent characteristics. Besides being photographed head-on against some flat, geometric, or calibrated backdrop, the subjects often appear tired, flustered, or disgruntled due to the physical, emotional, and jurisprudential ordeal that they have endured. They are sometimes accompanied in the photograph by another person—usually serving as a symbol of control or law enforcement—as seen in the round-up images or in the Carlisle arrival images.

Similar to the formulas suggested above, most of the boys in the first arrival photograph stand or sit facing front and shoulder-to-shoulder in front of the oddly calibrated backdrop provided by the geometric lines of the dormitory building. Also, Pratt's presence at the side of the group reads in such a context as the presence of not only a benign and paternalistic schoolmaster. More important, he serves as an enforcement official of some kind—reminiscent of a police officer keeping a lineup of suspects orderly during an identification or rogue's gallery photographic shoot. Further, Pratt's presence serves as a de facto prop, prompting the viewer to compare his civilized appearance with the implicit savagery of the boys. All such aesthetic characteristics feed into Tagg's characterization of institutional photography at this time. In being so photographed, the boys were not only objectified or repressed, they were *created* epistemologically for their various audiences.[39]

Most important, we see these emaciated figures in a context radically foreign to that from which they came or could have ever imagined. As Luther Standing Bear has stated, none of the boys leaving the reservation had any idea where he was going, how far it was from home, or what was going to happen to him on arrival. In fact, the boys' apprehensive parents conducted dramatic sacrificial potlatch-like ceremonies, because it was uncertain when or if the children would ever return. As he wrote:

> The next day my father invited all the people who lived near by to come to his place. He got all the goods down off the shelves in his store and carried them outside. Then he brought in about seven heads of ponies. When all the people were gathered there, he gave away all these things because I was going away East. I was going with the white people, and perhaps might never return; so he was sacrificing all his worldly possessions. Some of the other chiefs also gave away many things.[40]

With this in mind, it becomes clear that reactions ranging from sharp defiance to fear are appropriate in these early images, as this first generation of students fancied themselves having fallen victim to some mythic fate—off of the ends of the Earth.

Perhaps the criminological interpretation of these images is not in keeping with Choate's conscious intentions when making the pictures. But one need only recall several of the new arrivals were former prisoners from Fort Marion, whom Pratt considered to be the most vile offenders in the struggle for the frontier.[41] It was thus likely that the school's administration viewed at least some of the students not only as metaphoric prisoners, but as prisoners in a more literal sense who needed constant surveillance and containment. Although many of the noncombatant students were the descendants of respected reservation leaders such as Standing Bear, they too were not above suspicion in the minds of Pratt, the school's supporters, and the public. Many prominent and educated observers, as commentary by Harriet Beecher Stowe quoted in chapter 2 revealed, expressed fear, amazement, and morbid curiosity when first seeing the students in their indigenous appearance, an appearance that could easily connote danger.

4

Photography and Indoctrination II
The Before-and-After Portrait

Tom Torlino: A Photographic Odyssey

As I have discussed, Pratt's and Choate's collaboration in photographing the school's students was by most measures successful. The school, and indeed other boarding schools that began in Carlisle's wake, received increased funding and gained in enrollment for nearly twenty-five consecutive years. It is therefore helpful to return now to the before-and-after portraits of Tom Torlino that figures 3.4a and 3.4b show and to discuss the functions and limitations of the before-and-after portrait, because such portraits were among the most provocative and persuasive forms of argument that Pratt used.

The Torlino before-and-after portraits are by no means unique in nineteenth-century Anglo-American visual culture. Such imagery was used not only to represent the American Indian but also in a myriad of other contexts. Such contexts included those meant to represent cultural subalterns of all kinds: for example, African Americans, the poor, immigrants, and people living in colonized regions throughout the globe (see, for example, fig. 4.1). Historical evidence shows that such imagery became more widespread after many photographers adopted the collodion/albumen process, with its sharpness, detail, and relatively easy reproducibility. The mass distribution of such imagery, and the logic inherent in it, was thus partly contingent on technological developments in photographic reproduction.

Nevertheless, the comparative aesthetics of the before-and-after image can be dated to at least 1837–1839 with George Catlin's well-known *Pigeon's Egg Head Going to and Returning from Washington*, which figure 4.2 shows. The artist produced this double portrait in an illustrated album issued in 1849. In the bound album, titled *Souvenir of the North American Indians*, Catlin included the following caption next to the illustration:

> This chief, with several others from the remotest tribes, was con-
> ducted to Washington City . . . by the Govt [*sic*] Indian Agent, and
> their portraits were painted by the author . . . in their beautiful native
> costumes; and 18 months after . . . when he painted them again . . . in
> civilized costumes, the striking result of 18 months of civilization.[1]

Art historian William Truettner, in his introduction to the facsimile addition of Catlin's album, argues that the artist's rendering of this
young chief from the Assiniboin tribe suggests a skeptical attitude toward
the policies of assimilation. Truettner states that after the chief's stay in
Washington, he returned to his tribe in the upper Missouri River valley
and shocked his relatives with his paramilitary uniform and his erratic
behavior. Truettner points out that Catlin held the corruptions of white
civilization responsible for the chief's fall from grace among his people.[2]
The artist showed this in the image by replacing Pigeon's Egg Head's peace
pipe with a sword and representing the vices the young man picked up
during his trip: smoking and drinking alcohol. Catlin replaced the proud,
erect bearing of the first portrait with an off-center posture in a grotesque
mimicry of bourgeois Anglo-American social airs in the second.

It is not clear from surviving evidence whether Pratt knew of this specific image. However, Catlin's gallery, with illustrated albums of many of
his portraits, had won international renown by the 1840s. Given Pratt's
reformist sympathy with the Native American populations, it is likely
that he at least knew of Catlin and his work. Regardless of Pratt's specific
knowledge of this image, it is clear from the evidence that the general format of before-and-after imagery was becoming increasingly popular among
government reformers in the United States and Europe by the 1870s.

The logic of this type of portrait was essentially a positivistic logic of
improvement, with the "improvement" represented carrying a host of positivist associations, including evolutionist, aesthetic, and cultural. In addition, the notion of two side-by-side images of similar or the same subject
matter is a comparative tradition well known at the time in reformist circles
and subsequently, among present-day historians of the visual.

Specifically, the Enlightenment notion of "progress," or the progressive
and gradual upward trajectory of human existence in comfort, convenience,
productivity, health, affluence, and hygiene served as the philosophical backbone of most Victorian social reform. This idea was prevalent, whether the
reform was thought of as penal, educational, moral, or congenital. Importantly
for art historians, such a teleological rationale was inherent not only in the
modern disciplines of anthropology, sociology, and political science, but also

in the historiography of art history itself. In fact, this notion commonly informs how historians and critics are likely to read decontextualized side-by-side images in museums, galleries, publications, or academic presentations. Although the then-current social evolutionist conventions of the American School of Anthropology shaped how audiences would view the images at the time, modern art historical conventions may also have informed how following historians view such imagery.

Regarding cultural conditioning, one need only think of the famous Cimabue-Giotto, Early–High Renaissance, or High Renaissance–Baroque comparisons taught by art historians to consecutive generations of students of the discipline. Students are taught, for instance, to marvel at the vast aesthetic, technical, and cultural gains that the younger, advanced Giotto made over his allegedly backward-looking teacher Cimabue. The implication is, of course, that immeasurable value and originality are found in the improved work of the former as compared with the retardataire work of the latter. This is a positivistic logic, based on belief in a cultural improvement over time brought about by the genius of an individual artist. Such an assumption represents a modern individualist ethos; a characteristic of academic scholarship in the humanities for centuries. That such art historical notions inform the way we perceive comparative imagery is not surprising considering the time-honored pedagogical methods of the discipline. Significantly, its modern identity was formed during the Enlightenment and post-Enlightenment era in Europe under the influence of thinkers such has Auguste Comte and G. W. F. Hegel.[3]

Specifically, art historians writing under Hegel's influence, such as Heinrich Wölfflin, have long since inculcated a logic of side-by-side aesthetic comparison based on photographic reproduction to trace the trajectory, change, and improvement in art over various historical periods. It is significant that such comparative methods are modern in conception, dating at the earliest to Vasari, and most likely did not occur to Cimabue or Giotto in their own lifetimes.[4]

In this light, it is significant that Wölfflin often saw the shifting aesthetic periods of architecture, painting, and sculpture metaphorically in terms of biology and human corporeality. For example, he once wrote,

> To *explain* a style then can mean nothing other than to place it in its general historical context and to verify that it speaks in harmony with the other organs of its age . . . But the significance of reducing stylistic forms into terms of the *human body* is that it provides us with an immediate expression of the spiritual.[5]

In Wölfflin's view of the meaning of artistic style, we may detect a parallel aesthetic relationship of the human body and soul discussed earlier in reference to the phrenological portraits of Mills, and indeed to Puritan aesthetics more generally. Images of the human body, whether actual (as in painting and photography) or metaphoric (as in the "organic" elements of architecture) are often taken in qualitatively progressive terms suggestive of some cultural teleology. Art historians often imagine an "end state" of perfection in which all elements are in balance, both spiritually and aesthetically. More important for the current discussion, the art historical logic of aesthetic comparison/progress embedded in the views of side-by-side photographically reproduced images is not exclusive to the insular world of art history. In modern culture in general, especially in mass-mediated twentieth-century societies, such a visual logic is fundamental to both corporate advertising and political propaganda.

In this early instance of overt photographic propaganda, that Pratt self-consciously saw to it that the school's images functioned politically and propagandistically is obvious in the rhetorical framing of their possible meanings in his correspondence and in school publications. It is therefore understandable why a viewer of the past or present would be tempted to see these images as representing improvement, even if the viewer is at ideological odds with the politics of the image. Such transparent readings testify to Pratt's success as a visual propagandist. However, it is important to remember that such images may be read any number of ways—as degeneration, as unrelated to one another, or as simply representing the same subject in different clothes. Of course, Pratt and Choate warded off all of these possibilities, or misreadings, by their deft contextualization of text, rhetoric, and image.

Returning to the specific case of Torlino, it is important to recall that Pratt imagined the indigenous body as a tabula rasa onto which the will of civilization could be inscribed. And Pratt's use of such aesthetic logic was seemingly successful because it worked wonders as he succeeded politically in legitimizing his project. Further, and perhaps more surprisingly, this progressivist logic has been widely and unconsciously accepted by scholars looking at this image in recent decades. In fact, when writing about the Torlino before-and-after images, some of the most discerning historians gloss over consideration of it *as a photograph*. In so doing, they have missed a valuable opportunity to further critique the reasons for the political success of Pratt's ideological manipulations.

To highlight one example of such methodological oversight, let us consider the treatment of this image in the recent book on the topic by

American studies scholar Alan Trachtenberg. Like many before him writing about Carlisle, Trachtenberg uses the Torlino image as an obvious and transparent illustration of the school's assimilationist agenda. However, reading closely the image's caption in Trachtenberg's book *Shades of Hiawatha* reveals that he has in fact mislabeled it. He claims that it is a before-and-after portrait of Delos Lone Wolf, a student who attended Carlisle a full decade after Torlino.[6]

Other scholars, who have written otherwise important and penetrating critiques of Carlisle, have handled Choate's images in a similarly dismissive fashion, often taking Choate's work as being strictly illustrative rather than creative or manipulative in a photographic sense.[7] In methodological terms, I intend to conduct an aesthetic critique of these images and of the cultural logic of aesthetic comparison in the United States during this period. The power of this logic affected viewers during the nineteenth century and seemingly still holds sway over current historians' perceptions of these images.

I'll begin discussion of the image with reference to an exception to the logic of aesthetic comparison seen in the seminal work of Lonna Malsmheimer, a cultural historian who has studied Carlisle extensively. About the Torlino portrait, Malmsheimer notes that Torlino came to Carlisle from the Indian agency at Fort Defiance, a frontier military outpost near the then newly established Navajo reservation in New Mexico. He was the son of a high-ranking Navajo chief and traveled to the school with the sons of Manuelito, a principal leader of the Navajo people. Torlino arrived at the school in 1882 and remained at Carlisle intermittently until 1886 and thus was photographed both at his arrival and several years later, after a stay at the school. Because his before-and-after portraits were coupled with the survival of the negatives, Torlino's portraits are some of the most widely circulated and thus iconic images in the entire Carlisle archive.[8]

In analyzing the fallacies inherent in the logic of this imagery, it is helpful to consider more deeply both Torlino's personal history and the history of the Navajo people as a whole, two critical elements disavowed in this synecdochic[9] image. According to records, Torlino's exact date of arrival at Carlisle was 21 October 1882, nearly three years to the day after the arrival of the original Lakota Sioux group discussed in chapter 3.[10] By this point, Pratt had earned a reputation as a no-nonsense reformer. People in positions of power in Washington saw his mission at Carlisle as a success. Choate photographed Torlino with his fellow Navajo arrivals (see fig. 4.3). By this time, the "arrival" photographic session had become a ritual. Pratt subjected each group of new arrivals to it in his continual demand for newer, more updated images to serve as proof of the continuing success of Carlisle.[11]

In the original print of the photograph, which Choate mounted onto a cardboard backing, Torlino is visible on the lower left. He appears huddled, confused, downtrodden, sullen, and forlorn, as do all of his companions and nearly all the students photographed at such a moment during the previous three years of the school's history. Pratt would seize on the dirty appearance of the new arrivals as a signifier of their savagery. However, such an appearance can obviously be better credited to what must have seemed like an endless journey from the territories of the Southwest to the school in the mid-Atlantic. The trip would have included long walks in baking sun, bumpy rides in stagecoaches, the unfamiliar and shocking experience of the railroad, poor nutrition, and jeering crowds of curious white onlookers at nearly every station.[12] Luther Standing Bear describes the trials of the first such journey in depth in his autobiography, but the journey for the Navajos, coming from much farther south and west, would have taken roughly twice as long.

In the 1882 Navajo arrival portrait, we see the new students lined up in front of the bandstand, long a symbol of the center of school life, and something of an architectural symbol of power in the central quadrangle of the campus because of the structure's architecture and placement in the grounds. The bandstand was located in the middle of the campus, the centerpiece of the school's horseshoe-shaped configuration. On either side were the boys' and girls' dormitories, and Pratt's own residence was across the green. The bandstand was where the school's famous band practiced, and was the position from which Pratt and other officials could effectively survey the entire school population as the students milled about the quadrangle during the day.[13]

Pratt sits above the students with his arm leaning on the bandstand's balustrade and looks down on his new charges paternalistically. Again, Pratt's appearance in the photograph, with its staging at the bandstand, was intended to communicate an air of authority and control similar to that of the first pair of group arrival pictures of 1879. Such a composition is indeed simple but subtly suggests an unmistakable social and institutional hierarchy involving the students and their new "school father."[14]

Pratt selected Torlino and two of his male companions to pose for Choate for before-and-after portraits. Pratt correctly assumed that the images of these young Navajo men would serve to send the most dramatic message possible for such a format. This was because he was aware that the Navajos, coming from the far-flung regions of the Southwest, were the most likely of nearly any tribe to strike a wild and savage appearance in the eyes of his intended middle-class audience.[15] It is unnerving that Pratt so eagerly sold the allegedly "wild" appearance of Torlino and other Navajos to the public, given that his entire project was built on uplifting or dignifying the students. With such gestures, he came dangerously close to the tourist-promotional exoticism of such degrading spectacles as Buffalo Bill's Wild West Show.[16]

In Torlino's individual "before" portrait, Choate made the odd choice of decontextualizing Torlino from any background mise-en-scène whatever. In what would be a departure from the normal before-and-after formula, Torlino is set bust-length against a stark, washed-out background of vague locale, although the location was most likely Choate's studio in town. The photographer offers Torlino to the contemporary viewer as an ethno-graphic sample of the wildest of all tribal nations, the infamous Apache nation of the Southwest, of which the Navajos were a part. Torlino therefore was shown in what is ostensibly his original or savage dress: cloth headband, the famous long flowing hair of Apache men, a handwoven blanket sash over his shoulder, metallic earrings, elaborate necklaces, and dark suntanned skin.

In the "after" image, photographed in 1884 or 1885, Choate depicted Torlino as the polar opposite of his former savage self. His tired, worn expression was by then replaced with a seemingly confident gaze, his exotic jewelry was gone, his flowing hair was dramatically cropped, and he has donned a new, Victorian-era Euro-American men's suit with overcoat, cravat, and stiff-collared white shirt. Perhaps most strikingly, his skin tone had undergone a seemingly miraculous shift from its former dark brown to a much lighter tone.

In sum, Pratt and Choate intended such an image to serve as a signifier of the efficacy of the transformation. The side-by-side placement of the images encouraged the viewer to read from left to right, in the manner of an English-language text, with an implicit narrative at play. The format gives viewers the illusion that they have witnessed a miraculous change: The savage had evolved out of his previous darkness and into the light of civilization. Choate's manipulation of studio lighting is perhaps the most effective symbol in this interplay, because it altered the appearance of Torlino's skin from dark to light.

Perhaps even more disturbing is the presence in this image of what Fusco terms the "staging of evolutionary time." Fusco states that in ethnographic photography of the nineteenth century, it became common and indeed was mandatory for white photographers to use the before-and-after formula to give the viewer the impression that evolutionary time had advanced. In other words, the photographer played the role of God and Nature by theatrically staging savagery in the first image and civilization in the second—as if eons had elapsed instead of only months or years. Juxtaposing the two images gave viewers the sense that some miraculous evolution had taken place before their eyes. That is, a biological-cultural evolution was assumed to have taken place in only a few months or years, rather than in centuries. The apparent speed of this process therefore proved the wisdom and power inherent in white reformist agendas. This view found credibility, not least in the newly formed scientific evolutionist theories of racial and cultural development popular in the United States during the nineteenth century.[17]

However, this image masks as much as it reveals. Although Torlino was presented as the proof of Pratt's transformative powers, Bureau of Indian Affairs records suggest that he and other Navajo elites did not fare well at Carlisle. Malmsheimer points out that one of his companions, the son of the Navajo chief Manuelito, died at the school and the deceased student's brother returned to the Navajo reservation as a result.[18] Further, Torlino himself has a foggy and ambiguous record. It is important to remember that he did not arrive at Carlisle until the age of twenty-two, already a young man with a fully formed adult persona at the time of his arrival in 1882. Torlino returned to the reservation for an extended stay in 1884.[19] Pratt dreaded such extended leave because it indicated administrative failure. He obsessively feared his students would regress to their old ways if allowed to return to their reservations. Torlino did return to Carlisle in 1885, but then left abruptly on "departmental order" in 1886.[20] Such an order, given its "departmental" status, most likely emanated from the Department of the Interior, the federal agency charged with overseeing the Bureau of Indian Affairs, and thus Carlisle and all other Indian schools in the nation. The order would point to a serious problem of some sort with Torlino, something Pratt would want to avoid publicizing.

Despite this abrupt end to Torlino's short career at Carlisle, Pratt continued to reproduce images of him for both economic and political purposes in the school's papers for years to come. In fact, the school sold prints of Torlino's before-and-after portraits as part of subscription drives in the school's paper *Morning Star* in 1886 and used his arrival photograph as an illustration in the school publication *The Indian Helper* as late as 1897.[21] Despite Torlino's seeming problems, and the more severe problems of other Navajo students, Pratt continuously evoked their images in a perverse photographic afterlife to control both contemporary and later views of the school.

In discussing the most well-known images in Choate's repertoire, it is helpful to consider the history of the Navajo tribe as a whole. When so doing, the ahistoric character of these images becomes even plainer.

Despite the best efforts of Pratt and others to obscure or degrade the histo-ries of indigenous American tribes,[22] historians have luckily uncovered the long and complex histories of many of these peoples. To cite one example, Navajo historian Loretta Hall has written that the Navajo people have existed in the area that we today call the Southwest for nearly one thousand years; some sources place their arrival in the region in the eleventh century CE.[23] This is roughly eight hundred years before the United States took possession of the region in 1846.

Following the federal government's aggressive foray into Mexico dur-ing the Mexican-American War, the army soon met the Apache nation and the Navajos in particular. During this period, from 1864–1868, the military plundered Navajo livestock and burned most of their crops. Under the leadership of Kit Carson, the army placed the Navajos under siege, drove them out of their ancestral homeland of Canyon de Chelly (in what is now Arizona), and forcibly marched them to a de facto prison camp three hundred miles away. This event, known to historians as the Navajo Long Walk, and the resulting resettlement at a grim and inhospitable tract of land known as Bosque Redondo, cost thousands of Navajo lives. Once at their destination, many more Navajos died of starvation because the provi-sions they had from the army were inadequate and they could not grow crops in the new land. The federal government finally signed a treaty with them in 1868, giving them what would become their reservation comprising their original homelands in the Four Corners region.[24] These facts alone clearly refute Pratt's repeated offensive insinuations that the students who came to Carlisle had no real history and thus had a "valueless past."[25]

However, two details in particular belie Pratt's purpose in setting up these images as a polarized aesthetic comparison displaying some stunning progress from savagery to civilization. In the first image, Torlino dons both metallic earrings and an elaborate necklace. The items are not a sign of some resigned feral state or of the insularity of the Navajo people but are the result of colonial contact with the Spanish. The first Spanish incursion into Navajo lands occurred during the 1540–1542 expedition of the explorer Francisco Vásquez de Coronado. Cultural conflict and interchange went on between the colonial Spaniards and the Navajos for the entirety of the subsequent three centuries leading to the Mexican-American War and the resulting annexation of Mexican territory by the U.S. government. In fact, both metalworking and Christianity were known to the Navajos well before the Americans arrived.[26]

Thus, Torlino's metallic earrings are likely the result of advanced knowl-edge of metalwork. Further, Torlino's necklace consists of several striking symbols, with the clearly visible cruciform shapes being the most prominent. The large pendant cross with the parallel crossbars was a common Navajo religious symbol known as the dragonfly. In Navajo belief, this mythic creature was responsible for bringing crucial summer rains, allowing for the growth of crops. The smaller crosses with single crossbars may have had more than one connotation in Navajo culture. Scholar Alison Bird argues that these forms symbolically represent the morning star or other celestial bodies important in Navajo cosmology. Bird goes on to argue, however, that Navajo motivation for incorporating the cruciform shape into their attire was complicated by their difficult relations with the Spanish. She claims that crosses were initially worn in an effort to ward off religious persecution by placating Spanish missionary zeal. Further, Loretta Hall argues that although early attempts by the Spanish to convert the Navajos met only limited success, Catholicism eventually came to be a religion absorbed by many through cultural osmosis and was openly observed by some Navajos by the nineteenth century.[27]

Torlino's religious views prior to his arrival at the school remain unclear. Given the culturally complex and tumultuous environment in which he had been raised, his views may have ranged from outright acceptance or rejection of Christianity to a syncretic belief system practiced by some Navajos as early as the 1880s.[28] Regardless of Torlino's actual views, Pratt of course could not acknowledge Torlino's subjectivity in any complex way, because he needed the "before" portraits to read simply as pure savagery. Such in-depth knowledge might very well have been inconvenient for Pratt, because it would have rendered problematic the public reception of these images. A more dualistic reading was necessary in order for him to maintain the viability of his famous claim of "killing the Indian and saving the man."[29]

Finally, it is useful to consider the role of photography itself in Navajo culture in the nineteenth century. Anthropologist James Faris has written an innovative study on the topic that has opened the area to critical scrutiny. In tracing the history of photography in Navajo society, Faris claims that no photographs exist of Navajos before their internment at Bosque Redondo. Faris thus concludes that one must necessarily view nearly the entire history of Navajo photography as one embodying a disciplinary function. Essentially, the taking of photographic images of Navajos, mostly by white photographers, was an interaction symbolic of the former's domination by white American society.[30]

With this in mind, Faris has examined specific images of Navajos appearing as subjects in photography. Because of the early historical linkage of photographic imaging with political subjection, Faris states that when posed photographs of Navajos appear in the nineteenth century, the subject was most often forced to assume a specific pose. Faris points to many archival examples in support of this claim, one of which figure 4.4 shows, and sees the enforcement of the photographic interchange reflected in the downtrodden postures and sullen expressions of the unwilling subjects.[31] In figure 4.4, in a photograph likely made during their imprisonment at Bosque Redondo, the photographer forces the two young Navajo men to assume rather clichéd and transparent poses illustrating savagery, as they kneel and hold up bows and arrows.

One can only imagine, then, what effect the enforced days-long journey and the also-enforced ritual of arrival photographing must have had on Torlino's psyche. Torlino was old enough to have been alive during the Long Walk–Bosque Redondo incident of the 1860s. In fact, that violent cultural displacement and estrangement might possibly have constituted some of his earliest memories. This history, added to what Faris identifies as an "avoidance" reflex enacted by many Navajos in reaction to the presence of a photographer, must have made at least his initial experiences with photography nightmarish. Figure 4.5 illustrates this reflex. The anonymous photograph shows us a Navajo woman running for cover on seeing a photographer, a reaction Faris cites as common in Navajo culture.

The complex truth for the Navajo people, as well as for many other indigenous peoples, was that contact with whites had occurred long before Carlisle, and by the late nineteenth century most Native people had experienced at least some degree of cultural crossover. In this light, Pratt's absolutist polarization of savage versus civilization breaks down. As art historian Anna Blume has stated about the Torlino images, they display much more than Choate or Pratt intended.[32]

What is perhaps most disturbing about the before-and-after genre is the fact that evidence exists supporting the notion that Pratt and Choate were disingenuous in producing such images. It is one thing to cite the larger historical discourses that a person may or may not consciously absorb. It is another to be a willful propagandist, facilitating the abuse of image-making for repressive political purposes. In 1878, Pratt brought the original Fort Marion prisoners to the Hampton Institute and was recruiting new arrivals from reservations. He and General Samuel Chapman Armstrong, Hampton's founder, corresponded about the value of photography in promoting their respective political agendas. Armstrong wrote, "We wish a variety of photographs of the Indians. Be sure and have them bring their wild barbarous things. This will show whence we started." To which Pratt replied, "The argument will be all the better. 'Condition on arrival at Hampton.'"[33]

More intriguing still is an April 1880 letter written by Pratt to Carl Schurz, then secretary of the interior, and therefore a key federal overseer of the project. This letter complicates any characterization of Pratt as ignorant of indigenous affairs:

> I am most anxious to make a telling break on the Navajos, and goad the Presbyterians. The Navajoes [*sic*] furnish the most promising field for educational and industrial training of any Indians we have, and are only second to the Sioux in population. The Presbyterians who have had ten years to move upon this tribe are only now waking up to their responsibility. This is a Presbyterian Valley, and fifty Navajoe [*sic*] youth at this school will incite the whole church to work. I place the matter before you, with my opinion, that the 15 youth you have allowed from the Navajoes [*sic*] are too few; really weakness both ways, i.e., for success with the Indians and the Presbyterians.[34]

In this surprisingly frank letter, Pratt displayed an in-depth knowledge of both Navajo industrial skill and contemporary religious politics on the Navajo reservation. Further, Pratt clearly recognized the religious similarities between the Navajos and the residents of the Cumberland Valley (i.e., the "Presbyterian Valley"). Given such unlikely cultural overlaps, questions arise about why Pratt and many local residents were so eager to see the newly arriving Navajo contingent of October 1882, which included Torlino, as savage and wild rather than friendly. Further, it raises the point that, despite having at least a cursory familiarity with the complexities of the Navajo experience at this time, Pratt saw Navajo students in particular as desirable candidates for before-and-after portraits. Such intellectual duplicity suggests that Pratt was essentially playing into the prejudices of his target audiences by eschewing discussion of the particular experiences of each tribe or student.

These revealing letter exchanges offer the most significant insights into the degree of cynicism informing the practice of photography at the boarding schools. For at all such schools, including Hampton, photography and graphic reproductions of photographs were the key media in persuading the public that not only were such schools viable for congressional funding, but that the assimilationist project was moral and just. On one level, the Armstrong-Pratt correspondence suggests an ignorance of the extended history of indigenous tribes. Nevertheless, read with some of Pratt's other letters in mind, such as the letter to Secretary Schurz, what emerges is a willful and perhaps nefarious repression of that history in its true complexity in favor of the crude and simplistic "before-and-after" logic. Apparently for Pratt, "killing the Indian" entailed fetishistically evoking a visual cliché of Indianness while also photographically and thus metaphorically destroying that very Indianness in favor of an equally rigid and stereotyped Americanness.

It will be helpful here to consider another of Choate's before-and-after images in an effort to fully develop the idea of an intentionally and fetishistically evoked pan-Indian identity. As with Torlino's, such an identity could later be used as proof of the eventual and inevitable success of the civilizing process.

White Buffalo: The Body as Tourist Art

Choate photographed the newly arrived Cheyenne student White Buffalo in 1881, as figure 4.6 shows.[35] By 1881, white settlement and the treaties of the U.S. government had long since effectively fragmented the Cheyenne tribe into two main splinter groups, the Northern and Southern Cheyenne.[36] Similarly to the Torlino portraits, the image of the body of White Buffalo, a Northern Cheyenne, would become one of the most reproduced and commodified images in the history of the school. This can be attributed to the stereotypically and spectacularly "Indian" appearance of White Buffalo in the "before" photograph. One is struck by the elaborateness of the young man's clothing as well as by his distinctive long, prematurely gray hair. Choate reinforced the seeming authenticity of his appearance by titling the image "White Buffalo, Cheyenne, Nature Dress." As Pratt had noted in his correspondence with General Armstrong, photographing the Indian entailed the intentional guiding of the viewer's perception in particular directions. In this case, Choate subtly used the term "nature" to reinforce both the authenticity of the image and the preexisting stereotype of the Native American as "natural" and untouched by civilization.

Another reason for the popularity of White Buffalo's image was the uniqueness of his appearance, even among the incoming students. His graying hair clearly distinguished him from other young students and lent him an appearance undoubtedly considered even more exotic than that of his peers. In fact, judging from his indigenous name, White Buffalo might also have enjoyed a special status among his own people. According to scholars Richard Erdoes and Alfonso Ortiz, all Plains tribes shared a common veneration of the albino buffalo, an animal considered sacred. In fact, they coveted the albino buffalo hide as a sacred talisman that brought fortune to its possessor.[37]

It is thus possible that White Buffalo's name referred to this special creature, and that White Buffalo's appearance granted him a special status within his tribe. With these possibilities in mind, it is important to remember that when recruiting new students, Pratt wanted children who enjoyed the highest status within their tribe. These usually included youths who came from high-status families or who possessed extraordinary skills or characteristics. White Buffalo was therefore likely a prime discovery for Pratt, whose covert desire for the exotic was driven by a need to impress the viewing public and thus ensure further funding for his school. That White Buffalo's unique appearance could easily strike a white eastern audience as exotic could only bolster Pratt's claims of mastery over the savage. In this sense, White Buffalo's status in this image seems disturbingly like a zoological exhibit, rather than existential or human.

It is illuminating to compare the differences between the studio setting into which Choate placed White Buffalo and the one in which he photographed Torlino, who arrived in Carlisle only a year later than White Buffalo. Choate experimented with various props and backdrops. In Torlino's case, he blotted out the background in favor of highlighting of Torlino's perceived strangeness. Three years later, Choate chose to isolate Torlino's bust to allow the viewer to focus only on the change that had allegedly occurred. Such a treatment clearly isolated the subject and served to obscure any external or contextual elements other than those intended by Pratt and Choate.

In White Buffalo's "before" image, Choate set the youth in a much more elaborate studio environment. He is placed in a simulated Arcadia wearing what at first glance seems to be authentic Plains Indian dress—feathered warrior headdress, moccasins, buckskin suit, with long flowing hair and even a bow and arrow for good measure. Indeed, such a stereotypical appearance served as a form of aesthetic shorthand for untutored white audiences, to help them identify individuals from the Plains tribes, and even Native Americans more broadly.

The background and props clearly differ from the blank backdrop in the Torlino images. Choate chose to use several visual tropes common in nineteenth-century photography to exotic or natural subject matter. We see faux rocks on which the subject sits, hay and grass strewn artificially on the floor around the subject's feet, and a painted backdrop intended to evoke a generalized Edenic atmosphere. This is a setting undoubtedly intended to contextualize perceptions of White Buffalo as originating from an arcadian, precivilized past.

With Choate's pyrotechnical history-making in mind, it is important to consider more detailed and accurate historical realities when viewing this image. This is because this image would come to serve not only as an emblem of the rise from savagery to civilization, but would also be an important tool in the visual commodification of Indianness both at the school and in the country more widely.

In general historical terms, Cheyennes had the reputation of being one of the fiercest tribes in the entire Plains region. It was warriors from the Northern Cheyenne, with Sioux warriors, who soundly defeated army forces led by Lieutenant Colonel George Armstrong Custer at the famous Battle of the Little Bighorn in 1876. Custer's death during the battle was shocking for many because Custer had been a leading Union officer during the Civil War and had earned a reputation for battlefield savvy. The incident stunned the public and was reported widely in the press of the day.[38] The fact that Pratt was able to persuade a Northern Cheyenne youth to come to Carlisle only a few years after the incident could easily have served as helpful propaganda.

White Buffalo, a prominent member of the infamous Cheyenne tribe, was an important catch for Pratt, who had had great personal difficulty with more than one Cheyenne prisoner at Fort Marion a few years earlier. In fact, one of his prisoners, a young Cheyenne chief, committed suicide on the train on the way from Fort Marion to Hampton. The Cheyenne chief Grey Beard was one of few who had the courage to criticize Pratt face-to-face during the journey, and he tried to escape by jumping off the train while it was in motion. Grey Beard was shot and killed by an army soldier during his attempted escape.[39] Because of his difficult personal history with Cheyenne leaders, Pratt had a large stake in taming the young White Buffalo, an emergent leader of the tribe.

Further, Pratt and Choate intended the portrait to send a generalized view of Cheyennes that would have served to obscure the large-scale and problematic relations between the tribe and the federal government in the decades before the school's founding. After white settlement had driven the Cheyenne people out of their ancestral homelands in the Great Lakes region in the early nineteenth century, the U.S. Army attacked an encampment of Cheyennes and Arapahos on the banks of Sand Creek in southeastern Colorado in 1864. The incident became known as the Sand Creek Massacre and occurred when a group of Southern Cheyenne settlers refused to move from a piece of land earmarked for mining and development by the governor of the Colorado Territory. During an overnight raid, army forces led by Colonel John Chivington killed several hundred Cheyenne men, women, and children. Although the Cheyennes had staved off Custer's forces, the weight of these confrontations took their toll on the tribe's means of subsistence and allowed the federal government to force the scattered and weakened Cheyenne people onto government reservations.[40]

Given the radically altered way of life the Cheyenne people were faced with at the time of Choate's portrait, White Buffalo's dress in the portrait defies historical logic. The portrait's major selling point was the supposed authenticity of White Buffalo's appearance, and although it is true that traditional Cheyenne dress does in fact include a feathered war bonnet, buckskin cloak, and moccasins, by the early 1880s such articles were rare at best. In fact, white frontier traders sold similar items to tourists in such volume that the items couldn't have been authentic. Further, by this time, Plains Indian artisans began making simulated indigenous clothing for white brokers in exchange for subsistence wages.[41] Also relevant is the possibility that Choate himself owned a collection of this mass-produced Indian clothing in his own studio. Such a practice became increasingly important for photographers such as Choate and Will Soule, who wished to capture an image of authenticity in making images of Native Americans in indigenous dress.[42]

In short, authentic traditional Native American clothing was no longer being produced but rather was rapidly becoming a manufactured product of a cottage industry controlled by white entrepreneurs who were willing to exploit indigenous poverty to extract sellable artifacts. As scholar Marsha Bol has argued, the socioeconomic conditions affecting indigenous populations suggested the elimination of genuine ritual craft and its replacement by tourist art.[43] It is thus possible that Pratt or one of his agents purchased such regalia at a white-owned frontier trading post and had White Buffalo wear it as a costume for his portrait by Choate.

It is also important to consider the status of such clothing in Cheyenne culture. Even if this clothing had been authentic, that is, even if it had been produced by a Cheyenne artisan for strictly ritual purposes, White Buffalo's wearing it in such a context would have been an inappropriate gesture on his part. It is unlikely that he would have worn such an outfit for his journey east, given the widespread perception among the Indians that the students were going to meet some mysterious fate at the end of the world. Such clothing would have been appropriate at a tribal ritual, such as one to confer warrior status on a young man. In fact, the Cheyenne war bonnet was worn only by experienced warriors either in battle or during rituals. Being eighteen at the time of his arrival at Carlisle, it is unlikely that White Buffalo had reached warrior status among his people, despite his unique appearance.[44] Clearly, then, it seems that Choate was manipulating White Buffalo's appearance for purposes of photographic exhibition.

This manipulation of appearance ironically relates to the methods of display employed in Buffalo Bill Cody's famous Wild West shows of the 1880s and 1890s. Although Pratt was often on record as deploring these shows as gratuitous spectacles that degraded the indigenous performers, he and Cody employed oddly similar means. For instance, Cody would often have his actors don prereservation-era clothing in scenes to entertain white audiences in the United States and Europe. The war bonnet was an important part of this show, because mock battles were a fan favorite.[45]

Finally, a brief consideration of one of the props in the photograph, the bow and arrow that White Buffalo holds, further reveals the artifice of this image. The arrow was a sacred object to Cheyennes: they believed it to be a magical weapon given to the tribe by Sweet Medicine, a mythical ancestor figure. In their belief, arrows were endowed by Sweet Medicine with powers enabling their male hunters to more easily kill buffalo and therefore secure food, clothing, and shelter.[46] The arrow would have been both a ritual and a practical object to the Cheyenne hunter and warrior, and not a trivial object serving as a photographic prop. Thus, White Buffalo's possession of an arrow in this image would also have been an inappropriate gesture for the young man, given the status of the arrow and its religious associations in his culture.

All in all, White Buffalo was in a sense tamed by having his alleged authenticity exploited in the Anglo-American ritual of the photographic portrait. His existence has been degraded from an authentic, ritual-based one to that of an object of visual consumption, as if on display in a museum diorama. Any cultural authenticity had been and continued to be threatened by the federal government's reservation policies. Even at the start of his assimilation, White Buffalo was already, like Torlino, a compromised figure whose natural appearance served to further a propagandistic show.

White Buffalo's "after" portrait, which figure 4.7 shows, represents the culmination of his subjection and "civilization," with the camera once again providing immutable evidence of the success and irreversibility of the process. This image, like the Torlino "after" shot, was a distinctly modernized one, especially when considered in relation to the first image of White Buffalo. Choate dispensed with the elaborately planned backdrops and props and instead chose to focus solely on White Buffalo's bust. Like Torlino, White Buffalo assumed all the essential signifiers of a civilized persona: short-cropped hair, clean-shaven face, placid and confident bearing, and most important, the Victorian-era Anglo-American clothing. Such a formula was important for Pratt, because it decontextualized the subject and therefore repressed any visual hint of possible contradictions or psychic tensions that may have been at play.

Perhaps most important, the photographically isolated "after" version of White Buffalo best modernizes the subject and in so doing comes closest to successfully illustrating Pratt's mantra of "kill the Indian, save the man." He often echoed this statement when summing up his philosophy of assimilation. For Pratt, as for many other reform-minded leaders of this time, Indianness was incompatible with any definition of manhood, because the two states were polar opposites in moral, cultural, political, and pseudo-scientific terms. For Pratt, the Indian was a degraded creature whose degradation was both innate to indigenous culture *and* artificially expedited by then-current government policies of concentration. Pratt caused much controversy by vigorously disagreeing with the government's policy of concentrating Native Americans on reservations, because he felt such isolation would only further encourage their culturally retardataire characteristics. For him, inculcating the Protestant work ethic was the only way to "save the man," and thus ensure a place for the continent's indigenous inhabitants in modern society. As he often said, Native Americans had a "valueless past" that needed to be removed from their collective memory and character.

White Buffalo's second portrait was thus to serve as a portrait of him as a "Man" in the Enlightenment sense of the term, a new self in which the specter of the Indian has disappeared. French philosopher Michel Foucault has offered an oft-quoted yet helpful model with which to understand such concepts. According to Foucault, the distinctly modern conception of Man arose during the eighteenth century in central and western Europe and can be viewed as a foil to the medieval concept of the subject in aristocratic contexts. The new Man was a figure with powers of self-determination and capable of gaining knowledge and power without divine or monarchic sanction. In short, Man was an atomized and individualized figure newly liberated from the chains of superstition and subjection, capable of defining his own reality through the symbolic use of language.[47]

Although these features constitute the sociological traits of this new Man, it is important that Foucault goes on to discuss the representational nature of this new figure. In fact, the term "figure" can only be applied lightly to the Foucaultian Man, because it inherently lacks representational similitude to begin with. This is because Foucault argues for a symbolic and representational breakdown of the earlier, pre-Enlightenment use of language and thus visual symbols in modern Western culture. He argues that in modernity, words and images no longer neatly or logically coincide with some external reality. In this sense, Man is not so much an actual being as a form of representation, a figure neatly placed for the modern mass reproduction of knowledge more generally. Man is thus conceptual and theoretical and lacks a correlation with any person or persons in the real world. Man is an idea or designation made up exclusively for ideological dissemination. In this light, Man is a figure neatly suited to the new medium of photography in the nineteenth century. The original person or individual, in this case White Buffalo, is far less important than the symbolic value of his reproduced persona.[48]

Making such atomized and symbolically charged men was precisely what Pratt sought to do at Carlisle. He valued self-governance and self-reliance over what he perceived as the dependency and squalor fostered by life on the new reservations. He believed that in such contexts, indigenous peoples were encouraged to regress rather than progress into civilization. By taking the Indian out of a person and instilling a newer modern American identity of manhood into him, Pratt hoped to build a new generation of Americanized citizenry. In this equation, photography would play a central metaphoric and propagandistic role. By decontextualizing the bodies of his indigenous students, Pratt could visually make of them what he would. Through his deft manipulations of text and imagery, contemporary viewers were encouraged to in a sense play along and fit the various pieces of the puzzle together: yesterday, Indian; today, Man.

In White Buffalo's 1884 "after" portrait, it is thus unsurprising that he is presented in a classic minimalist photographic formula. He was thus necessarily shown in bust-length format wearing the garb of civilization: starched white collar, tie, and overcoat. He has cropped hair, in contrast to the wild White Buffalo of 1881. His gaze is set to focus confidently outside the picture's frame, a trope intended to suggest a sense of vision or intellect, and one often used in nineteenth-century bourgeois photographic portraiture. In other words, White Buffalo has now become a young man of focus and vision rather than the oddly out-of-place savage of the "before" image.

In taking White Buffalo out of any extended visual context, Choate made a more powerful if more subtle statement. By appearing without backdrop references, White Buffalo seems to stand alone as an autonomous man, no longer dependent on tribal superstition, tribal cultural affiliation, or government charity. Further, in being so self-contained, he obviously no longer carries the instruments of savagery, such as his bow and arrow, and becomes a visually more docile and contained figure. Both the suggestion of violence and the threat suggested by his "before" appearance have been effectively neutralized.

Apparently, White Buffalo's appearance as savage in the "before" picture was striking and desirable enough for Choate to make it the centerpiece of a montage cabinet card that figure 4.8 shows. Choate decided to mass-produce these cards and sold them for twenty cents apiece and two dollars for a dozen.[49] We again see that the intended savagery in White Buffalo's "before" portrait was desirable to a market of white consumers. As I've stated, in the nineteenth century, the vicarious consumption of the savage Other was a key ingredient in both perpetuating a profitable market for photography and continuing cultural expansionism into supposedly uncivilized regions around the globe.

In the montage, Choate chose to feature White Buffalo's savage self at the center of a concentrically arranged array of student portraits. The composition features various students, both male and female. Choate chose to display most in their "after" personae, that is, their postindoctrination appearance. It is interesting and perhaps a bit surprising that Choate chose one of the most wild-looking students in his "before" guise as the centerpiece for the composition. By featuring White Buffalo so prominently, however, Choate might well have intended the image to be read as a progressive chronological composition to highlight how far the selected students had evolved since entering the school. Such a reading is reinforced by the fact that several of the students, such as the young woman directly to the upper right of White Buffalo's head, wear not only their civilized clothing but specifically professional clothing. The young woman is wearing a nurse's uniform, nursing being one of the most common professions for young women graduating from Carlisle.

Choate here conveys the sense of civilized beings miraculously emanating from the wildness of their supposed origins through his darkroom legerdemain. In the style of all composite photographs, Choate artificially combined imagery and elements that do not necessarily have any logical connection outside the image itself. Although the necessary gaps and spaces existing between the various portraits on the board's surface may tacitly reveal this disconnectedness, they potentially contain a more positive meaning as well: One is in a sense encouraged to make connections for oneself. When viewed in the sense intended by Choate, these various busts, floating on the photographic surface, together form a logic that supports a vaguely metaphysical perception of the image. It is from this perspective that the civilized faces emanate from some misty feral past (represented by White Buffalo's presence), and in so doing serve as an abstracted photographic argumentation for Pratt's assimilationist mission.

Finally, in considering the facts of White Buffalo's biography after leaving the school, the inevitable contradictions and problems of life on the reservations serve to complicate the one-dimensional identity put forward in Choate's "after" portrait. Accounts of White Buffalo's life after graduation appear both in Pratt's autobiography and in several issues of various school publications. These publications routinely gave subscribers updates on the status of graduates. The readership would have consisted of a complex audience of current students, alumni, school administrators, government officials, and school donors. Pratt and various faculty members had general editorial oversight and took great pains to frame perceptions of the school's activities for such a diverse group of readers.

In the school's *Twenty-Fourth Annual Report* of 1903, printed in the school paper *Red Man and Helper*, Pratt noted with regret the startling news that White Buffalo had been accused of committing a triple homicide on the Northern Cheyenne reservation. Such a violent revelation was rare in these papers, which under Pratt's editorial influence usually glossed over any disturbing content and instead favored a saccharine version of the lives of current and former students. In his account of the incident, Pratt claimed that although White Buffalo was imprisoned, had confessed, and was awaiting trial, the murders never occurred. Instead, he stated that the *North American* of Philadelphia, the newspaper that had printed the story, had libeled White Buffalo. Pratt argued that such a story was politically motivated in order to discredit the work of the school and to degrade Native Americans more broadly. Interestingly, he went on to state that the paper's use of halftone reproduced photographs of the alleged victims of the crime were staged to fabricate evidence against White Buffalo. Ironically, he also chided the paper for reproducing one of Choate's "before" portraits of White Buffalo to make him look more "Indian," and thus more likely to have committed the crime.[50]

Such an appropriation of Choate's imagery would indeed have been an affront to Pratt, as he often used old student portraits in his propagandistic efforts to promote the school in newspapers. This dispute reflects in a sense the core of Pratt's struggle in visually representing his students. His intent was to have them appear newly civilized by juxtaposing the old and new photographic identities, but other institutions and publications, perhaps politically in opposition to his agenda, could just as easily appropriate school imagery to proffer the opposite effect. This easy appropriation discloses, if anything, the interchangeability of photographs more generally in the emergent American mass media of circa 1900, by then under the influence of halftone reproduction and mechanical typesetting. It discloses how easily Pratt himself could have made and controlled images of the students, and how others may just as easily have used them for other purposes.

The case of White Buffalo, like that of Tom Torlino, offers a murky and controversial if not tragic view of the afterlives of Carlisle students. Despite Pratt's continual efforts to dominate how the school was portrayed in its own publications, events of the outside world often contradicted him and shed a potentially skeptical light on the efficacy of the entire process of assimilation.

5

Publicizing the "Civilized" Savage

Phrenology, the Boarding School, and the "Red Man" at the White City

In considering the Carlisle Indian Industrial School as an institution of education, normalization, and improvement, it is important to view it not by itself but in relation to larger boarding-school discourse in the United States in the nineteenth century. Such institutions were theoretically complex in their founding philosophies, and their underlying assumptions about the appearance and thus the nature of the human body and mind were central to their establishment and legitimization.

The notion that phrenology and similar pseudoscientific bodies of knowledge played a central role in establishing the normal schools of the United States in the middle and late nineteenth century is one only recently developed by scholars. In his book *Head Masters*, education historian Stephen Tomlinson argues that phrenology played a key role in the notion that children of varying racial and socioeconomic groups ought to be "normalized" by a universal system of public education in the United States. Specifically, Tomlinson claims that the educational reformist agenda of Horace Mann (1796–1859) and others, traditionally viewed by historians as purely philanthropic or reformist, was informed by a phrenological view of the human mind and its capacities.

In weaving this argument, Tomlinson states that Mann and similar reformers of the antebellum era had wide-reaching influence on American education into the twentieth century. Further, he claims that their powerful notions of normalization and civilization were in turn heavily indebted to their personal relationships with noted phrenologists, including George

Combe.[1] Tomlinson's text is the first significant academic publication to link antebellum phrenology and Gilded Age reformism to education and racial improvement, ideas that were obviously central to the Carlisle project.

With boarding school imagery, the phrenological influences become plain when one considers the stated doctrines of Combe, Mann, and others on the topic of education. Tomlinson states that Combe often wrote that prisoners needed to be "reformed" through productive enforced labor, something that would reorient their phrenological faculties and allow them to return to society as socialized, civilized beings.[2] The notion of enforced productive labor as a mechanism for improvement clearly parallels Pratt's own agenda, as his subsequent use of photography both at Fort Marion and later at Carlisle suggest (see fig. 5.1). Although Pratt's aims were not "phrenological" in the orthodox sense of antebellum phrenology, it is evident that such thinking at least indirectly underlay his entire project. This may be ascertained by considering not only the school's emphasis on the supposedly uplifting aspects of civilized labor, but also Pratt's flirtation with anthropometrics. This interest continued into his final years at the school, when the anthropologist Franz Boas wrote him requesting anthropometric measurements of the Carlisle students, some of whom were included in a Carlisle pavilion in the ethnological section of the 1893 Chicago World's Fair (see fig. 5.2).[3] This assumption, that photographic aesthetics and anthropometric measurement were central to proving the efficacy of the government's assimilationist projects in publicized contexts such as the Fair, warrants closer examination.

To understand this provocative intersection of photography, anthropometrics, and public display, it is first necessary to consider the purposes of the 1893 Chicago World's Fair Columbian Exposition and how its aims related to ideas of race at the time. Historian Robert Rydell has written what is perhaps the most thoughtful theoretical analysis of the Fair. In his text *All the World's a Fair*, Rydell argues the Fair conveyed a utopian vision of American culture and its place in the emerging global economy. To this end, the organizers designed the section of the Fair that would be known popularly as the "White City," a temporary large-scale architectural installation that would represent a sanitized, ideal, and democratic vision of the United States of 1893 (see fig. 5.3). Rydell further argues that, given the dire state of political and economic affairs in the country in 1893, this characterization of an emergent democratic American economic empire must be viewed skeptically. If anything, such a representation of the cultural landscape was more reflective of the political fantasies of the Fair's bourgeois organizers than of any external reality.[4]

Also, one needs only to recall Albert Boime's argument in his *Art of Exclusion*. Briefly, Boime's thesis was that throughout the nineteenth century in the United States, chromatic metaphors such as "white," "black," or "red" served not only as formal classifications for artists and art historians, but also, and more importantly, as ideological signifiers. Boime goes on to argue that white stood at one end of the formal and thus ideological spectrum, in stark contrast to black and red, colors associated in many contexts with savagery, barbarism, and even spiritual evil.[5] From this perspective, the chromatic scheme, neoclassical architectural motifs, and rational layout of the so-called White City are clearly suggestive of the structure's status in the imaginations of both the Fair's organizers and its intended audiences.

Rydell goes on to point out that the Smithsonian Institution had a hand in the Fair's organization, because Secretary Spencer F. Baird's successor G. Brown Goode (1851–1896) was responsible for classifying the displays. In keeping with the Smithsonian's own methods of ethnographic classification, Goode chose a rationalized encyclopedic method with which to break down and make sense of the Fair's myriad national and international contributions. As Baird's assistant during Baird's years as the Smithsonian's second secretary, Goode specialized in genealogy and was thus adept at the visual systematization and rationalization of knowledge for museum audiences. At the Fair, he wished to systematize knowledge in a manner that would be comprehensible to all viewers, regardless of socioeconomic background.[6] This ambitious project required the deft and large-scale use of three-dimensional displays, photographic representations, and explanatory text.

Goode's most basic strategy in organizing the Fair was to divide objects into the fundamental categories of artistic and scientific knowledge. He clearly wished the Fair's audiences to perceive it as didactic and educational, in keeping with populist notions of the time regarding the purposes for and usefulness of such events. Conversely, the presence of more artistic content was seen by many civic reformers of the day as a means of morally uplifting the audiences who would attend the Fair. In this sense, the Fair's agenda of forwarding both scientific didacticism and moral uplift paralleled strategies common to the nation's large museums and art galleries.[7]

Despite these lofty aims, the concurrent existence of the Fair's Midway problematized a purist interpretation of the Fair's more respectable White City pavilions. In general, the Midway contained exhibits that were more lurid than the ostensibly didactic content of the White City. It featured displays in which non-European cultures were shown in an overtly degrading and stereotyped manner, thus eschewing any pretense of objective presentation. In sum, the Midway featured a carnivalesque, sideshow atmosphere, in contrast to the more staid and dignified atmosphere of the White City. The Midway thus became an irresistible temptation for the Fair's organizers, because it promised substantial economic return on investment. Further, Rydell argues that although the Midway did have scientific pretensions, its lurid merging of entertainment and education led to rather simplistic and stereotypical representations of non-European ethnic groups under the dubious umbrella of cultural representation. Such installations, usually promoting a view of indigenous people as either barbaric or childish, not only contradicted the government's ethnographic pavilions in the White City but also forwarded a crudely simplistic view of the evolutionary supremacy of Anglo-America.[8] Perhaps New York Senator Chauncey Depew put it most succinctly after visiting the Fair:

> There was about the Midway Plaisance a peculiar attraction for me. It presents Asiatic and African and other forms of life native to the inhabitants of the globe. It is the world in miniature. While it is of doubtful attractiveness for morality, it certainly emphasizes the value, as well as the progress, of our civilization. There are presented on the Midway real and typical representatives of nearly all the races of the earth, living in their natural methods, practicing their home arts, and presenting their so-called native amusements. The denizens of the Midway certainly present an interesting study to the ethnologist, and give the observer an opportunity to investigate these barbarous and semi-civilized people without the unpleasant accompaniments of travel through their countries and contact with them.[9]

Depew's quotation was both blunt and honest. Despite their "doubtful attractiveness for morality," he has assumed a representational legitimacy in the "real and typical" exhibits of the Midway. Through viewing the morally degraded Others of the "Asiatic and African" parts of the globe, he reinforced the Fair's dominant view of American society as being valuable and progressive in comparison. Such a comparative analysis of cultures, based on assumed aesthetic similitude, was the driving force of the Fair's attraction for Euro-American viewers.

The photograph that figure 5.2 shows, which is most likely the work of Frances Benjamin Johnston,[10] is not only the only surviving image of the Carlisle pavilion at the 1893 Fair but also played a key part in contemporary debates about representing the Native American. The internal tensions inherent in the Fair's mission were perhaps nowhere more obvious than in the organizers' tackling of this thorny problem. The representation of the Indian at the Fair stirred a good deal of resentment in Pratt, because he did not have direct control over the pavilion's initial arrangement. In his autobiography, he stated that he had to contend with entertainer William Cody's (1846–1917) alternative pavilion, placed just outside the Fair's entrance (see fig. 5.4). This entrepreneurial venture, which Cody famously dubbed his "Wild West Show," presented a gaudy Vanishing Race–type diorama of Native Americans, to which Pratt heatedly objected. Pratt felt that such a characterization would downplay the "advancing Indian civilization" by focusing on an "aboriginal and wild west feature" and would thus draw attention away from the school's accomplishments and focus it instead on the Indian's "valueless past." Although the Bureau of Indian Affairs endorsed Cody's pavilion, Pratt's deft political maneuvering provoked a compromise, and Carlisle received another pavilion of a more "progressive" nature, as seen in the Johnston photo.[11]

Cody, a Civil War veteran and Pratt's longtime nemesis in the arena of Indian representation, saw opportunity following the closing of the frontier in 1876. At the time, and to some extent still today, historians of the United States have lamented this "closing," brought about by a crackdown by the U.S. Army on the Sioux nation in what was then the Dakota Territory. The date of 1876 has been hailed as not only marking the nation's centennial anniversary, but also marking a turning point in serious organized indigenous resistance on the frontier.

In lieu of a physical frontier in the western reaches of the continent, historian Frederick Jackson Turner offered his famous thesis "The Significance of the Frontier in American History." This thesis, first delivered by Turner in Chicago to coincide with the Fair's opening in 1893, argued that the progressive conquest of lands and peoples in the American West was the cultural phenomenon that had defined the exceptional quality of the American. With the closing of the continental frontier in the 1870s, Turner worried about the future of the nation's character, because for him republican democracy emanated from the unhindered individualism of frontier competition.[12] Into this perceived vacuum, Cody and others offered melodramatic simulations of frontier drama and conflict, focusing on the "winning" of the frontier by Euro-American heroes over savage indigenous resistance to progress. Historian L. G. Moses has argued that such representations in effect quantified Native Americans and assigned them a neat role in American history—that of conquered and romanticized foe.[13] Such a teleological account would clearly serve to fix the indigenous tribes as unified under the rubric of a Vanishing Race.

Cody's show, which he opened in 1883 and ran for thirty years, did indeed offer a simplified and stereotypical version of events on the frontier.

Such performances both evoked and distanced the disturbing realities of frontier war and atrocity by assigning an evolutionist, teleological end to the question. Cody's narratives not only reinforced a sense of white American superiority over the inevitably doomed savages but also exploited postfrontier economic conditions. His native performers, ironically recruited either from the same reservations at which Pratt recruited for Carlisle or from the ranks of the criminals who in the 1890s still offered scattered resistance to white settlement, were often coerced through economic or political pressure to agree to perform.[14]

In the photograph from the National Archives that figure 5.5 shows, the photographer uses the familiar lineup composition seen in the Carlisle arrival images and the "round-up" photographs. The sitters bear the characteristic expressions of fear and sullenness, not unlike the Carlisle arrivals. It is important to recall that both groups were photographed against their will and that in both cases, the act of photographing was intended to be a gesture of both surveillance and subjection. This is apparent in this image in the fact that the detainees bear superimposed numerical designations— a practice introduced in the 1880s by law enforcement officials wishing to catalog criminal offenders (see also fig. 5.6).

This particular group, leaders of the 1890 Sioux Outbreak, were rounded up, photographed for government identification, and detained at the Fort Sheridan army encampment. Cody was attracted by the sensational press coverage of the outbreak, during which Sioux leaders tried to reintroduce traditional tribal dances, seen by many as an anachronism subversive of government rule on the reservations. He persuaded T. J. Morgan, then commissioner of Indian Affairs, to allow him to use the prisoners for his show. His reasoning was that such employment would both reform the wrongdoers and attract crowds eager for a heightened sense of realism in the performance.[15] Such governmental duplicity in exploiting conflict for the ends of commercial entertainment disturbed Pratt and others a good deal and drove his insistence on the presence of more legitimate counter-representations at the Fair.

In this ambiguous context, the Carlisle students were at least spared the overt degradation of a Buffalo Bill–style treatment, but they were put on display nonetheless as evidence of the efficacy of their civilization at the hands of Pratt.[16] Actual students and mannequins populated the Carlisle pavilion, producing an eerie effect. The mannequins are visible in the curio cabinet in the foreground of the Johnston photograph. Such figures may be seen as an unwitting metaphor for the manipulations of the boarding school wrought onto the bodies of the students. Such a rendering would parallel the alleged plasticity of the Indian body and mind, a notion promoted by Francis E. Leupp, the soon-to-be commissioner of Indian Affairs.

It is also significant that actual students, dressed in Carlisle's famous paramilitary uniforms, were sent to the Fair to display their advances for the American public. In the Johnston image, one such student appears in the left foreground, staring into the curio cabinet containing the mannequins. The young man is seemingly unaware of Johnston's presence as he meditates on the dark-skinned mannequins. These figures, one male and the other female, wear conventional late-Victorian middle-class Anglo-American fashions—something a student would likely wear in any number of Choate's "after" portraits. Given Johnston's characteristic method of tightly staging her school images and her preference for large-scale glass negatives at this time, it is more likely that the student was placed in the position at her direction. What results is typical of Johnston's boarding-school imagery. As in her more famous images from Hampton, one of which figure 5.7 shows, the newly converted indigenous American bears silent witness to his own cultural evolution, one brought about by the alleged beneficence of the federal government.

Recent scholarship on Johnston's Hampton album has focused on the sense of enforced didacticism in the images. Students of color, both African American and Native American, stare in awe at the living specimen of the past of indigenous American culture. The viewer, given a third-person perspective from across the room, is privileged in the sense that he or she views the scene in its entirety, and thus has a distanced vantage point which allows for the perceptual establishment of relations between the various figures. The dramatic disjunction of appearance between the student on display and the students viewing the display encourages one to evaluate the "vanished" Indian and his "civilized" counterparts. This is not unlike the perceptual journey suggested by the Fair's own juxtaposition of the "savage" pavilions of the Midway and the "civilized" pavilions of the White City.

In a slight variation on this theme, the young man in the Fair image serves as a de facto stand-in viewer of the pavilion. Through his presence, we are encouraged to meditate on the pavilion as a whole, also photographed from a distanced, totalizing perspective. The young student dwells on the "after" identities represented by the lifeless yet racialized mannequins, as if mesmerized by the miraculous appearance of their newly won cultural identities. Yet the assumed viewer, positioned well behind the young man, is allowed to see the bigger picture of government assimilation as a whole. Although the student serves as a visual segue into the pavilion, he sees only one cabinet—a museum rendering of his generation—whereas Johnston's viewer is given a greater panorama of the entire scene. In this way, the student's viewing is objectified by the camera, and the photograph's viewer marvels not only at the grandeur of the school's pavilion, but also looks on with approval as a student marvels at the cultural exemplars he sees.

Despite the ostensibly progressive content of the pavilion, as Tomlinson suggests, the specter of pseudoscience still loomed in the background of boarding-school discourse, as Carlisle and schools like it were affected by the ethos of phrenology's racial dispersion theories.[17] In the context of Carlisle's representation at the Fair, Franz Boas confirmed this in his letter to Pratt when he stated that he desired "a series of charts showing the distribution of the types of man and of the growth of children of various races and of the same race under varying conditions."[18] Obviously, the measurements for these charts were important for the government, because Pratt was ordered to comply with Boas's request by the commissioner of Indian Affairs. L. G. Moses has discussed the importance of these measurements, because they were a central aspect of the Fair's Anthropology Building. He states that the Fair's official guidebook encouraged visitors to view the "facial characteristics of Indian races" with an eye toward anthropometric comparison. In this light, Boas's request to Pratt for anthropometric measurements was in the spirit of fixing a comparative evolutionary racial scale. Although the gaudier representations proffered by the Fair subverted the intent of those submitted by the Bureau of Indian Affairs, both types of display nevertheless shared similar underlying aims of illustrating cultural supremacy.

This suggestion becomes more plausible when we consider that the purpose for such measurements was to produce lay figures, or mannequins, for the Smithsonian's galleries. The Smithsonian Institution thus may well have used the measurements to construct the mannequins used in the Bureau's official pavilion for Carlisle. An intended aesthetics of evolutionary comparison was thus a central characteristic of how white patrons were supposed to see the indigenous bodies within the displays, whether those displays were deemed valid (in the White City) or lurid (along the Midway).

Further, from this perspective, the logic of the staple before-and-after photographs that served as a cornerstone in Pratt's propaganda is a predictable outcome of applying phrenological knowledge to the problem of secular education. Both Mann and Combe had thought of secular education in evolutionary terms, because it would serve to uplift the most degraded of the general population. This category, consisting of those most in need of reeducation, soon became an umbrellalike model and included the blind, the deaf, the criminal, the insane, and the racially subaltern.[19] The moral uplift of the normal school was applied broadly, and was intended to reform all deviants and effect a marriage to decent civilization.

Clearly, it was deemed necessary by those in power that visual evidence of cultural evolution, based at least covertly on the principles of phrenology and anthropometrics, was necessary to prove the effects of this new scientific education on subalterns. The road from savagery to civilization could be neatly summed up in two side-by-side images informed by the ethos of comparative anthropology. Whether it was for the Fair or in the context of a printed album, Anglo-American audiences sought the opportunity to view the savage Natives beside the elevated Natives of the school assimilation programs.

Frances Benjamin Johnston, Hampton, and the Carlisle Album

It is likely that Pratt first met Frances Benjamin Johnston (1864–1952) at the 1893 Fair while Johnston was employed by the Smithsonian to document the event for the federal government's official report. Apparently, their first meetings were positive, because eight years later Pratt would commission Johnston to illustrate the school's annual catalog. Pratt's hiring of Johnston was significant, because it showed his desire to reach and impress larger audiences in his tireless campaign to publicize the assimilationist agenda. Given that John Choate was still the school's quasi-official photographer until his death in 1902, it would seem that Pratt harbored a need to engage a photographer whose reputation superseded that of the provincial Choate.

By the turn of the century, Johnston would have qualified, as she had become not only one of the nation's leading photographers but also an important ambassador for American photography in international contexts. These credentials made Johnston by far the most well-known photographer ever to photograph any of the government's Indian boarding schools. It is therefore necessary to consider her career in some depth and the Carlisle album that is within her oeuvre, and to place her subjectivity into the context of American cultural debates of the time.

Coming from a well-to-do family in Washington, D.C., Johnston's interest in art began early, when she began to study drawing as a child while at the Notre Dame Convent in Maryland. Her first real step toward a serious career was a stint at the prestigious and coeducational Académie Julian in Paris in 1883. The Académie, founded in 1868 by French painter Rodolphe Julian, was extremely liberal for the time both in its admission policies and its pedagogy. It famously admitted female students, and instructors conducted coeducational nude life drawing classes. The institution therefore attracted women and foreign students, many of whom were excluded from older, more established academies in France and other countries.[20] In fact, many other Americans attended the Académie over the years, including John Singer Sargent, Robert Henri, Thomas Dewing, and John Henry Twachtman.[21]

Johnston went to Paris with the ambition of becoming a fine artist, and initially continued to pursue her ambition on returning to the United States. In 1885 she enrolled at the Art Students League in Washington, D.C. Johnston scholar Bettina Berch claims that Johnston's first move into photography occurred while she was still studying at the ASL. Another female student, Elizabeth Sylvester, convinced Johnston to pursue a career in magazine illustration, a field more open to women at the time.[22]

With her interest shifting to photography, Johnston managed to secure an apprenticeship to study the medium under Thomas William Smillie (1843–1917), a photographer who worked at the Smithsonian Institution from 1870 until his death in 1917. Her apprenticeship under Smillie was her first systematic study of the medium and was a significant counter-influence to the academic aestheticism taught at the Académie. Smillie had been hired as the Smithsonian's first full-time staff photographer in 1870 by the Institution's first secretary, Joseph Henry. In this position, Smillie was responsible for systematically photographing all aspects of the Smithsonian's collection for archival purposes. Smillie held his post under Baird's secretarial tenure and was named head photographer for the newly established Section of Photography in 1883. It was around this time as the new section's head photographer that he likely trained the young Johnston. Smillie held influential positions in the Smithsonian's hierarchy until his death in 1917.[23] It is thus fair to assume that his photographic method was not only influential for decades but in a sense defined the government's official documentary style during this period.

When viewing some of Smillie's surviving images, both his participation in then-current trends in ethnographic photography and his influence on Johnston's later work become clear. In addition to his tasks at the museum, Smillie was also responsible for accompanying government surveys to the West and photographing Indian delegations that came to Washington. His group compositions, of which figure 5.8 is a typical example, are quintessentially ethnographic. They are frontal, iconic, tightly framed, and shot at eye level, with strong side lighting flooding the subjects. Indeed, many of Johnston's later images at Hampton and Carlisle would bear the stamp of these formal tropes. Further, Johnston's two sources of early training—one in a fine arts milieu and another in an ethnographic milieu—would form a tension in her work that would make interpretation of that work difficult for decades.

Additionally, photography historians often characterize the 1880s as a "second revolution" during which the medium and its applications broadened dramatically. Photography took on more recognizable, modern forms because of expanding technologies such as halftone reproduction, handheld cameras, faster exposure times, industrialized printing, and roll film.[24] It was during this decade that Johnston came to early maturity as a professional photographer.

The newly opened entrepreneurial atmosphere in the publishing and photography worlds suited Johnston. In 1889, shortly after her study with Smillie, she received her first professional commission to produce an article for the popular periodical *Demorest's Family Magazine*. In what would become a trademark of her diverse skill and business acumen, Johnston executed photographs for the article, titled "Uncle Sam's Money," and wrote the article's text. The article, written about currency production at the national mint in Philadelphia, was illustrated by two zinc engraving reproductions of her original prints, one of which figure 5.9 shows.[25] Apparently, Johnston's skill with both pen and camera, coupled with the magazine's high circulation, was enough to attract the attention of many in the field of photography.

Although the mint photographs are her earliest known work, their technical polish is unmistakable. Clearly, the young painter-turned-photographer learned her new trade quickly. This is all the more impressive when one considers that on her first assignment, Johnston did not own her own photographic equipment. In fact, she approached Eastman Kodak founder George Eastman through a family connection the following year and requested a camera. Eastman, who had founded his company in 1881, was the leading photographic entrepreneur in the United States at the time. He agreed to give Johnston a camera, provided she work as his agent in Washington.[26] Eastman's activities were not only extraordinary in photography, but in a sense were typical of the entrepreneurial capitalist ethos that governed the nation's economy during the closing decades of the century. It is thus helpful to view Johnston as a player in this larger competitive game of free agent–style capitalism.

Johnston's employment by Eastman in the early 1890s further cemented her reputation as a skillful technician and genuine entrepreneur in the field. The correspondence between the two suggests that Johnston's ambition and independence was at times a bit much even for Eastman to bear. Records indicate that Johnston serviced and billed many of Eastman's most important clients and conducted a wide variety of business transactions, including providing camera equipment and printing services for the Interior Department, the Agriculture Department, and the Smithsonian. Although she was successful both in drumming up new business and in perpetuating preexisting business on Eastman's behalf, the latter occasionally betrayed a hint of mistrust of Johnston's practices and even accused her at one point of price fixing.[27]

Despite these early career conflicts, Johnston was successful in establishing a signature photographic method in the *Demorest's* series and other early assignments. One can sense her deft handling of large-format glass negatives and intensive lighting, her extreme attention to detail, and the odd stillness for which her work is perhaps best known. The feeling of suspension is intriguing when one considers that much of Johnston's work before 1910 dealt with corporeal subject matter, often in industrial contexts.

Most important for recent scholarship, many of these images, which were often completed on government or private institution commission, focus on the presence of both female and African American participants within the emergent industrial labor system. Historian Shawn Michelle Smith has noted that in much of Johnston's work, these characteristic social and institutional dynamics were ever present and thus underlie her work's ostensibly diverse content.[28]

Her ethnicity, socioeconomic background, and support from the government clearly would have given Johnston a sense of empowerment, access, and thus photographic control in imaging such people. It is therefore perhaps unsurprising that she often chose to focus heavily on groups normally unrepresented in images of labor at the time. As several art historians have noted, in American visual culture during this period of rapid industrialization, middle-class artists construed labor as a sexually and racially encoded activity. This has been interpreted as connoting a fascination with a sense of gritty "manliness," usually projected onto a labor force represented as chiefly (although not exclusively) white and male.[29]

In this context, Johnston's representation of a more diverse labor force stood apart and would foreshadow her later work at Hampton and Carlisle. However, as Smith notes, although Johnston may have been a potential advocate for culturally marginal groups, her class status nevertheless requires us to view her images cautiously, with an eye toward how she participated in establishing visual hegemony.[30]

With this in mind, I would like to consider Johnston's work of the turn of the century, a period in which she focused on the most hegemonic of all contexts, the public education system. Shortly before coming to Carlisle in 1901, Johnston embarked on a series of commissions to document some of the nation's most challenging education projects, both public and private. In December 1899, Hollis Burke Frissell, the second president of the Hampton Normal and Agricultural Institute in Hampton, Virginia, invited her to carry out an extensive series of photographs of the school, an example of which figure 5.10 shows. Hampton, a boarding school at which young African American and Native American students studied economically useful trades such as agriculture, carpentry, teaching, and domestic services, was founded in 1868 by Pratt's army colleague Samuel Chapman Armstrong. An officer during the Civil War, Armstrong wished to establish an institution that would aid the newly freed black population of the South in integrating into the national population during the difficult period of Reconstruction.[31]

These printed images, originating from Johnston's trademark large-format glass-plate albumen negatives, were to serve two important purposes, for the school in particular and also the nation. First, some were distributed in illustrative form to Hampton students, parents, faculty, and potential donors through publication in several contexts, including the school's periodical *Southern Workman*.[32] Second, a selection of the images was to travel to the 1900 Paris Exposition Universelle. Therefore, the two original intended audiences were domestic and international. Although the domestic audiences were clearly racially mixed, the overriding agenda for making the images was nonetheless to forge a perception of the "progress" made by freed slaves and their children in the South since the Civil War. As Smith notes, such an agenda was nationalistic in bent and assumed an Anglo-American cultural identity for which the students needed to strive.

At Paris, Johnston curated the display of her own work and that of twenty-eight other female American photographers. The Hampton images made up only a portion of the entire show and were housed in a section of the Exposition titled Palace of Social Economy of American Negro Exhibition. The organizers intended this exhibition to show the efficacy of American government policy on the touchy topic of race relations as well as the ascension of the black American since the war to potentially skeptical international audiences.[33]

That such a reading of these racial images was important to the political establishment of the time is clear when one considers the context in which Johnston made the photographs. As Smith contends, this was an era during which white supremacist terror was reaching a fever pitch in the United States. To counteract such violent racial and class warfare, both the government and private institutions launched large-scale projects of cultural assimilation, establishing not only boarding schools but also public museums, soup kitchens, halfway houses, libraries, and other philanthropic institutions. In a manner similar to that of Carlisle, Hampton was one such school, whose purpose was to homogenize the black and indigenous populations. The students were to enter the mainstream of Anglo-American social and economic activity through the repetitive performance of cultural rituals and acquisition of "relevant" cultural knowledge.[34]

With this in mind, it is therefore unsurprising to witness Johnston's photographic solution to the problem of shaping public perception of African American life. One tactic entailed Johnston placing two images side by side, such as the photographs that figures 5.11 and 5.12 show. The tactic is similar to that used by Choate in the 1880s, and the implication is that the viewer ought to read the images as temporal/cultural before-and-after shots. Thus, in figure 5.11, or the "before" image, Johnston presented a seemingly transparent scene of rural squalor and immobility. It is known that besides making images at the school, Johnston ventured into the rural Virginia countryside and chose particular houses and families to photograph. Obviously, she chose locations and people that she thought were most likely to display the primitive state of the Southern black, before the arrival of reformist institutions like Hampton. Indeed, the scene is disturbing and most likely intended to remind Anglo-American and African American viewers alike of the pitfalls of cultural and political regression.

From this standpoint, the second image in such a sequence suggests a sense of liberation from the previous squalor and immobility of slavery. The differences between figures 5.11 and 5.12 could not be more stark—manicured landscaping versus an uncultivated and bleak landscape, Victorian construction versus a makeshift shack, and two hygienic young girls obediently posing on the front lawn versus the downtrodden, inattentive, and unkempt residents of the shack. This final dichotomy needs further consideration.

In nearly all of her "after" or end-state images from Hampton, Johnston's subjects conveniently appeared in front of the camera, seemingly obediently and attentively. This quality lent an eerie tension to her work that is characteristic of her boarding-school imagery as a whole. On the one hand, the images offered seemingly transparent views into the incidental day-to-day goings-on of the school and in the lives of school alumni. Clearly, the viewer was to marvel at how far the African American had traveled since emerging from the degradation of slavery. On the other hand, the still appearance of all the images of course betrays the technological limits inherent in her use of large-format glass-plate negatives. Because this method required a multisecond exposure, the clarity of her images can only result from self-conscious posing by her subjects. Whether the figures seem obedient and attentive, or sullen, disconnected, and inattentive, the same method applies. And as I mentioned earlier, Johnston enjoyed a relationship of authority with both groups, whether those groups were visually coded as "liberated" or "regressive."

It is therefore reasonable to assume that Johnston actively directed her subjects to assume a particular demeanor in front of the lens to accentuate the polarizing effects of side-by-side imagery. Thus, the "primitive" images of rural blacks are not necessarily more authentic than the images of the more obviously rigidly posed students of the school, and vice versa. Just as Choate's studio techniques actively produced Indianness, Johnston's engagement of her subjects produced "blackness" in varying degrees of retrogression or advancement in culturally evolutionist terms.

Following Smith's argument a bit further, the dominant characteristic of people in both photographs is their disavowal of the photographer's presence and their failure to return the camera's gaze. This characteristic not only legitimizes the images as transparent windows into reality but also assures the viewer (especially white viewers) that Johnston's own cultural and photographic authority remain intact or pure, and have not been compromised by her contact with the black men in the images.[35] It is precisely this disavowal of the photographic situation per se that allows the viewer to overlook Johnston's obvious formal tropes and read the images as genuine.

The seeming invisibility of the photographer's presence therefore allowed Johnston, like Choate, to engage in extensive aesthetic manipulation without losing the veneer of ethnographic documentation. In the famous pair of photographs that figures 5.13 and 5.14 show, Johnston juxtaposed two black families in interior domestic scenes.[36] In contrast to the more light-diffused and symmetrical "after" shot, in the "before" image the asymmetry of the composition perversely reinforces a sense of unaffectedness—despite the stiffness of the poses of the couple at the table. Their asymmetrical positioning, taken with the makeshift appearance of the room, the low ceiling, shoddy construction, and flooding sunlight entering from the window on the far right all lend the image a credible sense of primitiveness. Yet on reflection, this capturing of a primitive quality stems more from European artistic convention than from any lived experience most viewers would have had with such a situation.

Indeed, one is not hard pressed to think of the presence of such themes and compositions in the mainstream history of European art. Such themes are found in the seventeenth-century Dutch interiors executed by Vermeer, the eighteenth-century didactic genre paintings of Greuze, and nineteenth-century American genre scenes such as those painted by Eastman Johnson.

Often, genre paintings made a tacit argument to the viewer. They are to be taken as authentic scenes offering a view into gritty day-to-day realities with their use of aesthetic convention made subordinate to their intended representational rawness.

Judging from the positive reception these images received in 1899–1900, Johnston was clearly successful in conveying a sense of primitive premodern squalor in the "before" images. A famous commentary on the Paris Exhibition images came from W. E. B. Du Bois, who went so far as to suggest that the authorship of the images was in fact only partly Johnston's. Du Bois, along with Hampton graduate Booker T. Washington, assisted in compiling the selection for the exposition. In his commentary, he asserted that the images were in a sense authored by the students themselves, whose improved appearances in the "after" images indicated a sense of black empowerment and thus at least partly dictated the terms of the photographic engagement. Although this assertion does challenge the one-sided interpretation of the images as manifestations of a "white supremacist gaze,"[37] it nevertheless preserves the fundamental positioning of the images in a discourse of documentary transparency.

These images have been praised mainly for their aesthetic refinement as recently as 1966, when the Museum of Modern Art reprinted a selection of Johnston's images for a MoMA exhibition catalog of her Hampton work. Judging from the catalog's text, curator John Szarkowski selected those images he judged most artistic. In his essay, Szarkowski stated that he appreciated the social and historical factors involved in making the forty-four selected images. Nevertheless, he wished to go beyond such considerations and "discover" them as pictures; something that, as his choice of words imply, he felt had not been discerned previously. Further, he stated that Johnston's original sequencing of the images in the Paris Exposition album signals the presence of her own "personal vision and characteristic style" in the Hampton series and in her photography more generally.[38]

Despite the freshness of his interpretation, Szarkowski nevertheless loses sight of issues of race, power, gender, class, and authorship in his insistence on the aesthetic merit of Johnston's work. Although the images do betray a strict concern for composition and lighting, his analysis fails to flesh out *how* Johnston used aesthetics in the service of ethnographic documentation and the establishment of a dominant white nationalism during the Gilded Age. To this end, it is helpful to consider Johnston's work at Carlisle and the various functions that work served.

Concurrently with her high-profile accomplishment at Hampton, Johnston embarked on another ambitious project in 1899. She again tackled the problem of photographing children in institutional contexts when the city of Washington, D.C., commissioned her to document the educational methods of the city's public school system. The city wished to publicize its reputedly progressive public education system and thus hired Johnston to make a series of images that would accompany the Hampton images to the Paris Exposition. Although the school system was integrated at this time, Johnston's images forward a view of racial segregation, as individual images include either all-white or all-black subjects.[39] The image that figure 5.15 shows, of female students ostensibly exercising during a gym class, was another standard compositional formula often seen in Johnston's school imagery. The girls hang from a large climbing apparatus flattened against the far wall of the room. Because their faces are hidden, their uniforms are identical, and their hairstyles and hair color are also nearly identical, the girls seem transfixed, frozen, and interchangeable—akin to scientific or museum specimens. This style was in keeping with Johnston's and the city's agenda. Johnston clearly wished to forgo individual identification or portraiture in favor of highlighting the system itself and its effects on the student body, as it were. In this sense, this is a chillingly industrial image, whose formula she would repeat at Carlisle many times. Whether the person in the image is male or female, black or white, one senses the subordination of the body and the will to the newly emergent standardized public education regime in the country, a system that prepared children for a lifetime of repetitive industrial labor.

After meeting Johnston at the World's Fair, Pratt sought to secure her esteemed services to promote his mission at Carlisle. Johnston initially wrote to the Bureau of Indian Affairs in December of 1900 requesting a commission to photograph the school grounds and the students. Oddly, the bureau balked and refused to allocate funds for a Carlisle project.[40] It was at that point that Pratt personally hired Johnston to carry out the series in March 1901.

For Pratt, the project was suffused with personal sentiment. This is evident in the surviving correspondence between him and Johnston. Judging from the tone of the letters, Johnston had become close to Pratt and his entire family. Further, she seems to have accepted a total payment of only $250 for the entire project, in contrast to the $1,000-plus in expenses she commanded from the Hampton administration.[41] This is significant in the making and thus the reading of these images. The tension in Johnston's work—between a discernible empathy for subaltern people not usually photographed and an intensive insistence on a suspended, distanced photographic style—surface when one views the Carlisle images.

The Carlisle images are currently scattered in various collections. The two main repositories are the Library of Congress and the Cumberland County Historical Society in Carlisle, Pennsylvania. Pratt selected only eighteen of Johnston's more than one hundred original negatives for publication, and they were subsequently published in 1902 in an illustrated catalog. Significantly, despite the closeness of their personal relationship, Pratt rarely credited Johnston with the catalog's illustrations in public. This treatment echoed his treatment of Choate during their twenty-three-year collaboration. In fact, he mentioned Johnston's name publicly only once in reference to the catalog, in the 18 September 1901 issue of *The Red Man and Helper*, one of the school's several literary organs:

> Many inquiries are made concerning the establishment, methods, aims and results of the school, together with queries as to the use made of education by those who go out from us.
>   To meet these I have arranged to issue something in the nature of a catalogue or annual, giving the points of general interest.
>   From the first we have kept as careful an office record of every student as our work would permit, but our numbers are too great for a catalogue of all. I shall therefore include only all the graduates and a few special students who left the school before we began to graduate pupils.
>   A committee is now at work on this booklet which will be illustrated with some of Miss Johnston's pictures and ready for publication as soon as plates are procured.[42]

In the album itself, Pratt neglected to mention Johnston's name once, even though by 1901 she enjoyed an international reputation. Pratt kept control of the original negatives and used them repeatedly in school publications before his departure from the school in 1904. The album itself was supposed to print in a run of 2,500 copies in 1902.[43] Considering Johnston's lack of editorial control over the images and her relatively meager $250 commission rate, it was as if she and Pratt had reached a tacit agreement about her limited authorial role in making the images. It is thus helpful to think of the images in the album in two senses with respect to authorship. First, the manner in which Johnston posed, framed, and shot the images, and second, how Pratt edited and reprinted the images in the catalog and subsequent contexts. Pratt opened the catalog with a section titled "The Carlisle Idea," containing excerpts from various speeches and editorials he had delivered and written during his tenure as superintendent of the school. Pratt seemingly wrote and edited this preface, and it thus lends the impression to the reader that the catalog is entirely his work. The opening excerpt, reprinted from correspondence between Pratt and an army superior on his capture of the Fort Marion prisoners in 1875, is typical of Pratt's assimilationist rhetoric and sets the tone for the entire catalog:

> The young men in this party (the Indian prisoners) while undergoing this banishment should be educated in English, trained in our industries, and brought in contact with our civilization as much as possible, for sooner or later they will be returned to their tribes and after all they are not so culpable as their old leaders, being more like soldiers acting under orders.[44]

Pratt's obsession remained consistent from the time of the Fort Marion detainment in the 1870s through the end of his tenure at Carlisle in 1904. He wished to take the "salvageable" younger generations of indigenous warriors and uplift them beyond the savagery of their forebears. Through systematic exposure to all things civilized, beginning with the English language and Christianity, and moving on to applicable trades, the indigenous youths were to be transformed into civilized citizens of the republic. Then, on returning to their reservations, they would spread the beneficial influence of the civilizing process to all others, thus disbanding the older tribal ways of communal ownership and paganism.

Given his central concern with inculcating industry as a key goal of the Carlisle experience, it is curious that Pratt chose the image that figure 5.16 shows as the first in the catalog's sequence. Johnston presents an idyllic scene characteristic of white bourgeois leisure. The full bloom of the trees and fullness of the surrounding lawn indicate that Johnston made the image after her first trip to the school in March. As Bettina Berch has noted, Johnston needed to reshoot several of the images, because some of the shots failed to meet Pratt's aesthetic expectations.[45] Their correspondence reveals that Johnston made later trips to Carlisle, in May and June of 1901, again presumably to reshoot for the catalog.[46]

Simply titled "Croquet," the image features several female students casually yet conveniently arranged before the camera. The figures mainly occupy the middle ground and background of the scene, because Johnston chose to give a more sweeping view of the school's quadrangle. The feeling of leisure and ease is balanced by the presence of a male groundskeeper on the far right, who is watching over the young women as he attends to his duties. This "overseer" trope was to become typical in nearly all of Johnston's images (see also fig. 5.1), because a faculty or staff member is usually present. Further, the angle of view circumscribes the students neatly into the architectural fold of the campus grounds, as Johnston offers no vision of

the world *beyond* the campus. This latter point is compositionally significant when one considers the layout of the school's architecture. Carlisle
scholar and curator Barb Landis has argued that the concentric geometric arrangement of the school grounds served as a panoptic architectural
device, intended to contain the students physically as well as perceptually.[47]
Indeed, from most points within the school's still-remaining central area,
to this day one cannot see beyond the rectangular arrangement of buildings, which creates an environmental sense of containment (see fig. 5.17).

Further, the content of the picture strikes an odd note when viewed in
light of Pratt's insistence on military-style training and regimentation. The
performance of a leisure activity reserved at this time for the bourgeoisie is
misleading. The types of trades taught to young women at Carlisle—chiefly
nursing, cooking, and domestic service—although economically viable during this era, was not bourgeois or even petit bourgeois in socioeconomic
terms. The students, even the most successful ones, were destined for lives of
skilled or semiskilled labor and thus socioeconomic servitude. Such a representation is little more than an absurd form of socioeconomic masquerade
and is seemingly illogical when viewed in this light.

However, juxtaposing images of students at work and students at
leisure served larger ideological purposes at Carlisle under Pratt's strict
regime. For instance, the album contains a wide array of representations of
the indigenous body, ranging from a group portrait of the school's famous
band, which figure 5.18 shows, to scenes of young male students engaged in
athletic activities in the school's gym, which figure 5.19 shows. Pratt inter-
spersed such scenes of athletic and cultural pursuits with perhaps more representative scenes depicting varying degrees of skilled and physical labor, as
in figures 5.20 and 5.21. All such representations, whether depicting "work"
or "leisure," need to be considered in terms of an emergent industrial order.
The writings of Italian philosopher Antonio Gramsci are helpful in fleshing
out a deeper meaning for such a genre of images.

In his famous collection of philosophical tracts *The Prison Notebooks*,
written between 1929 and 1935, Gramsci outlined the principle methods by
which powerful institutions subjected large masses of the human population
to industrial economic and productive control. In general, Gramsci argued
that every aspect of a worker's life—from his time on the job to his ostensibly "leisure" time—required regimentation and regulation by the state.
This was to ensure the most efficient and competitive national economy
possible, one in which the working classes were in a sense *always* at work.
For Gramsci, this entailed not only the familiar bourgeois division of time
into work versus leisure hours, but the complete and total mechanization of

the worker's mind and body throughout each minute of every day. In fact, Gramsci saw the American industrial system—in particular the practices of industrialist Henry Ford (1863–1947)—as demonstrating this ethos.[48]

Specifically, Gramsci contended that in the American industrial system as it emerged in the early twentieth century, one could make out a shift from an economy based on competition between individuals to one based on corporate hegemony and state economic planning. In this newer form of capitalism, it was incumbent upon both the corporation and the state to effectively regulate workers' thoughts and behavior. This was to be carried out not only in the factory through mechanical, repetitive tasks but also outside the factory in the form of moral, social, and even sexual regulation. In other words, the worker was told not only when to awaken and go to work but also whom to associate with, how much to eat and drink, how often to go to church, and how often to engage in sexual congress. In this sense, the worker's neighborhood and family lives reinforce his or her "work ethic." Gramsci terms this the rationalization of work.[49] When one recalls Pratt's strict regimentation of the students' work, study, and leisure-time activities each school day into hourly segments, Gramsci's characterization seems all the more relevant.

Additionally, the *specific* types of labor depicted in the content of these images should not be taken for granted. In figure 5.21, which Pratt titled "Coping Stone Fences," we can sense the inculcation of a skill that would serve multiple purposes. Not only are the boys being taught a "useful trade" according to Pratt's pedagogical mandates, but they are learning in effect an entire cosmology. The notion of dividing land into geometrically demarcated *private* plots was of course the central aim of the Dawes Act of 1887. The purpose of this act was to both break tribal bonds among reservation residents and promote stationary agriculture over nomadic hunting and gathering. The ideological destruction of indigenous cultural forms was central to the entire assimilationist agenda. The compelled performance of such Anglo-American rituals was to serve as proof of the mental and physical submission of the students to Pratt's regime.

When viewing such photographs, it is important to consider not only the place they held within the visual culture of the institution but also the content of individual images. As discussed earlier, images of labor were prominent in American art during this period, and often took part in the changing discourses surrounding labor in the industrializing economy. In addition to being prominent in American art in paintings executed by Thomas Anshutz and others, newer images of labor often reflected a more scientific view of work based on the segmenting and mechanizing of human movement. This new aesthetic was, of course, distinct from earlier images of labor, which romanticized the early industrial laborer in the picturesque "Vulcan at the forge" figure.⁵⁰ Johnston's images rest awkwardly in this visual discourse on labor. The content of her images of students at work varies widely, and the public reception of her oeuvre complicated the matter due to the wide array of readings of her work—from strictly scientific or documentary in tone to pictorial.

Pratt's intended audience consisted of two primary groups. Most prominently, he was trying to reach and persuade government officials in Washington and various school contributors and patrons. Second, he courted favor with prominent indigenous chiefs, many of whom had children at Carlisle. With this in mind, and to follow up on the "scientific" aspects of Johnston's work, we will consider the photograph titled "Boiler House" (see fig. 5.20). The photograph's content is perhaps the first element that would strike contemporary audiences. Members of both groups Pratt wanted to reach would likely have perceived the labor the image depicts as alien to their own experience.

Two male students engage in a form of work lodged midway between the preindustrial manual labor of shoveling and the more mechanized repetitive labor increasingly characteristic of the early twentieth century and its machines. They are clearly dwarfed by and thus compositionally subjected to the dark, metallic, and imposing boilers that loom above their stooped bodies. Similarly to the convention used in the "leisure" image of the young women playing croquet, the white faculty member on the left serves as both a narrative and compositional overseer. He is the visual evidence of the school's authority, ensuring that the young men comply with orders and complete their task competently and safely. Johnston catches the young men in midtask, bent over and in the act of throwing coal into the machines. Such menial tasks were important to Pratt, because student laborers largely powered the campus's infrastructure. This provided Pratt with an endless supply of de facto slave labor, and even made the school's industries profitable.⁵¹

In the larger cultural contexts of the newly emergent industrial labor, Johnston's work anticipates the chronophotographic studies used to promote the labor theories of American industrial engineer Frederick W. Taylor (1856–1915). An industrial management theorist often cited by Gramsci, Taylor wrote prolifically on the topic of worker efficiency in factories. In his famous essay "The Principles of Scientific Management," Taylor proposed that to increase worker productivity and thus the mutual profits of shop owner and worker, managers needed to adopt a new form of work-time surveillance. Essentially, the minute analysis of a worker's physical movements was important in ensuring conservation of time and energy, greater productivity, and thus greater corporate profit. Taylor felt that American workers had traditionally been too wasteful in their work movements. The new "scientific" manager would be able to watch a worker engaged in tasks and then offer a critique of that individual's relative efficiency in terms of movement.[52] Essentially, Taylor wished to speed up and in a sense mechanize the American labor force, in keeping with the dramatically changing demands of the mechanized industrial workplace.

Not coincidentally, Taylor's notion of increased efficiency through the minute analytic breakdown of physical motion was something also of interest to photographers during the Gilded Age. Such would at least indirectly influence Johnston's own perception of the human body as a subject for photography. Perhaps most well known in this vein are Eadweard Muybridge's early experiments in chronophotography. Muybridge often focused on the minute, moment-to-moment details inherent in the seemingly unconscious daily routines of his subjects. Although his images were most often clearly staged, they were nevertheless accepted by many at the time for their perceived scientific legitimacy.

It was not long before the scientific uses of chronophotography were applied to the workplace. Beginning in the 1890s, corporations hired Taylor to improve shop performance through the analysis of both worker movement and the architectural design of factory floors. Some of Taylor's followers, such as Frank Gilbreth (1868–1924), were hired to make visual recordings of worker movements. What resulted was the photographic application of Taylor's scientific management principles, known then as the "chronocyclegraph." In his time-lapsed photographs, Gilbreth affixed small light bulbs to workers' hands and photographed them as their hands moved while performing a specific task. What resulted was a visual graph, which could then be put to use as a model for less efficient workers.[53] Essentially, employers sought to segment and atomize space and time with such a practice.

Art historian Mark Antliff has offered a helpful and provocative explanation of the cultural effects of such a view of the space-time continuum. He argues that in applying the quantification of space and time to industrial production, Taylorism succeeded in fragmenting the organic labor-based production of premodern eras into a series of repetitive tasks and expedited worker movements to as great a degree as possible. The result was that the organic manufacture of whole objects by single skilled artisans became subordinate to mass production. Work tasks became repetitive and standardized and workers became interchangeable, like parts in the new machines of the factory.[54]

It was precisely the social and psychological atomization and individuation brought on by such work conditions that Pratt wished to show with labor images in the Johnston album. It must be remembered that what Pratt wanted to prove more than anything was that the Indian could be forcibly "civilized." This meant that previous primitive or tribal habits and associations had to be broken through such mechanistic regimentation. Although Johnston's images are not chronophotographic in literal technique because they are made by different photographic means, the ethos of work-time surveillance is clearly in place nonetheless. Also, a depiction of the human body at work that was based on standardization and calibration would have served Pratt conveniently in two other closely related ways.

First, it served to reinforce the worldview proposed by the Dawes Act of 1887. As I have discussed, this act of Congress segmented the frontier, opening land up for speculation and development. Areas once open to nomadic migration and range hunting not only were divided into confining reservations but could then be divided further into smaller parcels by order of the president. The act reduced indigenous inhabitants to low-grade tenants, because it allotted at most 120 acres for each family. Once the families were on the parcels, the government typically assumed that they would adopt Euro-American methods of agriculture and livestock raising as an alternative to the "roving" lifestyles of their tribal forebears.[55] Second, it served to hasten the destruction of traditional Native American crafts and fundamental views of nature in the race toward industrial labor standardization.

That these principles were also central to Pratt's mission is proven in another of Johnston's images, which figure 5.22 shows. In this image, titled by Pratt "Farm Scene," Johnston offers not an image of industrial labor but a slightly more surprising image of traditional agriculture. A young male student poses with horses and hoe in a cultivated field. This student was possibly photographed during a stint in the Carlisle "outing" program. This program sent students to live with a white family to be immersed in mainstream American culture and apply the trade they had learned at the school. Interestingly, the youth acknowledges Johnston's presence as he gazes directly at the camera, which lends him a slightly more independent aura than does the posture struck by the subservient boiler-room workers. Johnston's camera was elevated, because her viewpoint is roughly parallel with the heads of the two horses and spans out over the youth's head, thus giving the viewer a panoramic view of the entire field. Such a commanding view of the field's totality signals that Pratt wanted some of the images in the album to suggest a greater degree of independence for the students depicted. Such professional autonomy and sense of economic self-determination were two things that he felt would most quickly Americanize the Indian and rescue him from his "valueless past."

Such an image and the notions it embodies were of course central to the American cultural mythos of the "independent farmer." This mythical male figure, whom art historian Sarah Burns has characterized as the "ideal American citizen," was often credited with taming the wilderness and making it hospitable for human settlement and cultivation, thus representing the apex of possessive individualism. This "noble yeoman," unpretentious and self-sufficient, often found his way into American art throughout the nineteenth century and came to stand for everything good and wholesome in the culture through his benign mastery of the land (see fig. 5.23).[56] In this sense, the student's direct gaze, upright commanding posture, and tight rein over the domesticated animals participate in this important cultural mythology. Although Pratt was interested in producing docile workers, he was also interested in imposing Western-style economics on the formerly tribal cultures of the Native American. This scene is thus a stand-in metaphor for the more general aims of boarding-school education: to steer the Indian away from perceived sloth and dependence on government handouts and toward a greater independence.

Oddly though, not all is well in Johnston's version of the Yankee Farmer. Although she succeeds in setting up a composition that suggests a stark individualism, this starkness overtakes any sense of attainment. Although the young farmer is clearly posing rather than tilling the field, Johnston fails to include conventional signifiers of a bucolic balance between agriculture and unfettered nature. The aridness of the composition, if not the land itself, is reminiscent of another of the images from her Carlisle series, the even starker depiction of young male students picking potatoes in a field seen in figure 5.1. Significantly, Pratt failed to include this latter image in the catalog; perhaps its vision of subjection was too overt. The boys are too obviously engaged in enforced and seemingly futile labor at the hands of an authoritatively gesturing male faculty member.

Johnston's yeoman does seem more independently engaged than his fellow students in the potato-picking image. However, he also plies his skills in an equally bleak setting—a setting that Johnston takes pains to emphasize by shooting out over his head. There are no farm animals in the pasture, no barefoot children, no adoring spouse, and no quaint antebellum homestead to represent the fruits of his labor. In fact, foliage is conspicuously absent from this landscape, appearing only as an irrelevant cluster of trees in the far background. All of this raises the question of why a professional image-maker of Johnston's skill chose such a scene to represent the concept of the "independent farmer." Cultural logic would indicate that such bucolic representations of farming were no longer read as unproblematically "real" in this era of increasingly industrialized agriculture. Perhaps Johnston simply opted for a grittier sense of realism in this modernized farm scene, and thus chose to forgo visual gratuities. Despite these troubling paradoxes, clearly Pratt believed the image would read as positive by his mainly urbane white audiences, and that the sense of autonomy would outstrip the sense of desolation.

These oddly ambivalent pictorial devices become more significant when one considers that most Carlisle graduates failed to reach this particular kind of American cultural independence. Most who returned to the reservations were largely unsuccessful in tilling the land they found awaiting them on return from the school. In fact, David Wallace Adams has noted that by 1899, of the 3,899 students who had attended the school, only 209 had graduated. Of those, an even smaller percentage found a combination of health, prosperity, and autonomy.[57]

Pratt's scheme for inculcating agricultural skill in the male students was largely a failure. This is unsurprising when one considers that the reservations to which most of the students would return were in arid and inhospitable parts of the continent, such as the deserts of the Southwest and the Badlands of the Dakotas. Equally as destructive as the territorial seizures of the reservation system were the effects such dislocations had on Native Americans' cultural relationship to nature.

In figure 5.24, Johnston sets the scene away from the school quadrangle in a less determinate location—likely in the countryside near the school grounds. A female faculty member conducts a "Nature Lesson" with a group of third-grade students. Although one or two students acknowledge the photographer's presence, the majority poses in a semicircular formation, in dutifully rapt attention. The teacher lectures to the students about some aspect of the natural environment around the school as she holds up a floral specimen for the students to see. It is noteworthy that in American art and culture during this time, "nature" was commonly deployed as an antimodernist trope—something pure or fantastic—a foil to the cities and factories, as in figure 5.25. Further, the stereotype of the Native as Noble Savage—a figure in greater harmony with the natural world—was central to how Euro-Americans regarded indigenous peoples for centuries. It was an idea perpetuated by some of the most prominent trends in American painting in the nineteenth century, including the Hudson River School.

Looking at "Nature Lesson," it is therefore odd that the Indian students were thought to need a lesson from an Anglo-American instructor on the aspects of nature as part of their curriculum. In a sense, this type of image, which cultural historian Ella Shohat has termed a representation of a colonizing "didacticism,"[58] displays an "enlightened" European didactically instructing the "ignorant" natives in the facts of life. However, the display becomes complicated when one considers the cultural stereotype of the Native American as more "natural" than the European. Such visual performances were not uncommon at Carlisle.

In another image by Johnston titled "Reading Class," this time inside one of the school's classrooms, as figure 5.26 shows, a faculty member teaches the students *their* own history. A young male student stands to read a passage while absorbing the fundamentals of the English language. The students are being reeducated on their own cultural history through the linguistic and ideological lenses of the school. Indianesque craft objects decorate the walls, apparently serving as visual aides in the teacher's lesson. These accoutrements, consisting of various textiles, a buckskin shirt, and drawn illustrations of a teepee, are overseen by a portrait of the nation's "founding father," George Washington. It is as if Pratt believed, and wanted to show, the notion that as well as needing indoctrination into the emerging order of mechanized work and atomized property, students also needed a Eurocentric reeducation about their own past, ironically thought "valueless" by Pratt and most others. Sadly, such patronizing and condescending pedagogy was often a requirement, and by the early twentieth century, the younger generation of students no longer had knowledge of their ancestral language or crafts.[59] Ironically, these lessons were increasingly offered at the boarding schools even though actual tribal practices such as Ghost Dances[60] were outlawed on the reservations. The government feared their performance would spur rebellion as it had during the Sioux Outbreak of 1890.

Pratt and other patrons perceived Johnston's images as having a documentary viability during the course of her long career, yet one senses an underlying concern on his part that her images might be read "incorrectly." It was largely for this reason that he held tight editorial control over the album and remained concerned about framing the images with skillfully worded captions. Taking his obvious political agenda into account, Pratt's concern was understandable. Johnston's reception varied around this time in her career (circa 1900).

Given Pratt's scant public mention of Johnston during the compiling, publishing, and distributing of the album, a certain reluctance to acknowledge her as the author of the photographic illustrations was obvious. Indeed, taken as a whole, the photographs function more as an illumination of the album's text than as documents intended to stand alone in any aesthetic sense. In short, it was as if Pratt wished to make the photographer and the processes of production invisible to public perception. This treatment was of course by 1901 standard for Carlisle photographers. Despite Pratt's efforts to impose a documentary-type view on the images, Johnston's reputation at the time was more complex, as Pratt undoubtedly well knew, given their close personal association. In fact, Johnston's fame and ambition assured her access to several different institutional contexts at this time, perhaps most notably the elite confines of Pictorialism.

Pictorialism was a culturally and technically progressive movement in photography around the turn of the century. Its appeal was transatlantic; adherents came not only from the Anglo-American world but also, notably, from Germany. In general, what bound these diverse practitioners of the medium together was a desire to raise photography to the level of the fine art of painting. This entailed stressing the artist/photographer's manual intervention in the image's fabrication, rather than emphasizing the cold mechanical and chemical processes of conventional photography. In the United States, the Pictorialist ethos was advocated by F. Holland Day, who sought to infuse his images with literary and artistic legitimacy by using platinum printing and elaborately staged tableaux. In figure 5.27 we see the photographer himself posing as Christ, with two scantily clad male models serving as Roman centurions. American audiences often deemed such an image suspect, as the artistic pretension and homoerotic undercurrents fell well outside what was considered proper subject matter for the "scientific" medium.[61]

Undeterred, Day and many of his colleagues persisted in creating these elaborate scenes to free the medium from what they saw as the banality of the newly emergent amateurism promoted by Kodak's point-and-click ethos. A commonly used solution to the perceived problem of this industrialization of photography was the insertion of, or making visible, the author of the image. Day did this not only through innovative print techniques but also through inserting his body into the theatrical guise of Christ. For others, such as Pictorialist Edward Steichen (1879–1973), the individualistic, creative authorship in photography was assured not only through self-portraiture but also by simulating a painterly surface with tactile printing surfaces such as gum bichromate. Steichen summarized the agenda of Pictorialism in a brief article for the first edition of *Camera Work*, a magazine dedicated to promoting photography as art form in the United States:

> A manipulated print may not be a photograph. The personal intervention between the action of the light and the print itself may be a

blemish to the purity of photography. But, whether this intervention consists merely of marking, shading and tinting in a direct print, or of stippling, painting and scratching on the negative, or of using glycerine, brush and mop on a print, faking has set in, and the results must always depend upon the photographer, upon his personality, his technical ability and his feeling.[62]

In typical form, Steichen summed up the platform of the Photo-Secession, a radical Pictorialist group he founded with fellow photographer Alfred Stieglitz (1864–1946) in New York in 1902. This group was mainly concerned with promoting radical photography and art for American audiences. As Steichen's commentary suggests, the group was more concerned with the personality and feeling of the artist/photographer than with the mere scientific applications of the medium. It was in this spirit that the independently wealthy Stieglitz financed *Camera Work*'s publication as the group's official literary organ from 1903 until 1917. Stieglitz also financed the Little Galleries of the Photo-Secession at 291 Fifth Avenue in Manhattan, which served as the group's official exhibition space from 1905 until 1917.[63]

The aura of cultural ferment brought about by the emergence of Pictorialism in the United States in the 1890s naturally attracted attention in the world of photography, and eventually attracted Johnston. In fact, Johnston corresponded with members of the movement for many years, beginning with Gertrude Käsebier as early as 1892. Apparently the admiration was mutual. In a letter dated November 7 of that year, Käsebier not only congratulated Johnston on her professional successes in the *Demorest's* article but also informed Johnston that Stieglitz himself had caught wind of the assignment.[64]

Stieglitz was indeed enthusiastic about Johnston's work, especially during the early years of their association. This is clear in their personal correspondence, as Stieglitz often wrote glowingly about Johnston's work:

> When you were here, I spoke to you about an insert I would like to have of yours, for "Camera Notes." For the purpose, I would like you to send me one of your negatives with a print, or a *reversed* transparency which should measure *within* 5 x 7¼ inches. The choice of subject, I shall leave to you. At the same time, I would like a few prints for halftone reproduction, as your exhibition which we hope to have here early in the fall will be fully reviewed.
>
> Our new quarters are beautiful and I'm sure you will like them. "Camera Notes" is a big success. The next number is now on the press and I shall send you a copy as soon as it is ready.[65]

This letter shows that as early as 1898, a year before her documentary work at Hampton, Johnston was already active within the social and professional circles of American Pictorialism. *Camera Notes* was the periodical published by the prestigious New York Camera Club, and Stieglitz was serving as editor at this time.[66] Obviously, Stieglitz and others saw the Washington-based Johnston as much more than a provincial amateur, because exhibition at the club and reproduction in the journal were both sought-after professional honors. Stieglitz apparently anticipated significant public interest in Johnston's show, as indicated both by his desire for half-tone reproductions of her work and his comment "will be fully reviewed."

Although clearly Johnston made most of her living throughout her career in carrying out "documentary" work, her self-fashioned public image was more complex, as suggested by the correspondence above. This is no small issue, because the battle lines in photography in the United States circa 1900 were drawn between "scientific" and "artistic" photography, and "professional" and "amateur" photography. Johnston surpassed nearly all American women in her genuine status as a professional. Yet her position in the debate was a bit more equivocal when it came to the scientific-artistic dichotomy. It was as if she sought to occupy both camps to drum up as much recognition as possible for herself.

This self-fashioning was deft, and included both visual advertising and written text. Some of the more famous of Johnston's advertising images, intended to characterize her professional status, were executed for her by her friend William Mills Thompson (1875–1944), a prominent illustrator in Washington at the time. In Thompson's illustrations, which Johnston often photographed and then distributed as calling cards (see, for example, figs. 5.28 and 5.29), it is obvious the photographer was acutely aware of her status within the prevalent professional discourse surrounding the medium around the turn of the twentieth century.

In the first illustration, the figure representing Johnston has its back to the viewer and dominates the foreground of the composition. Dressed in fashionable New Woman attire and carrying the tools of her trade, the photographer assertively faces a seemingly boundless landscape topped by the symbol of a setting sun. The motif of the sunset was prominent in American art at this time, often suggesting expanse, opportunity, forward progress, and other such ideas associated with the growing economic and political power of the nation during the era of continental expansion. Although the idealized landscape suggests a sense of the romantic or adventurous, the textual designation of Johnston's trade as "Photographic Illustration" clearly anchors her practice in a more utilitarian discourse of photographic documentation.

In the second image, which Johnston photographed in the cyanotype format that she also used for some of the Carlisle images, the photographer faces the viewer wearing similar New Woman fashion. In this case, Thompson includes a large palette with the tripod and camera—an overt reference to the artistic quality of Johnston's work. Thompson here seemed less concerned with conveying specific professional data, and thus the image reads more as a sketch or informal portrait of Johnston. Thompson's production of sixteen small illustrations within a brief period during 1896, the photographing of at least one of them, and the inclusion of the photographer's name in prominent print all indicate that the portraits were intended for a wider audience.[67]

Johnston ambitiously tried to control her public persona through such imagery. References to the sun, the painterly palette, the mobile camera, and the like were tropes also used by Muybridge and Choate in their own advertising. By appealing to both aesthetic craft and reportage, she was by all accounts successful in courting various patrons, from the nation's political elites to prominent periodicals to the leaders of the Photo-Secession to institutional bureaucrats.

Although Pratt clearly approved of her work, he nonetheless maintained rigid control over the Carlisle negatives as well as over editing the catalog. In this respect, it is intriguing to consider that Johnston made many more prints than the number that appeared in the final catalog. In fact, the Library of Congress Division of Prints and Photographs currently holds one cache of 107 of her Carlisle prints in both gelatin silver and cyanotype format. Significantly, none of the ninety-six printed cyanotypes found their way into the catalog in reproduced form.[68]

Pratt did comment on the cyanotypes in his correspondence with Johnston. In one letter to her, he noted that he and his staff have received the "blue prints" and would soon be selecting from them for inclusion in the final publication.[69] It is tempting to speculate that the blue-tinted appearance of such prints were considered too "artistic" for inclusion in the catalog, which was of course intended to read as a straight "illustrative" document on the school's curriculum. Further, the content of many of her prints clearly superseded anything Pratt likely had in mind for documenting the school's programs.

For example, in the print that figure 5.30 shows, Johnston chose to focus on a female faculty member's quiet leisure moment. The woman sits reading, ignoring the camera. In this "room of her own," Johnston shows this woman in a portrait that at the time would likely have been read as a bit unconventional—a literate woman, unaccompanied by a man, inside her own eclectic studiolike accommodations enjoying leisure reading. This literate, independent, and comfortably appointed woman is reminiscent of Johnston herself as seen in her famous self-portrait of 1896 (see fig. 5.31). Although the image of the teacher clearly lacks the overtly self-parodic quality of the more famous self-portrait, the underlying idea of the intellectually independent New Woman links them. Art historian Elizabeth Hutchinson has argued that representations of studio space in visual imagery were increasingly important for photographers as well as artists at this time in American cultural history. She claims that the studio space was taken as reflective of the subject's persona and had a larger cultural cachet. The public saw those with eclectically designed studios as well-traveled, sophisticated, and bohemian—all important for a successful photographer or artist. Further, a well-appointed studio communicated a sense of individuality—something at self-conscious odds with the increasingly standardized interior spaces produced by industrially mass-produced architecture.[70]

With this in mind, it is interesting to consider the image in figure 5.32, which did make its way into the catalog and provides a marked departure from many of Johnston's other prints. Titled "Individual Lesson in Instrumental Music," the image shows just that—a female student at a piano receiving personalized instruction from a female faculty member. The scene is in a singularly appointed room—one filled with an array of furnishings and items that suggest the private quarters of a faculty member rather than a room intended for public use.

Apparently Pratt considered some of the more intimate interior scenes acceptable, as they indicated a more personalized relationship between faculty members and students. Further, although Pratt viewed instruction in the fine arts and music as less utilitarian than the school's more well-known industrial training, it was nevertheless included in the curriculum: The school's band was part of his proof of the cultural and intellectual fitness of his students.[71]

A Photographic Native Voice at Carlisle

Another significant part of the aforementioned "fitness" of the student body entailed proving both the intellectual attainment and physical strength of individual students. Such students would serve as models for Carlisle, both aesthetically and socially. Within this array of bodily representations, it is necessary to consider the existence of a native voice that took part in the photographic archiving of the Carlisle curriculum. In this sense, the 1895 catalog, illustrated in part by photographs taken by student John Leslie, offers a rare glimpse of images made by a cultural Other in this flurry of institutional representation.

Native American practitioners of photography were rare in the nineteenth century, and thus Leslie's images offer a potentially uncommon vision of the boarding-school experience. Leslie, a member of the Puyallup tribe in Washington State, attended Carlisle in the 1890s, graduating in 1896. He began studying photography in 1894 as part of the school's outing program, which was the backbone of Pratt's agenda, because he believed that total immersion in white culture would most effectively break the tribal bonds of the students. By this standard, Leslie apparently thrived in the program. It is known that he studied under both John Choate and John Andrews, another local photographer. His images bear a noticeable imprint of Choate's compositional influence. In fact, the school newspaper at the time, *The Indian Helper*, quipped that Leslie was Choate's "right hand Indian man."[72] Significantly, Leslie was regarded as one of the school's most promising students; the paper went on to state that Leslie would have "some fine pictures some of these days" and that he was the "most taking man on the grounds."[73] Pratt thought so highly of Leslie's acquired skills that the school sold some of Leslie's local landscape photographs at the campus and through mail subscription to school patrons and parents for ten cents each. He also went so far as to include an exhibition of Leslie's student work at the 1895 International Exposition in Atlanta.[74] Pratt thus saw Leslie as an exemplary student, a model of the newly professionalized Indian. This view is confirmed by Leslie's biographical information after leaving Carlisle. He returned to the Pacific Northwest following his graduation in 1896 and quickly became a successful professional photographer. He worked in both Washington and British Columbia, where it was reported by the *Helper* that he was "doing well in the photography business. In three weeks he took in $40.00."[75] He was listed as a professional photographer as late as 1915 in that year's school catalog, well after Pratt's tenure as superintendent had ended. Dozens of Leslie's photographs, with some by Choate and Johnston, illustrated the 1895 catalog, titled *United States Indian School, Carlisle, Pennsylvania*.[76]

In reviewing the catalog, what strikes one at first are the similarities and differences in the images of Choate, Leslie, and Johnston.[77] In fact, some of Leslie's images are at first glance quite different from Choate's and Johnston's. Often, students either overtly acknowledge the photographer's presence, as in figure I.6, or are strewn about much more casually than one generally sees in the work of the Anglo-American photographers, as in figure 5.33. In the latter image, Leslie offers us a view of the school's central quadrangle from a second-story window in one of the campus buildings. The casualness of the composition and the seemingly random arrangement of figures would suggest a significantly different view of the student body. Here, there is a lack of ordering of the human body. This is different from Choate's panoramic views of the school, which place a greater emphasis on the militaristic spatial arrangement of the students within the campus grounds, as in figure 5.34.

Nevertheless, despite such visible differences, what is striking about Leslie's contributions to the catalog is the degree to which the photographer had seemingly internalized the representational mandates of the school's photographic ethos. For example, in figure 5.33, although the students strike a more spontaneous posture in the image, they are nonetheless rigidly segregated by gender, something characteristic of the Anglo-American images. More important, Leslie's take on the campus grounds and the relationship of the human body to them is not "subversive" in any real sense, because the figures are still easily enclosed by the militaristic concentric architecture. As I've noted, the layout of the school's buildings and their architecture and the subsequent photographic images of that architecture forward a perception of enclosure in both students and viewers.

This is unsurprising when one considers the guiding ethic of Carlisle and all such Progressive Era reform institutions in the United States at this time. The discipline of photography, like all others taught at the school, entailed assuming specifically defined cultural roles by the students. Thus, in this anonymous photograph of figure 5.35, the slightly older student on the right dons a middle-class business suit becoming a practitioner of the trade of photography. In the tableau, he appears to be making a photographic after-type portrait of a younger student who dons the school's more familiar paramilitary male uniform while sitting rigidly and apprehensively in the chair. Clearly, the school's administrators wished to continue promoting the notion of a smooth, unproblematic journey from barbarism to professionalized citizen in which the older students could serve as living exemplars for the younger, incoming students. Adapting Euro-American representational strategies proved crucial in this effort.

Imaging the "Manly" Native Body

The array of representational formats in Carlisle imagery is complex. Images range from depictions of industrial labor to agricultural labor to classroom instruction to leisure-time activities. This diversification raises questions about how the students and their educations were perceived and why Pratt felt it necessary to balance depictions of work and leisure. These representations were made not only by a diverse array of photographers but also appeared in a wide assortment of formats, including the print media of the day.

Part of the answer to these questions lies in the school's publicly stated pedagogical aims. In the rear of the 1902 catalog, Pratt wrote out an extended list of the school's pedagogical offerings and methods. Under headings such as "Carpentry," "Blacksmithing and Wagonmaking," "Tinsmithing," "Printing," "Domestic Science," "Laundry Work," and "Athletics," Pratt extolled the relative benefits of each type of instruction. For example, on the topic of "Physical Culture," he wrote:

> The department of physical training preserves the health of the individual; builds up the body by means of selected exercises; promotes correct habits of standing and walking; corrects improper posture and abnormalities; and while furnishing a relaxation from the more arduous duties, improves the co-ordination of mind and body . . . [78]

In terms that resonate with the attitudes of Theodore Roosevelt, Pratt often endorsed physical training, especially for male students, as a way of both improving and normalizing the indigenous body and mind. This was also a way of proving the relative fitness of the Native American in relation to the young Anglo-American men of the more established Ivy League colleges. It was in this latter vein that leisure-time pursuits such as football would become a central part of his project, and in some respects become *as* important as the seemingly more "serious" industrial training. He thus supported and even promoted athletic matches pitting Carlisle's male athletic teams against those of the nation's top colleges.[79] Pratt clearly aimed to prove the notion that racial supremacy à la the eugenics movement was invalid, and that Carlisle's population was as "fit" as those of top schools. Nevertheless, his continual need to engage in such contests would seem to be a tacit acknowledgment of the continuing dominance of eugenicist assumptions about race among even the country's academic elite at the time. For as historians such as David Wallace Adams have noted, at this time athletic competition symbolically represented racial conflict.

In fact, the question of latter-day pseudosciences and their relationship to bodily representation was, as I have discussed, a specter with which Pratt had to reckon throughout his tenure at the school. While the rigid, calibrating sense embodied in the Johnston images suggest that this issue persisted during Pratt's tenure at the school, other publicity images more overtly engaged the issue of eugenic "fitness." The school's concern for proving the fitness of its students culminated in representations of the figure of Jim Thorpe and other stars of the school's football program.

Pratt launched the well-known Carlisle football program in 1893 at the request of male students wishing to test their capabilities against other, predominantly Anglo-American, colleges. That male students initiated this movement is significant. Their commitment to football shows the degree to which they held self-awareness of the masculine "proving" rituals of Anglo-American culture. Although Pratt did approve of a program, his commitment to it was shaky in the early years, because one student broke a leg during a game.[80] Pratt threatened to revoke the program, fearing negative publicity for the school but was persuaded to keep the program by the enthusiastic participants. In fact, Pratt's need to continually prove the fitness and thus cultural and social viability of his students led him to overlook potential negative consequences of the violent sport. That Pratt and others did in fact see the game as a metaphor for real-world competition and even warfare is indicated by his telling public statements on the school's program:

> The Indian is not dead yet, but alive and able to compete with the world, if allowed to use his god-given faculties. "A fair field and no favor" is all he asks and he will render a good account of himself, whether in business, music, art, education or athletics.[81]

This is one of the most revealing and frank statements Pratt made during his tenure at Carlisle. In this brief quote, he lays bare the cultural and psychological confluence of athletic competition and social and professional success. Further, Pratt's "field" metaphor was significant for its perception of sport during this era, as many conflated the athletic field and its physical struggle and violence with the larger cultural fields of politics and the professions. This is reminiscent of Theodore Roosevelt's dictum about athletic training and rough phallocentric physical contact. Roosevelt saw them as confirmation of American manhood and as a cultural antidote to the perceived physical and psychic flatulence brought on by the conspicuous consumption of the Gilded Age.[82]

With this in mind, let us turn to several widely publicized images of Carlisle athletes. The first is a series of newspaper illustrations from 1896 of several stars from the Carlisle football team, two of which figure 5.36 shows. The illustrations appeared in the 1 November 1896 edition of the *New York Journal*. They illustrated an article by the writer Stephen Crane, who reported on a football game between Carlisle's team and that of Harvard University. The players are posed in stereotypically rigid athletic positions. According to the illustrations' caption, each drawing was made after a "snap shot photograph." Therefore, the young men represented were subjected to yet another instance of the ritual of photography in the service of cultural agendas. Assuming these images did indeed originate from photographs, they make up perhaps the oddest and most uncharacteristic renderings of students ever made under Pratt's time at the institution. Clearly, a different visual trope is used in this case and one is again given to wondering why such images were made and how they would have been perceived by the public.

Such imagery, highlighting the athleticism, competitive fitness, and virility of the male form, was in fact common in the United States during the late Victorian era (see, for example, fig. 5.37). As Jackson Lears has argued, the period saw a rise in what he terms the "martial ideal." This notion was predicated on the assumption that a middle-class masculine identity was under threat of dissolution because of the increasingly intense demands of bourgeois domesticity and the industrial marketplace. As a solution, Lears claims that many men, especially Anglo-American bourgeois men, sought to reaffirm a masculine selfhood by engaging in a "cult of violence." For Lears, this worship of physical violence and physiological conflict was manifest largely in literary and other representational contexts. It was thus a simulacrum of "Spartan virtue" intended to ward off the bodily and psychic softness brought on by bureaucratized work and commercial luxury.[83]

Significantly, the use of literary text and imagery in Crane's article serves to create a similar atmosphere of primal, mythical contact between Harvard's minions of "civilization" and the "red men" against whom they were pitted in the contest. The article appeared under the headline, "Harvard University Against the Carlisle Indians," and opened with a rhetorical flourish typical of Crane. The writer stated that because of Carlisle's loss, there was "sorrow in the lodge of Lone Wolf." It was as if in referring to the famous chief, Crane was drawing a logical connection between a loss in a particular football game and Native American sorrow more generally. Crane set a dramatic tone for the contest when he wrote:

> Fifteen thousand people expected a surprise. They were there to observe how the red man could come from his prairies with a memory of four centuries of oppression and humiliation as his inheritance, with dark years, perhaps utter extinction before him, and yet make a show of the white warriors at their favorite sport.[84]

Clearly, Crane framed the game as "more than a game," as David Wallace Adams has put the matter in reference to the cultural perception of Carlisle athletics. As Adams has noted, many in the white media and public saw interracial athletic contests as metaphors for frontier warfare between white settlers and the indigenous population.[85] Crane's use of the term "white warrior" may be interpreted not only as a manifestation of the more general discourse on "manliness" but also a more specific metaphor for racial war. It was as if it were the duty of Carlisle's team to avenge "four centuries of oppression and humiliation" in one afternoon.

Returning to the illustrations, on one level their inclusion was clearly a nod to the athletic skill and prowess of the Carlisle players. Crane's text, seemingly intended to read as deferential to the efforts of the Carlisle team, attempted to frame the images positively. And yet the static nature and partial to full nudity of the figures clearly superseded anything Pratt would have considered appropriate for his students in public display. For Pratt, physicality was not an end in itself but was just one among many skills needed for success in civilization. In that sense, it is significant that such revealing imagery never surfaced in the publicity photographs made under Pratt's direct control at the school. What is highlighted here seems to be pure physicality as an end in itself. As David Wallace Adams has noted, however, publishing such images was a gambit, as many in white audiences had ambivalent views of Indian success. For some, semi- or fully nude young indigenous men recalled the savagery of their ancestors on the frontier, while others perceived their athletic skill as valid proof of good public policy toward the Native American.[86]

Such ambivalence of intent and reception is present when considering the striking image in figure 5.38 of Carlisle's most famous athletic star, Jim Thorpe. Although made several years after Pratt left the school, this unique photograph compositionally echoes the *New York Journal* illustrations. Thorpe stands with his back to the camera, wearing nothing but an athletic supporter. He has clearly been told how to pose, because his posture is self-conscious and artificial. He is not even "athletically" posed but rather is posed in a manner given to pure exhibition. Thorpe biographer Robert Wheeler has written that this image, probably made in 1912, was intended for "a panel of experts, physicians, mathematicians and others using only the most accurate of measuring devices [who] measured Jim's body 42 different ways."[87]

Not only a standout at Carlisle, Thorpe went on to win several medals at the 1912 Olympics. Following his return from the Olympics, Thorpe was hailed by one of the school's newspapers, *The Red Man*: "It should mean much in awakening among Indians a desire for greater physical and mental perfection, and for more care in guarding the health and increasing the strength of Indians everywhere."[88] Following the games, Thorpe was often cast as a national treasure, and someone whose "perfection" might serve as an inspiration to Indian youth nationwide.

Despite the positive responses to his victories, many observers were perplexed by Thorpe's astonishing athletic accomplishments. The photograph was made on Thorpe's return from the games, and as Wheeler suggests, the image served anthropometric purposes. Clearly, government officials were unable to explain or rationalize Thorpe's unprecedented success in multiple sports, and thus turned to anthropometrics in an effort to rationalize it. This image therefore exists at a sticky representational crossroads. Although Thorpe was admired by many white Americans for his skill and seemed for many to embody the "improvements" wrought by his training at Carlisle, these photographs indicate that he was viewed nonetheless as an odd curiosity. He was a "natural wonder" whose existence defied the eugenic conventional wisdom still prominent in the United States circa 1910.[89] Given this cultural logic, it is therefore predictable that Thorpe's observers turned to anthropometrics to make sense of the stature of this national treasure. This incident is reminiscent of Franz Boas's use of anthropometrics twenty years earlier in his effort to explain the "distribution of types of man" for the Ethnological Exhibition at the Chicago Fair.[90] It also speaks to the persistence of eugenic science as a paradigm for conceptualizing race in the United States well into the twentieth century.

Conclusion

The Johnston catalog was released in early 1902, arriving on the heels of the school's published annual report in September 1901. Pratt thus saw the timing of its release as politically important in the way Choate's portraits were important in the school's initial publicity in the 1880s. Perhaps even more important were the abruptly shifting cultural and political winds in Washington. Following President McKinley's assassination in Buffalo in September 1901, Theodore Roosevelt, a new young leader, came to power in the White House. Whereas McKinley had been a supporter of the boarding schools, Roosevelt's own position on the "Indian question" was initially less well known to Pratt and others.

Pratt's uncertainty about the school's future in the face of the ever-shifting political tide in Washington was one factor driving his concern with publicity and thus the photographic framing of life at the school. His uncertainty with the new administration was not unwarranted, as events would soon show. In a letter from October 1901 intending to court the political favor of the new president, Pratt's uncertainty is borne out in his uncharacteristically patronizing tone:

> I watched with no little interest and with very considerable hope your beginnings as governor in regard to the Indians of New York. It was evident to me that you intended in some way if possible to break up the hindering conditions of their reservation life. This leads me to believe that you will be anxious to do the same for all Indians, now that have come under your care . . . send your most careful and intelligent observer to penetrate every corner of Carlisle and its every feature

> ... and I am sure you will be convinced that there is great room for
> improvement, and that stoppages entirely within your power can be
> made and buildings up accomplished while you are President that
> will far more speedily absorb and citizenize the Indian than all that
> we are doing . . . I am absolutely at your service. I believe in your
> "Strenuous Life" and feel sure that for the Indian as well as in every
> other cause you will do vast good for all people.[1]

Given the political climate of the moment, the Johnston catalog may
be seen as an attempt on Pratt's part not only to perpetuate the ideology of
cultural assimilation but also to preserve his increasingly precarious hold on
Carlisle. Despite his efforts, larger cultural shifts occurring in the country
around 1900 further discredited his rigidly assimilationist agenda, and even
challenged his core belief that the Indian had a "valueless past."

Elizabeth Hutchinson has convincingly argued that at this moment,
the nation's ruling elite had a change of heart toward indigenous populations. She has stated that as the *reality* of frontier conflict faded in the
1890s, the Anglo-American population picked up a romantic longing for
an "authentic" and essentialized pan-Indian culture. In a material sense,
this shift from racial hatred to paternalistic condescension manifested in
what she terms a "craze" for Native American material goods. Indian craft
objects such as textiles, baskets, figurines, masks, and the like were sought
after as collectible items—items that carried a preindustrial or "revitaliz-
ing" aura for those collecting them.[2] In other words, such material cultural
production, which had by circa 1900 reached the status of self-consciously
mass-produced tourist art, was endowed with a talismanic quality by the
middle-class northeastern Anglo-Americans who collected the items. In
this newer milieu, Pratt's one-sided system of repressing all signifiers of a
lingering Indianness lost favor, leading to his resignation under pressure as
superintendent in 1904.

The Limits of Assimilationist Representation

In retrospect, Pratt's project of photographic transformation was one that
could only have been accomplished under a specific set of historical and
cultural circumstances. At the time, the side-by-side comparison of photographic portraits projected an aura that could best be appreciated in the
nineteenth century: They held the authority of science and objectivity. This
use of photography was thus an exercise of power over the bodies of others. In hindsight, however, it becomes clear through a critical historical
analysis that the logic of such imagery was contingent on then-emergent

technologies. This was another factor beyond Pratt's control that would eventually lead to the discrediting of his assimilationist agenda.

The facile placement of two images side by side in print form was something that could maintain an absolutist sense of credibility only in a brief historical window. Specifically, the era of the collodion/albumen photographic process represents the only time during which such comparisons garnered a near-unquestioning faith in their truthfulness. Collodion's features of reproducibility, high levels of detail, subtle tonal gradations, and attractive final printing format combined to abet a perception of credibility and continuity in the minds of contemporary viewers. This remained the case as long as such wildly realistic and easily disseminated photographic images were still a novelty. Because of the medium's perceived legitimacy, photographs claiming to show the passage of time or evolutionary "progress" necessarily contain a self-referential logic that establishes a sense of their truth and objectivity. The workings of this logic are of course undone by the act of juxtapositioning and the seeming flawlessness of the representational form. As media critic Marshall McLuhan has written about the logic of photographic representation:

> Syntax, the net of rationality, disappeared from the later prints, just as it tended to disappear from the telegraph message and from the impressionist painting ... the direction of the syntactical point of view from outside *onto* the painting ended as literary form dwindled into headlines with the telegraph. With the photograph, in the same way, men had discovered how to make visual reports without syntax.[3]

As McLuhan argues, photography can *only* show us one moment in time. Nevertheless, the photograph, like typeset headlines, benefits from this representational short-circuitry and oddly attains a higher status in the representational order of things. It is this fundamentally irrational or perhaps fetishistic quality of the photograph as a medium that allows for both its terseness *and* viability.

Beyond the historical preponderance of collodion/albumen, Pratt was shrewd in co-opting the even more revolutionary and complex representational technologies of halftone reproduction and mechanical typesetting. In the end, it was perhaps the school's newspapers, with their deft juxtapositioning of reproduced photographic portraits of students within complexly formatted layouts, that were most effective. Pratt's use of all of these technologies effectively forged a mass-propagated lie about the true nature of the school and the lives of its students. Because of illness, delinquency, and even death, most of them never graduated.

It is important, though, to see Pratt's manipulations in a larger historical context. Perhaps his efforts were doomed to failure from the start. What
was at issue in such photographs was not so much a cultural concern for living indigenous Americans but for *desirable* representations of them. In this
sense, Anglo-American taste would ebb and flow well beyond Pratt's own
tenure at the school. Even before he resigned in 1904, ambivalence about
the material culture and subsequent visual representations of Native society
was afoot. While Pratt and others were obsessed with the idea of civilization, prominent countercurrents were running through middle-class conventions of taste. Not only were these countercurrents distastefully revealed
in the Wild West Show spectacle, but they were also thoroughly institutionalized in more legitimate contexts by the late nineteenth century.

Evidence of this cultural hybridization surfaced in the work not only of
photographers and illustrators, but also occasionally even in the work of the
nation's leading fine artists, such as Thomas Eakins (1844–1916). In the portrait of ethnologist Frank Hamilton Cushing that figure C.1 shows, Eakins
rendered what was then a popular and symbolic figure in American cultural
discourse: the adventurer-scientist. Beginning in 1876, Cushing worked as
an ethnologist for the Smithsonian Institution. In 1879, he embarked on a
four-year tour of Zuni lands in New Mexico. His purpose was not simply to
observe the indigenous tribe on its reservation but to live among its people.
Indeed, Cushing was successful in establishing credibility within the tribe,
because he was appointed by tribal leadership to several honorary positions
of leadership.[4]

Middle-class white society subsequently perceived him as an eccen-
tric who shirked civilized life for the more "authentic" life of the Zuni. He
amassed a great collection of objects during his travels that play a central
symbolic role in this portrait. Executed in Eakins's Philadelphia studio in
1895, the painting nevertheless lends an atmosphere of exoticism, for Cushing
wears several articles of Zuni clothing, most of which were made for him
during his stay with the Zuni. In fact, the portrait backdrop was constructed
within the artist's studio and was intended to evoke a Zuni pueblo.[5]

Such imagery clearly contradicts the central tenets of assimilationism
and is indicative of the "Indian Craze" discussed by Elizabeth Hutchinson.
What Pratt and company spent decades trying to repress, many in the
entertainment and scientific communities exploited for various cultural,
political, and economic reasons. Just at the moment when assimilationism
most aggressively sought to prove the supremacy of Anglo-American civilization over that of the Native American through deconstructing the latter
civilization, many embraced or exploited the signifiers of Native American

material culture. The reasons for this paradox are complex. Several historians have argued that as Native Americans came to represent less of an actual threat on the frontier, a nostalgia concurrently arose that simplistically romanticized their supposedly more "authentic" and "simple" way of life. Such premodern simplicity was commonly seen by middle-class intellectuals and consumers as a healthy antidote to the duress of modern acceleration.[6] In this context, Pratt's "modernizing" agenda would prove too unromantic, and even distasteful.

Perhaps Frederick Jackson Turner was correct when he argued in 1893 that to be American is to need newer and newer frontiers, newer and newer challenges. If the challenge is not posed domestically by indigenous residents, then other obstacles are sought and found, as one sees in the nation's subsequent history. In this sense, the future status of American society and its resulting representations even today seem to be very much in doubt. In a country in which Anglo-Americans have ceased to make up a majority and the desire to democratize the Third World has outstripped the economic capacity to continue nation-building, one is given to wondering how much longer the by-now overextended frontier ethos will endure as a national political ideal. In obsessively seeking to uplift Others, we run the risk of destroying ourselves. Perhaps, then, this is the prophetic lesson of Carlisle.

Notes

Introduction

1. In deploying the terms "Other" and "Otherness" throughout this study, I intend them to be understood in the manner originally suggested by Edward Said in his famous work *Orientalism*. Said, a postcolonial scholar, critiques representations of colonized subjects as nineteenth-century Euro-American literature depicts them. Specifically, Said argues that such literary characterizations, often constructed with Islamic or Central Asian cultures in mind, tend to marginalize and fetishize what he terms the "Others" who appear in them. In this context, Western writers may be seen to eroticize and infantilize persons from such colonized regions in an effort not only to evoke sensual fantasy and feelings of superiority in the reader, but also to unwittingly reinforce relations of colonial socioeconomic and cultural domination. Notably, Said goes on to argue that the textual fabrication of these Others was ironically more reflective of Euro-American desires, aspirations, and fears than it was of any material cultural reality within the colonized world. For more on Said's conception of the Other, see *Orientalism* (New York: Vintage Books, 1978).

2. Albert Boime, *The Art of Exclusion: Representing Blacks in the Nineteenth Century* (Washington, D.C.: Smithsonian Institution Press, 1990), 1–2.

3. See Brian Wallis, "Black Bodies, White Science: Louis Agassiz's Slave Daguerreotypes," *American Art* 9 (1995): 38–61.

4. David Wallace Adams, *Education for Extinction: American Indians and the Boarding School Experience 1875–1928* (Lawrence: University of Kansas Press, 1996), 21–24.

5. Alan Trachtenberg, *Shades of Hiawatha: Staging Indians, Making Americans, 1880–1930* (New York: Hill and Wang, 2004), xiv–xvi.

6. Erving Goffman, "The Mortified Self," in *The Goffman Reader*, ed. Charles Lemert and Ann Branaman (Oxford: Blackwell Publishers, 1997), 55.

7. Max Weber, *The Protestant Ethic and the Spirit of Capitalism*, trans. Talcott Parsons (New York: Scribner and Sons, 1958).

8. Adams, *Education for Extinction*, 56.

9. Antonio Gramsci, *Selections from the Prison Notebooks*, trans. Quintin Hoare and Geoffrey Nowell Smith (New York: International Publishers, 1971), 301–6.

10. Joel Pfister has helpfully characterized this process in Marxist terms as the "proletarianizing" of the students. See Joel Pfister, *Individuality Incorporated: Indians and the Multicultural Modern* (Durham, N.C.: Duke University Press, 2004).

11. Anne McClintock, *Imperial Leather: Race, Gender, and Sexuality in the Colonial Conquest* (New York: Routledge, 1995).

12. Richard Henry Pratt, *Battlefield and Classroom: Four Decades with the American Indian, 1867–1904*, ed. Robert M. Utley (New Haven, Conn.: Yale University Press, 1964), 214–15.

13. Theodore Roosevelt, *The Strenuous Life* (New York: Review of Reviews Co., 1910), 26–27.

14. Wayne Craven, *Colonial American Portraiture: The Economic, Religious, Social, Cultural, Philosophical, Scientific, and Aesthetic Foundations* (Cambridge: Cambridge University Press, 1986), 9.

15. Lewis Henry Morgan, *Ancient Society: Or, Researches in the Lines of Human Progress from Savagery Through Barbarism to Civilization* (New York: H. Holt, 1878).

16. Typically, Pratt rejected essentializing notions of race, as he shrewdly discerned the fact that in order for Carlisle to succeed, he needed to prove the notion that Indian youths could indeed change over time. Traditional racial pseudoscience posited that racial characteristics were innate, dictated by either a deity or Nature. Therefore, variously defined racial groups were set in terms of their varying "capacities."

17. Pratt, *Battlefield and Classroom*, 136–38.

18. Samuel G. Morton, *Crania Americana, or a Comparative View of the Skulls of Various Aboriginal Nations of North and South America* (Philadelphia: J. Dobson, 1839). I will consider Morton's text in much greater depth later.

19. Johnston executed this series at the Hampton Institute in Hampton, Virginia, in 1899. Hampton was a boarding school founded by Union Army General Samuel C. Armstrong in 1868. Like Carlisle, the school was founded on the principle that African American and Native American students could improve their lot in life if given a viable education and allowed to compete. Johnston was asked to document the school's grounds and activities. The Hampton Institute's motives for hiring her were similar to those of Pratt at Carlisle.

20. Frederick W. Taylor, *The Principles of Scientific Management* (New York: Harper and Brothers, 1911). I will explore Taylor's philosophy of industrial shop management, often termed "Taylorism" by historians and economists, in greater depth later. Essentially, Taylor recommended that plant managers minutely track the bodily movements and gestures of their employees in an effort to curb these movements so as to best facilitate work-time productivity. Some, like Gramsci, argue that Taylor's principles were also applied indirectly by the forces of industrial capitalism to workers' leisure time through advertising, mandated consumption, sexual regulation, and other techniques that served to structure the ostensibly "leisure" time and activity of the proletariat. The "leisure" time of Carlisle School students was also closely surveyed by school administration.

21. By critical theory, I refer primarily to the wave of Franco-American theoretical analysis that has been deployed in the field of American art history with increasing frequency in recent decades. I will elaborate further upon the work of specific scholars and critics below.

22. Michel Foucault, *Discipline and Punish: The Birth of the Prison*, trans. Alan Sheridan (New York: Vintage Books, 1977), 195–228.

23. Roland Barthes, *Camera Lucida*, trans. Richard Howell (New York: Hill and Wang, 1981), 40–59.

24. Carol Armstrong, *Scenes in a Library: Reading the Photograph in the Book, 1843–1875* (Cambridge, Mass.: MIT Press, 1998). See especially her introduction.

25. See, for instance T. J. Jackson Lears, *No Place of Grace* (New York: Pantheon Books, 1981); Sarah Burns, *Inventing the Modern Artist: Art and Culture in Gilded Age America* (New Haven, Conn.: Yale University Press, 1996); Kathleen Pyne, *Art and the Higher Life: Painting and Evolutionary Thought in Late Nineteenth-Century America* (Austin: University of Texas Press, 1996); Alan Trachtenberg, *The Incorporation of America* (New York: Hill and Wang, 1990).

26. See Peter Wood and Karen Dalton, *Winslow Homer's Images of Blacks* (Austin: University of Texas Press, 1988); Hugh Honour, *The Image of the Black in Western Art*, 4 vols. (New York: Morrow, 1976); Boime, *Art of Exclusion*; Wallis, "Black Bodies."

Chapter 1

1. Francis E. Leupp, *Annual Report of the Commissioner of Indian Affairs* (Washington, D.C.: GPO, 1905), 2, quoted in Adams, *Education for Extinction*, 19. Italics added.

2. I am indebted in this study to the Lockean conception of the "tabula rasa." British philosopher John Locke (1632–1704) has often been credited by historians of the United States as being the primary source of the democratic, middle-class American ideal of the "self-made man." Essentially, Locke argues that human beings share a unifying nature—we are all born with a mind that is a blank slate, and the workings of our senses subsequently determine what is imprinted on our individual minds. This idea is often contrasted to the older aristocratic notions of divine predetermination, which posited that people were made one way or another by God and thus could not change the fundamental nature of their existences. Locke's characterization of identity as being self-determined rather than predetermined is thus seen as a catalyst for the revolutionary political thinking of the eighteenth century that led both to a more democratic perception of the self and to the establishment of the United States. However, I will maintain in this dissertation that Locke's notion was gradually co-opted and transformed by the political and cultural elite of early republican America. Specifically, the reform-minded founders of the nation's modern institutions—asylums, prisons, hospitals, and common schools— chose to use the blank slate metaphor in the establishment of a newer order of repression. This "new order" was certainly more liberal than the older aristocratic order of Europe but was nonetheless based on hierarchical assumptions regarding the capacities and qualities of the mind. In the "republican" or "democratic" context of the United States, these hierarchies were established by positing a cultural normalcy

that was based on Anglo-American bourgeois values. For more on the tabula rasa, see John Locke, *An Essay Concerning Human Understanding, in Four Books* (London: E. Holt and T. Basset, 1690).

3. It is important to remember that the "survey" document would become increasingly significant in the coming decades for the U.S. government. Such documents—eventually accompanied by paintings, illustrations, and photographs—were often perceived by the leadership in the East as the first step toward recognizing and thus laying some claim to the vast and mysterious territories of the continent. In this sense, one may see Jefferson's *Notes on Virginia* as the first in a line of American exploratory surveys, ranging from Lewis and Clark to the Hayden Survey and beyond. In a sense, they all represent the "scientific" cutting edge of the Frontierist ethos.

4. Thomas Jefferson, *The Life and Selected Writings of Thomas Jefferson*, ed. Adrienne Koch and William Peden (New York: The Modern Library: 1998), 208–9.

5. Ibid., 308.

6. Ibid., 238–39.

7. Ibid., 237.

8. Benjamin Henry Latrobe, *The Journals of Benjamin Henry Latrobe, 1799–1820: From Philadelphia to New Orleans*, ed. Edward Carter III, John Van Horne, and Lee Formwalt (New Haven, Conn.: Yale University Press, 1980), 171–72.

9. George Catlin, in *Sources and Documents in the History of Art Series: American Art, 1700–1960*, ed. H. W. Janson and John McCoubrey (Englewood Cliffs, N.J.: Prentice Hall, 1965), 93–95.

10. Frances K. Pohl, *Framing America: A Social History of American Art* (New York: Thames and Hudson, 2002), 138. Pohl links this association with the then-popular notions of pantheism, or of the existence of God in nature. She derives this notion from Enlightenment-era concepts of the "Sublime" as a key aspect of nature. Referring to the English philosopher Edmund Burke, Pohl states that many in the United States felt a sense of awe, reverence, and even terror when presented with the vastness of nature and the frontier. This perception entailed a necessary romanticized rejection of the encroachments of tourism, settlement, and other implements of expansionist capitalism that were by then already cutting into the frontier. She notes that in some of Cole's paintings, it was even necessary for him to alter the actual appearance of the place because campsites, staircases, and other visual evidence of human encroachment were present. Cole would characteristically refuse to include such things in a painting, in order to proffer a perception of "purity" in the landscape.

11. In deploying this term, Pohl seems to be following Albert Boime, who famously evoked the phrase in his important book *The Magisterial Gaze: Manifest Destiny and American Landscape Painting, c. 1830–1865* (Washington, D.C.: Smithsonian Institution Press, 1991).

12. Pohl, *Framing America*, 138.

13. Charles Colbert, *A Measure of Perfection: Phrenology and the Fine Arts in America* (Chapel Hill: University of North Carolina Press, 1997), 243.

14. Ralph Waldo Emerson, *"Nature,"* 1836, in *The American Tradition in Literature,* ed. George and Barbara Perkins, 8th ed. (New York: McGraw-Hill, 1994), 464.

15. Catlin, 1832, *Sources and Documents,* 94.

16. Colbert, *Measure of Perfection,* 242–53. I will expand upon this shortly.

17. The reference to Darwinism in the 1830s is admittedly a slight historical stretch. However, although Darwinism per se was only in its embryonic form at this time and would not reach maturity until the 1850s, earlier pre-Darwinian evolutionist conceptions of history had by this time been forwarded in Europe and subsequently disseminated in the United States. The historical systems and methods of both Goethe and Vico, with their emphasis on a "stages of Man" model of history, may be said to represent the early evolutionist thought in the West by this date.

18. Colbert, *Measure of Perfection,* 242–53.

19. Johann Gaspar Spurzheim, *Outlines of Phrenology* (London: Treuttel, Wurtz, and Richter 1829), 3.

20. Colbert, *Measure of Perfection,* 2.

21. Hayes P. Mauro, "Johann Caspar Lavater," in *Encyclopedia of the Romantic Era, 1760–1850,* ed. Christopher John Murray (New York: Fitzroy Dearborn, 2004), 656–58.

22. Colbert, *Measure of Perfection,* 2–4, 7; also Roger Cooter, *The Cultural Meaning of Popular Science: Phrenology and the Organization of Consent in Nineteenth-Century Britain* (Cambridge: Cambridge University Press, 1984), 70–71.

23. Franz Joseph Gall and Johann Gaspar Spurzheim, *Recherches sur le Système Nerveux en Général, en sur celui du Cerveau en Particulier* (Paris: F. Schoell and H. Nicole, 1809). See especially Gall's introduction to this text for his general principles.

24. Gall, *Recherches,* 3–4.

25. John Davies, *Phrenology: Fad & Science: A 19th Century American Crusade* (New Haven, Conn.: Yale University Press, 1955), 7–8.

26. Ibid., 8–9; Colbert, *Measure of Perfection,* 8–10.

27. For example, see Caldwell's verbose defense of phrenology in his article "Phrenology Vindicated," published in the journal *Christian Examiner* in November 1834. Caldwell was a well-known moralist who believed that various aspects of medical "science" could be deployed to cure vices such as gambling. In this sense, he may be seen as a forerunner of the progressive reformers later in the century such as Eliza Farnham, Marmaduke Sampson, Horace Mann, and Richard Henry Pratt himself. That his conception of the term "science" was broader than that accepted by many of his peers apparently did little to shake Caldwell's faith in the pseudoscience of phrenology. See also Davies, *Phrenology,* 13 and Colbert, *Measure of Perfection,* 11.

28. The Central Phrenological Society was the first such group in the United States, founded by Bell, Biddle, and others in 1822. See Colbert, *Measure of Perfection,* 11 and Davies, *Phrenology,* 13.

29. Colbert, *Measure of Perfection,* 11–12. Colbert argues that Dunlop's text bears the influence of Francis's enthusiasm for phrenology.

30. Davies, *Phrenology,* 9.

31. Spurzheim, *Outlines of Phrenology*, 20–22; Colbert, *Measure of Perfection*, 13.

32. Davies, *Phrenology*, 26.

33. George Combe, *The Constitution of Man* (Hartford, Conn.: S. Andrus and Sons, 1842), 3.

34. Immanuel Kant, *Critique of Pure Reason*, ed. and trans. J. M. D. Meiklejohn (London: G. Bell, 1887).

35. Combe, *Constitution of Man*, 22–28.

36. Cooter, *Cultural Meaning of Popular Science*, 120–22.

37. Colbert, *Measure of Perfection*, 20–22.

38. Ibid., 20–21.

39. Craven, *Colonial American Portraiture*, 3–28.

40. I've taken biographical information about Morton from the website of the American Philosophical Society, the institution that houses the archive of Morton's papers. See American Philosophical Society, "Samuel G. Morton Papers," http://www.amphilsoc.org/mole/view?docId=ead/Mss.B.M843-ead.xml;query=;brand=default.

41. Ibid.

42. It was precisely such reasoning that informed the attitudes toward the poor that Pratt and other boarding school administrators held, who sought to "improve" the underclass via strenuous training in bodily hygiene and moral training. Similar tactics were deployed at Hampton, Tuskegee, and Hull House.

43. American Philosophical Society website, "Samuel G. Morton Papers."

44. For Morton, the definitions of race and nation were closely related. He saw them as being defined in a twofold manner—through physical characteristics and through language. Those who shared both could be categorized as belonging to the same nation. Those who shared the former were part of the same race. See Morton, *Crania Americana*, preface.

45. Ibid., 292.

46. On Camper and the convergence of aesthetics and anthropological discourse, see Miriam Claude Meijer, *Race and Aesthetics in the Anthropology of Petrus Camper (1722–1789)* (Amsterdam: Rodopi, 1999).

47. George Combe, "Phrenological Remarks on the Relation Between the Natural Talents and Dispositions of Nations, and the Development of their Brains," in Morton, *Crania Americana*, 269–72.

48. Ibid., 273–75.

49. Ibid., 271; Morton, *Crania Americana*, preface.

50. Morton, *Crania Americana*, preface.

51. Ibid.

52. Ibid.

53. Brian Wallis, "Black Bodies," 38–61.

54. I use the term "eugenics" here to refer to the scientific notion that character traits and mental faculties are genetically transmitted from one generation to the next. In the late nineteenth century, this school of thought was prominent among the

Anglo-American intellectual elite. It was best represented in the teachings of Francis Galton (1822–1911), whose work on the topic was read widely on both sides of the Atlantic. His principal work on the topic was his *Inquiries Into Human Faculty and Its Development* (London: Macmillan, 1883).

Chapter 2

1. Morton, *Crania Americana*, preface.

2. George Combe, *Phrenology Applied to Painting and Sculpture* (London: Simpkin, Marshall, and Co., 1855), 3–4.

3. Henry T. Tuckerman, *Book of the Artists* (New York: G. P. Putnam and Sons, 1867), 584.

4. Charles Colbert, "Clark Mills and the Phrenologist," *Art Bulletin* 70, no. 1 (March 1988): 136.

5. Ibid., 135.

6. Ibid.

7. Anonymous untitled obituary, *The Art Amateur* 8, no. 3 (1883): 56–57. The dollar amount referred to is presumably in 1853 American dollars.

8. Stephen A. Douglas, "Oration of the Hon. Stephen A. Douglas on the Inauguration of the Jackson Statue, January 8, 1853," in *The Inauguration of Mills's Equestrian Statue of Andrew Jackson, at Washington, January 8, 1853* (Washington, D.C.: GPO, 1853), 3. Italics added.

9. Combe, *Phrenology Applied*, 7.

10. Pratt, *Battlefield and Classroom*, 1–2.

11. Ibid., 5.

12. The term "Five Civilized Tribes" referred to the Cherokee, Chickasaw, Choctaw, Creek, and Seminole tribes. These tribes were dubbed "civilized" by white anthropologists because of their adaptation to Euro-American cultural practices, including plow agriculture, animal husbandry, parliamentary forms of governance, and in some cases anglicized clothing and religious practices. Prior to being forced onto Indian Territory in the 1830s by Andrew Jackson and other military and political leaders, they inhabited the Southeast portion of the country. For more about Victorian anthropological conventions that led to the tribes' categorization as "civilized," see Morgan, *Ancient Society*.

13. Pratt, *Battlefield and Classroom*, 116, 213–14. Pratt blames the "hatred and greed" of early settlers for the conflicts with Native American tribes.

14. Ibid., 92.

15. Letter from Richard Henry Pratt to General John Eston, 23 January 1883, Richard Henry Pratt Papers, Yale Collection of Western Americana, Beinecke Rare Book and Manuscript Library, Yale University.

16. The Dawes Act, passed by Congress in 1887 under the auspices of Senator Henry Dawes of Massachusetts, was designed to allot small parcels of land to specific individuals living on reservations. Whereas the Fort Laramie Treaty effectively immobilized the indigenous population, the Dawes, or General Allotment, Act

served to atomize the tribes and thus break traditional tribal bonds, which were often based on shared property. The Dawes Act initially excluded the "Civilized" tribes, but eventually was renegotiated so as to include virtually all major tribes. The renegotiation of the act in 1893 was designed to negate the authority of tribal government in favor of state and federal government. See Archives.gov., Teaching with Documents, "Maps of Indian Territory, The Dawes Act, and Will Rogers' Enrollment Case File," The National Archives, http://www.archives.gov/education/lessons/fed-indian-policy.

17. Pratt, *Battlefield and Classroom*, 105. Pratt writes that the Indian prisoners could not have received fair trials on the frontier due to the ferocity of the sentiment against them. It was thus decided to solve the problem of conflict by transporting the alleged instigators to an off-site location indefinitely.

18. Ibid., 113–14. The fatality associated with the trip occurred during the extended train ride to Fort Marion, which covered hundreds of miles. Several incidents of violence erupted among the captives. In one case, a Cheyenne warrior named Grey Beard attempted to escape by jumping from the train while it was in motion. He was subsequently shot and killed by armed guards. According to Pratt's account, Grey Beard had confronted him earlier in the trip and objected to the fact that the prisoners had been shackled and taken from their families.

19. Ibid., 116–35.

20. Foucault, *Discipline and Punish*, 170–94.

21. Harriet Beecher Stowe, "The Indians at St. Augustine," *The Christian Union* (April 1877).

22. Spencer F. Baird to Richard Henry Pratt, 21 May 1877, Pratt Papers.

23. I use the term "index" here in a sense similar to how the term is most often deployed in current art historical and art critical discourse. The indexical representation is one that bears the actual physiological imprint of the subject being represented, and in this sense is the most immediate and lifelike of all forms of visual representation. Because of this link to the physical presence of the original object, the indexical representation is often deemed the most authentic or credible in realist art or scientific illustration. Thus, photographs, fingerprints, handprints, footprints, and life masks are the most indexical by this definition. For more on the definition of the concept of the index, see Carol Armstrong, *Scenes in a Library*, Introduction.

24. For more about Baird's biography, see William Healy Dall, *Spencer Fullerton Baird, a Biography* (Philadelphia: J. B. Lippincott, 1915).

25. Heck, J. G., *Iconographic Encyclopedia of Science, Literature, and Art*, ed. and trans. by Spencer F. Baird, vol. 2 (New York: Rudolph Garrigue, 1851), 707–9; Heck, *Iconographic Encyclopedia* 3:123–26.

26. Spencer F. Baird to Richard H. Pratt, 12 June 1877, Pratt Papers.

27. Spencer F. Baird to Richard H. Pratt, 14 June 1877, Pratt Papers.

28. Spencer F. Baird to Richard H. Pratt, 26 November 1877, Spencer F. Baird Papers, RU 26, vol. 180, Smithsonian Institution Archives.

29. For more on the museum's founding ethos, see the Smithsonian's web pages, which discuss the institution's history: Smithsonian Institution Archives, Institutional

History Division, http://www.siarchives.si.edu/sia/ihd.html. See especially the pages on Baird's role: Pamela M. Henson, "Spencer F. Baird's Vision for a National Museum," Smithsonian Institution Archives, Institutional History Division, http://siarchives.si.edu/history/exhibits/baird/bairdhm.htm.

30. H. H. Arnason, *The Sculptures of Houdon* (New York: Oxford University Press, 1975), 73–75.

31. Thomas Jefferson to William Henry Harrison, 12 January 1785, in *Houdon in America*, ed. Gilbert Chinard (Baltimore: Johns Hopkins Press, 1930), 6.

32. Colbert, *Measure of Perfection*, 228, 236.

33. See Henson, "Spencer F. Baird's Vision," http://siarchives.si.edu/history/exhibits/baird/bairdhm.htm.

34. Spencer F. Baird to Richard Henry Pratt, 28 July 1877, Pratt Papers; also, Richard Henry Pratt to Spencer F. Baird, 20 July 1877, Pratt Papers.

35. Pratt, *Battlefield and Classroom*, 136–37.

36. For more on Palmer and other members of the Smithsonian's preparators, see Department of Anthropology, "Anthropology Conservation Laboratory: Focus on Leadership," National Museum of Natural History, http://anthropology.si.edu/conservation/focus_on_leadership1.htm.

37. Collection history card addendum, November 1956, accession nos. 6020 and 7540, National Museum of Natural History, Smithsonian Institution, Washington, D.C.

38. David Hunt, personal communication with the author, August 2005.

39. National Museum of Natural History, *Proceedings of the National Museum*, vol. 1 (Washington, D.C.: GPO, 1878), 201. Italics added.

40. In his 12 June 1877 letter to Pratt, Baird requested not only facial casts, but also casts of extraneous body parts such as hands and arms. This would seem to indicate a desire for greater realism in the diorama and also a desire for more detailed anthropometric measurements.

41. Lewis Henry Morgan, *Ancient Society, Or, Researches in the Lines of Human Progress from Savagery through Barbarism to Civilization* (London: MacMillan, 1877; Marxists Internet Archive Reference Archive, 2004), chap. 3, http://www.marxists.org/reference/archive/morgan-lewis/ancient-society/index.htm.

42. See Spencer F. Baird to Richard Henry Pratt, 23 January 1878, Pratt Papers, and response from Pratt outlining the crimes, Richard Henry Pratt to Spencer F. Baird, 9 February 1878, Pratt Papers.

43. *Proceedings of the National Museum*, 1878, 1:211.

44. For more information on Bertillon and on the linkages between anthropology, criminology, and portraiture, see Sandra Phillips, "Identifying the Criminal," in *Police Pictures: The Photograph as Evidence*, ed. Sandra Phillips, Mark Haworth-Booth, and Carol Squires (San Francisco: Chronicle Books, 1997), 11–31.

45. Phillips, "Identifying the Criminal," 11–31.

46. Clark Mills to Spencer F. Baird, 15 July 1877, Baird Papers.

47. For more on these general topics, see William Truettner, ed., *The West as*

America: Reinterpreting Images of the Frontier, 1820–1920 (Washington, D.C.: National Museum of American Art and Smithsonian Institution Press, 1991).

48. Clark Mills to Spencer F. Baird, 31 July 1877, Baird Papers.

Chapter 3

1. Coco Fusco, "Racial Signs, Racial Marks, Racial Metaphors," in *Only Skin Deep: Changing Visions of the American Self*, ed. Coco Fusco and Brian Wallis (New York: Harry N. Abrams, 2003), 16.

2. Ibid., 21.

3. Ibid., 37–38; see also Homi K. Bhabha, *The Location of Culture* (New York: Routledge, 1994), 85–93 for a discussion of mimicry and colonialism.

4. Richard Henry Pratt to Rutherford B. Hayes, 25 January 1880, Pratt Papers.

5. Richard Henry Pratt to Thaddeus Pound, 14 January 1880, Pratt Papers.

6. Even Pratt admits some discord in his autobiography. He states that at first, a number of young male students mutilated their new Western-style clothing as a form of protest. However, he assures us that after an initial verbal scolding, nearly all acquiesced. See Pratt, *Battlefield and Classroom*, 118. In fact, more extreme incidents of physical restraint and violence, illness, desertion, and malnutrition abounded at Carlisle and other early boarding schools. I will explore this issue in greater depth later.

7. According to Pratt's autobiographical account, despite some congressional resistance, he accomplished the essential tasks necessary to get the school off of the ground within a matter of days, if not hours. He claims to have convinced the secretary of the Interior, the secretary of War, the commissioner of Indian Affairs, and key members of Congress of the wisdom and viability of the project within the course of a day or so. See Pratt, *Battlefield and Classroom*, 213–17.

8. Adams, *Education for Extinction*, 26–27.

9. I will discuss these dramatic portraits in greater depth shortly. As I alluded to in the Introduction, they were used to convince school patrons, government officials, and indigenous leaders of the school's efficacy in transforming the children. These dramatic portraits were generally intended to set up a stark aesthetic comparison between the appearance and thus assumed ontological nature of the child upon entering Carlisle and the child's renewed appearance and character several months or years later. The implication, of course, was that Pratt's educational ideology was responsible for the positive turn from savage/barbarian to citizen.

10. Adams, *Education for Extinction*, 27.

11. Richard Tritt, "John Nicholas Choate: A Cumberland County Photographer," *Cumberland County History* 13, no. 2 (1996): 77–78.

12. Ibid., 79; Naomi Rosenblum, *A World History of Photography* (New York: Abbeville Press, 1997), 196.

13. Robert Haas, *Muybridge: Man in Motion* (Berkeley: University of California Press, 1976), 13–24.

14. Virtually all scholars who have studied Carlisle agree on these exact dates for the initial images.

15. The School's central quadrangle was flanked by the two dormitory buildings, with Pratt's residence perpendicular to the two buildings. This created a tightly enclosed horseshoe configuration. The school's famous bandstand, a symbol of conformism and unity, stood in the middle. There was thus a rigid, geometric architectural configuration that facilitated a sense of entrapment and surveillance. Michel Foucault highlights such a centered geometric configuration in his discussion of panoptic penal architecture, designed during the Enlightenment to place prisoners under either constant surveillance or the psychological threat of constant surveillance. The upshot of this psychology of surveillance was the making of "docile" or subservient penal bodies. In other words, the prisoners were to be subjected via institutionalized paranoia and fear rather than direct physical coercion. He defines this as the prime mechanism of "enlightened" penal reform during the eighteenth and nineteenth centuries, contrasting it to the supposed brutality of the ancient and medieval exercise of power. An obvious allusion may thus be drawn between Foucault's panoptic penal structures and the architecture of other reformist institutions of Modernity, especially schools. For further discussion, see Foucault, *Discipline and Punish*, 170–77, 195–209.

16. William Henry Fox Talbot, "Some Account of the Art of Photogenic Drawing, or, The Process by Which Natural Objects May Be Made to Delineate Themselves without the Aid of the Artist's Pencil," in *Art in Theory, 1815–1900: An Anthology of Changing Ideas*, ed. Charles Harrison, Paul Wood, and Jason Gaiger (Oxford: Blackwell Publishers, 1998), 249–55.

17. Pratt, *Battlefield and Classroom*, 121.

18. Luther Standing Bear, *My People, the Sioux*, ed. E. A. Brininstool (Boston: Houghton Mifflin, 1928), 125.

19. Ibid., 131.

20. Antonia Valdes-Depena, "Marketing the Exotic: Creating the Image of the 'Real' Indian," in *Visualizing a Mission: Artifacts and Images of the Carlisle Indian School, 1879–1918*, ed. Phillip Earenfight (Carlisle, Pa.: The Trout Gallery, Dickinson College, 2004), 35–41.

21. Rosenblum, *World History of Photography*, 198–99.

22. Oliver Wendell Holmes, "The Stereoscope and the Stereograph," in *Art in Theory*, 668–72.

23. Interestingly, the reform-minded Holmes held sharp and derisive views on the continent's indigenous inhabitants. He wrote that the new social reformist ideas of the nineteenth century were not readily accepted by the "lower classes" of people in the country, thus making their implementation problematic. He cited Native Americans as a group typically incapable of accepting such "progressive" thought, due to their inherently "feral" nature. See Holmes, *Pages from an Old Volume of Life* (Cambridge, Mass.: H. O. Houghton, 1883), 325–26.

24. Soule was among the white photographers who photographed prisoners at Fort Sill during the period of 1869–1874, concurrently with Pratt's original tenure in the Indian Territory. For general information on Soule, see Russell Belous, *Will Soule, the Indian Photographer at Fort Sill, Oklahoma, 1869–74* (Los Angeles: Ward Ritchie Press, 1969).

25. Aleta Ringlero, "Prairie Pinups: Reconsidering Historic Portraits of American Indian Women," in *Only Skin Deep*, 183–91. Ringlero rightly sees such imagery as therefore failing as ethnography, as the assumed "authentic" appearance of many of these women was the result of studio pyrotechnics.

26. I will take up the topic of gender in Carlisle imagery in greater length later in this study.

27. Orson S. Fowler, *The Practical Phrenologist* (Boston: O. S. Fowler, 1869), 87–88.

28. For more on Fowler's audiences, see Davies, *Phrenology*, 47–48, 50, 52–57.

29. Ibid., 87–88.

30. Fowler's choice of the caption "Indian Chief" underneath the illustration bespeaks his assumption that such a generalized designation is adequate for his readership. In other words, such a simplistic stereotype effectively conveys the essential identity of this racial "type," as if all indigenous peoples were interchangeable and tribal distinctions were irrelevant.

31. In keeping with this conspicuously pseudoscientific logic, Fowler discusses the figure of "Haggarty, a Murderer" slightly later in the book. Fowler's criminal character predictably displays similar phrenological traits to those seen in his illustration of the "Indian Chief" character. Both have flat crowns, or tops of the skull, and both have a marked narrowing near the top of the sides of their respective skulls. In the case of the "Murderer," this is indicative of low moral character and outbursts of gross violence against others. See Fowler, *The Practical Phrenologist*, 87–88, 110.

32. Jacob Riis, *How the Other Half Lives* (New York: Dover Publications, 1971), 48–59.

33. Trachtenberg, *Shades of Hiawatha*, xxii. On the status of the Italo-Slavic immigrant as evolutionarily inferior, see also Ysabel Rennie, *The Search for Criminal Man: A Conceptual History of the Dangerous Offender* (Lexington, Mass.: Lexington Books, 1978).

34. Phillips, "Identifying the Criminal," 18–22.

35. John Tagg, *The Burden of Representation* (Minneapolis: University of Minnesota Press, 1993), 76, 80, 85.

36. Ibid., 77.

37. Linda Poolaw, "Spirit Capture: Observations of an Encounter," in *Spirit Capture: Photographs from the National Museum of the American Indian*, ed. Tim Johnson (Washington, D.C.: Smithsonian Institution Press, 1998), 169.

38. Tagg, *Burden of Representation*, 64–65.

39. Tagg, following Michel Foucault, is careful to note the multidimensional qualities of police, hospital, and school photographs. He insists that they were intended as positive rather than oppressive. That is, they were intended to display or prove the progress made by the student at various points in his or her school education. Foucault termed this ritualistic, repetitive form of surveillance "examination." See Tagg, *Burden of Representation*, 82–83; Foucault, *Discipline and Punish*, 184–94.

40. Standing Bear, *My People*, 125.

41. For a detailed account of the alleged frontier atrocities and crimes, see Pratt, *Battlefield and Classroom*, 1–103. It should be noted that this extended account covers the period of 1867–1875 and is by no means one-dimensional. Pratt recognizes the duplicity in frontier war and discusses atrocities committed by both sides as well as the political complexities of land allotment.

Chapter 4

1. George Catlin, *Souvenir of the North American Indians*, facs. ed. (London: 1849; Tulsa, Okla.: Gilcrease Museum, 2003), 52.

2. William Truettner, "Vanishing with a Trace: Art and Indian Life in the Gilcrease Souvenir Album," introduction to Catlin, *Souvenir*, xxi, xxvii.

3. Comte speaks of three phases of human mental development: the Theological, the Metaphysical, and the Scientific. The earlier phases represent knowledge gained via superstition or other forms of inexact logic. The Scientific phase represents man's highest attainment because it is based on empirical knowledge. One can view Pratt's conception of "proper education" as one progressing out of the superstitious mindset of the blanket Indian and into the higher realm of modern civilized knowledge based on systematic scientific observation. In this sense, the before-and-after photographs are intended to convey not only a physical but a mental morphing—from the doldrums of nativist belief into the light of modern Western scientism. See Auguste Comte, "The Nature and Importance of the Positive Philosophy," in *The Positive Philosophy of August Comte*, ed. and trans. Harriet Martineau, 2 vols. (London: John Chapman, 1853), quoted in *Art in Theory*, 151–55. Hegel postulated that the visible, aesthetic qualities of the artwork reflected the work's history and the history of human artistic achievement more generally. Thus, if one were to look at images from differing times, one could ascertain the degree of artistic development within both the work and the given civilization and era. This idea is instructive, because Pratt obviously intended the photographs to signify the various states of Tom Torlino at varying times in his own existence. These states—whether the "original" state of savagery or the "improved" state of civilization, were of course inscribed onto Torlino's body by Pratt, Choate, and the school administration. See G. W. F. Hegel, "Lectures on Aesthetics," in *Introductory Lectures on Aesthetics*, ed. and trans. Bernard Bosenquet (London: Kegan Paul, 1886), quoted in *Art in Theory*, 58–69.

4. Heinrich Wölfflin, *Renaissance and Baroque*, ed. and trans. Kathrin Simon (London: Fontana, 1964). One could also apply this to the stylistic shifts of the period cited by Wölfflin: Early Renaissance to High Renaissance, or High Renaissance to Baroque. Although he disavows the notion that any one individual could be solely responsible for these seismic aesthetic and cultural changes, he does repeatedly cite exemplars such as Raphael, who for him embody these epochal shifts.

5. Ibid., 29–34.

6. Trachtenberg, *Shades of Hiawatha*, 43. I want to note here that I admire Professor Trachtenberg's work very much. I am simply pointing out that this famous image has often been perceived as transparently illustrative and therefore taken for

granted by many scholars. Although Trachtenberg and many others have justifiably attacked Pratt's logic of assimilationism, I want to take a slightly different tack and deconstruct the very representational codes taken as "given" by previous critics of Carlisle.

7. Even David Wallace Adams, probably the most important historian of Carlisle in recent years, chooses not to refer to the image in his text, although he uses it as a de facto illustration for his critique of Pratt's assimilationism. See Adams, *Education for Extinction*, 100–112. Again, I want to emphasize that I admire Adams's work very much, and simply wish to point out methodological differences between us.

8. Lonna Malmsheimer, "Imitation White Men: Images of Transformation at the Carlisle Indian School," *Studies in Visual Communication* 11, no. 4 (1985): 65–66.

9. I deploy the term *synecdochic* here in the sense explained by Joseph Childers and Gary Hentzi. In their explanation of the literary critical terms *metonymy* and *synecdoche*, Childers and Hentzi argue that each term refers to the usage of a sort of linguistic or visual metaphor by a person or institution in the effort to explain or characterize something. In this sense, metonymy is a figure of speech that substitutes the name of something for the name of another thing closely related to it. Thus the use of the word *Washington* to refer to the U.S. government. Synecdoche is the use of a fragment in speech (or visual representation) as a stand-in for the whole. Thus, in this context, these two momentary photographic images stand in for "Tom Torlino" the human being—his character, his life, his aspirations, his beliefs, his personal and ancestral histories. What is implied in the use of metonymy and synecdoche is that a relationship of contiguity exists between the fragment and the whole. Thus, in the first image, Torlino is supposed to be perceived as embodying savagery in its totality, and in the second he is taken to embody civilization and all it implied for contemporary audiences. See Joseph Childers and Gary Hentzi, eds., *The Columbia Dictionary of Modern Literary and Cultural Criticism* (New York: Columbia University Press, 1995), 187–88.

10. Bureau of Indian Affairs, "Carlisle Indian Industrial School: Descriptive and Historical Record of Student," file 1327, no. 872, RG 75, National Archives.

11. In the sense of the continual photographing of newly arriving students, the terms "ritual" and "indoctrination" become operative. By ritualistically photographing successive generations of newcomers, Pratt in a sense photographically branded them, and in so doing confirmed and further legitimized his project. The photographs may thus be seen as the death toll for the pre-Carlisle cultural identities of the new students and metaphors for the enforced cultural initiation to which they were to be subjected. For an in-depth discussion on the ritualistic role of photography in modern penal institutions, see Foucault, *Discipline and Punish*, 187, 191, 194. He characterizes photography as producing an "ignoble archive" that produces the "sciences of Man," fosters "domination" of the body, and serves therefore as a "ritual of truth."

12. For greater details about a typical journey of this kind, see Standing Bear, *My People*, 125–32.

13. The bandstand often served as a symbolic object of surveillance and authority. This perception was often put into print in one of the school's early publications, *The Indian Helper.* As the title suggests, the paper was intended to be a

patronizing, boosterish publication that fostered school spirit and enthusiasm for the assimilation process. Issues of the *Helper* generally started off with a poem or column written by the so-called "Man-on-the-Bandstand," an ambivalent and anonymous authority figure whose hyphenated name was intended to mimic anglicized Native American names. The real person behind the "Man-on-the-Bandstand" was actually female: Marianna Burgess, one of the school's original faculty members. Her pseudonymous column was intended to convey a vaguely authoritative and moralizing message to its readership, which consisted mostly of students and school patrons.

14. Pratt often signed personal correspondence to his students with the title "Your School Father." Such a gesture undoubtedly communicated Pratt's authority to the students, who had been raised with centuries-old paternalistic traditions and were unaccustomed to hearing a white man presumptuously assume the role of father in their lives.

15. Malmsheimer cites local newspaper reaction to the appearance of the arriving Navajo. The *Daily Evening Sentinel* wrote that the group was "as dirty a crowd as one would wish to see . . . dirty . . . greasy . . . wore a scared look." She also notes, significantly, that Pratt marketed images of Navajo students in one of the school papers, the *Morning Star*, offering free prints of Torlino to new subscribers, "one showing a Navajo in his still wilder native dress, and the other after two years in the school." See Malmsheimer, "Imitation White Men," 64–65.

16. Pratt repeatedly decried the demeaning nature of this spectacle, then becoming wildly popular with audiences in both the United States and Europe. He was careful to rhetorically distance himself, his views on Indian education, and the school's activities from such "entertainment." Despite this conscious intention, he nevertheless shrewdly perceived the political and economic value of exploiting the "Indianness" of his arriving students. For a revealing reference to the Buffalo Bill show and its relationship to his own project, see Pratt, *Battlefield and Classroom*, 120–21.

17. See Fusco, "Racial Signs," 21, 32–33. Fusco argues that such a representational scheme gained credibility as traditional Judeo-Christian explanations of racial difference receded in the face of more modern scientific explanations. Thus, the notion that human beings could speed up the evolutionary process of other human beings became appealing as monogenesis was increasingly replaced by polygenesis and later social Darwinism. In this sense, the overtly racist pseudoscience of the antebellum era was updated, but the newer sciences still carried the presumption of white evolutionary superiority.

18. Malmsheimer, "Imitation White Men," 66.

19. Bureau of Indian Affairs, "Carlisle Indian Industrial School," file 1327.

20. Ibid.

21. *Morning Star* 6, no. 9 (April 1886): 3; *The Indian Helper* 12, no. 22 (March 1897).

22. Pratt, *Battlefield and Classroom*, 303–4.

23. I use the designation CE in this instance instead of the traditional AD. In recent art history textbooks, such as that by Marilyn Stokstad, the designation CE, ("of the common era") is deemed preferable to AD (anno Domini, "in the year of

the Lord"). The latter designation is increasingly viewed by Stokstad and others as a throwback to a more eurocentric era in the discipline's history. Ironically, however, the CE designation does nothing to overturn the basic numerical conception of historical time of the Julian and Gregorian calendars. Marilyn Stoksad and Michael Cothren, *Art: A Brief History*, 4th ed. (New York: Prentice Hall, 2009).

24. Loretta Hall, "Navajo," in *The Gale Encyclopedia of Native American Tribes*, ed. Sharon Malinowski and Anna Sheets, vol. 2 (Detroit: Gale, 1998), 217–18.

25. Pratt, *Battlefield and Classroom*, 303.

26. Loretta Hall, "Navajo," 220, 223.

27. Hall, "Navajo," 220, 223; Alison Bird, *Heart of the Dragonfly: The Historical Development of the Cross Necklaces of The Pueblo and Navajo Peoples* (Albuquerque, N. Mex.: Avanyu Publishing, 1992), xvii, 137, 139.

28. Leonard Dinnerstein, *Natives and Strangers: A Multicultural History of Americans* (New York: Oxford University Press, 2003), 178.

29. Richard Henry Pratt, "The Advantages of Mingling Indians with Whites," in *Proceedings and Addresses of the National Education Association, 1895* (Washington, D.C.: National Education Association, 1895), 761–62.

30. James Faris, *Navajo and Photography: A Critical History of the Representation of an American People* (Albuquerque: University of New Mexico Press, 1996), 53.

31. Ibid., 65.

32. Anna Blume, "In Place of Writing," in *Plains Indian Drawings 1865–1918: Pages from a Visual History*, ed. Janet Berlo (New York: Harry N. Abrams, 1996), 44. For more on the general history of the Navajo from Spanish contact through the nineteenth century, see Robert A. Roessel, *Dinétak* (Rough Rock, Ariz.: Navajo Curriculum Center, 1982).

33. Samuel C. Armstrong to Richard Henry Pratt, 26 August 1878, Pratt Papers; Richard Henry Pratt to Samuel C. Armstrong, 7 September 1878, Armstrong Papers, Hampton Archives, Hampton University, Virginia; Richard Henry Pratt to Samuel C. Armstrong, 13 October 1878, Armstrong Papers.

34. Richard Henry Pratt to Carl Schurz, 8 April 1880, Pratt Papers.

35. Bureau of Indian Affairs, "Carlisle Indian Industrial School," file 1327.

36. Ann Boyd, "Cheyenne," in *The Gale Encyclopedia*, 2: 221. The splitting of the Cheyenne, who were originally one large tribe from the Great Lakes region, was a gradual process with complex causes. By the 1830s, the split had occurred and is thought to have been brought about by the incursion of white settlement into the upper Midwest, the ancestral homeland of the Cheyenne. This drove the tribe south and west, and in this process they broke apart. In 1867, the U.S. government gave the Southern fragment a reservation in the Oklahoma Territory, effectively codifying the split. The Northern group received a reservation in Montana in 1884.

37. Richard Erdoes and Alfonso Ortiz, ed. *American Indian Myths and Legends* (New York: Pantheon Books, 1984).

38. For more on the Battle of the Little Bighorn, see Richard G. Hardorff, ed., *Cheyenne Memories of the Custer Fight: A Sourcebook* (Spokane, Wash.: Arthur H. Clark, 1995) and Paul A. Hutton, ed., *The Custer Reader* (Lincoln: University of Nebraska Press, 1992).

39. Pratt, *Battlefield and Classroom*, 112–14. Pratt writes of his conversation with Grey Beard, recounting that the chief asked him how *he* would like to be chained up and taken from his family. Pratt confides to the reader, "It was a hard question."

40. Boyd, "Cheyenne," 222.

41. Marsha Bol, "Defining Lakota Tourist Art," in *Unpacking Culture: Art and Commodity in Colonial and Postcolonial Worlds*, ed. Ruth Phillips and Christopher Steiner (Berkeley: University of California Press, 1999), 224–25.

42. Ringlero, "Prairie Pinups," 188. See also Joanna Cohen Scherer, "You Can't Believe Your Eyes: Inaccuracies in Photographs of North American Indians," *Exposure* 16, no. 4 (1978): 6–19.

43. Bol, "Defining Lakota Tourist Art," 216–17.

44. White Buffalo's date of birth is stated on his student card, now part of the Records of the Department of the Interior and Bureau of Indian Affairs archives in the National Archives and Records Administration, Washington, D.C.

45. Bol, "Defining Lakota Tourist Art," 216.

46. Boyd, "Cheyenne," 225–26.

47. Michel Foucault, *The Order of Things*, ed. and trans. R. D. Laing, rev. ed. (New York: Vintage Books, 1973), 303–43.

48. Ibid., 304–6.

49. Laura Turner, "John Nicholas Choate and the Production of Photography at the Carlisle Indian School," in *Visualizing a Mission*, 14–19.

50. Richard Henry Pratt, *Twenty Fourth Annual Report, Red Man and Helper*, 14 August 1903. See also Pratt's account of the incident in *Battlefield and Classroom*, 334–35.

Chapter 5

1. Stephen Tomlinson, *Head Masters* (Tuscaloosa: University of Alabama Press, 2005), 215–38.

2. Tomlinson, *Head Masters*, 234.

3. Franz Boas to Richard Henry Pratt, 8 June 1891, Pratt Papers.

4. Robert Rydell, *All the World's a Fair* (Chicago: University of Chicago Press, 1984), 39, 45. Rydell points to the economic panic of 1893 and the brutality of Jim Crow in support of his claim that the Fair's message about the United States contradicted the actualities of racial and class strife.

5. Boime, *Art of Exclusion*, 1–2.

6. Rydell, *All the World's a Fair*, 43–45.

7. On the ideology of moral uplift in museums, see Carol Duncan, *Civilizing Rituals: Inside Public Art Museums* (New York: Routledge, 1995).

8. Rydell, *All the World's a Fair*, 40.

9. "None Can Compare with It," *New York Times*, 19 June 1893.

10. Richard Tritt, personal communication with the author, August 2004. Tritt

is the current photography curator at the Cumberland County Historical Society in Carlisle, Pennsylvania, the institution that holds the most extensive archive of Carlisle material. Also, Judith Fryer Davidov points out that Johnston was one of the government's official photographers, and had been hired to document government pavilions at the Fair. Apparently, Johnston's images were selected above others to illustrate the government's official report on the Fair. See Judith Fryer Davidov, *Woman's Camera Work* (Durham, N.C.: Duke University Press, 1998), 77.

11. Pratt, *Battlefield and Classroom*, 303–4.

12. Frederick Jackson Turner, "The Significance of the Frontier in American History," in *Rereading Frederick Jackson Turner*, ed. John Mack Faragher (New Haven, Conn.: Yale University Press, 1998), 31–60.

13. L. G. Moses, *Wild West Shows and the Images of Native Americans, 1883–1933* (Albuquerque: University of New Mexico Press, 1996), 11–12.

14. Ibid., 108–12.

15. Ibid., 108–12.

16. This is not to say that Pratt never paraded his charges around, either metaphorically or literally. In fact, on many occasions he took students with him to prominent events, including the Fair, and had them march in formation or recite poetry or sing songs, in an effort to exhibit their newly acquired civilization.

17. Tomlinson, *Head Masters*, 231–34.

18. Franz Boas to Richard Henry Pratt, 8 June 1891, Pratt Papers

19. Tomlinson, *Head Masters*, 215–64, 268–85.

20. For details of Johnston's early life, see Pete Daniel and Raymond Smock, *A Talent for Detail: The Photographs of Miss Frances Benjamin Johnston, 1899–1910* (New York: Harmony Books, 1974).

21. For more on the Académie Julian, see J. David Farmer, "Overcoming All Obstacles: The Women of the Académie Julian, An Exhibition Organized by the Dahesh Museum," *The California Art Club Newsletter* (April/May 2000), http://www.californiaartclub.org/newsletter/articles/article_julian1.shtml.

22. Bettina Berch, *The Woman Behind the Lens* (Charlottesville: University of Virginia Press, 2000), 14–15.

23. For more on Smillie, see the Smithsonian's website, specifically the archives pages: Smithsonian Institution; Archives, Manuscripts, Photographs Catalog; Smithsonian Institution Research Information System, "Thomas William Smillie ca 1900," http://siris-archives.si.edu/ipac20/ipac.jsp?uri=full=3100001~!97189!0, and Merry A. Foresta, "Photos for All Time," *Smithsonian.com* (April 2004), http://www.smithsonianmag.com/arts-culture/photos-for-all-time.html.

24. Rosenblum, *World History of Photography*, 442–53.

25. Daniel and Smock, *Talent for Detail*, 39.

26. Berch, *The Woman Behind the Lens*, 15–16.

27. Container 28, reels 21–22, Papers of Frances Benjamin Johnston, Manuscripts Division, Library of Congress.

28. Shawn Michelle Smith, *American Archives: Gender, Race, and Class in Visual Culture* (Princeton, N.J.: Princeton University Press, 1999), 169–70.

29. On the industrial worker and visions of masculinity in American art, see Randall C. Griffin, "Thomas Anshutz's *The Ironworkers' Noontime:* Remythologizing the Industrial Worker," *Smithsonian Studies in American Art* 4, nos. 3–4 (1990): 129–43.

30. Smith, *American Archives*, 170–71.

31. For general background on Armstrong and Hampton, see Robert Francis Engs, *Educating the Disenfranchised and Disinherited: Samuel Chapman Armstrong and the Hampton Institute, 1839–93* (Knoxville: University of Tennessee Press, 1999).

32. Daniel and Smock, *Talent for Detail*, 95–96.

33. Berch, *The Woman Behind the Lens*, 39. See also Jeannene Przyblyski, "American Visions at the Paris Exposition, 1900: Another Look at Frances Benjamin Johnston's Hampton Photographs," *Art Journal* 57, no. 3 (1998): 60–68.

34. Smith, *American Archives*, 172–76.

35. Smith, *American Archives*, 170. Smith links the importance of Johnston's perceived legitimacy and "purity" to the stereotypical and irrational fear of black engagement with white womanhood.

36. I base this assertion of an intended juxtaposition on John Szarkowski's placement of these images side by side in the 1966 Museum of Modern Art (MoMA) edition of the album. Szarkowski claimed to have been following Johnston's original ordering of the images.

37. Smith deploys this term in characterizing Johnston's Hampton work. See Smith, *American Archives*, 169. On the Du Bois commentary, see Przyblyski, "American Visions," 67.

38. John Szarkowski, *The Hampton Album* (New York: Doubleday Books, 1966), 5–9.

39. Berch, *The Woman Behind the Lens*, 42.

40. Ibid., 56.

41. Richard Henry Pratt to Frances Benjamin Johnston, 17 July 1901, Johnston Papers. See also Berch, *The Woman Behind the Lens*, 48.

42. Richard Henry Pratt, "A New Illustrated Catalogue," *The Red Man and Helper* 17, no. 10 (1901): 4.

43. Richard Henry Pratt to Frances Benjamin Johnston, 6 July 1901, Johnston Papers.

44. Richard Henry Pratt, "The Carlisle Idea," excerpt from 1902 illustrated catalog (Carlisle, Pa.: Carlisle Indian Industrial School, 1902).

45. Berch, *The Woman Behind the Lens*, 56–57.

46. Richard Henry Pratt to Frances Benjamin Johnston, 13 May 1901, 3 June 1901, 6 June 1901, Pratt Papers.

47. Barb Landis, curator, Cumberland County Historical Society, personal communication with the author, August 2004.

48. Gramsci, *Selections*, 279–87.

49. Ibid., 301–6.

50. On this topic, see Randall C. Griffin, "Thomas Anshutz's *The Ironworkers' Noontime*."

51. For more on the philosophy of labor at North American Indian boarding schools, see Ward Churchill, *Kill the Indian and Save the Man: The Genocidal Impact of Indian Residential Schools* (San Francisco: City Lights Books, 2004), 44–51. Churchill argues that such labor practices, in addition to being enforced, led to profitability for the school, thus further exploiting the labor of the children. Additionally, he points to the serious health risks to children in the course of such backbreaking labor.

52. Frederick W. Taylor, *Principles of Scientific Management*. See the introduction and first chapter for a greater elaboration of his ideas.

53. Mary Warner Marien, *Photography: A Cultural History* (New York: Harry N. Abrams, 2002), 217.

54. Mark Antliff, "Fascism, Modernism, and Modernity," *Art Bulletin* 84, no. 1 (2002): 160–61.

55. Adams, *Education for Extinction*, 17.

56. Sarah Burns, *Pastoral Inventions* (Philadelphia: Temple University Press, 1989), 11–19, 99–109.

57. Adams, *Education for Extinction*, 63.

58. Ella Shohat, *Unthinking Eurocentrism: Multiculturalism and the Media* (New York: Routledge, 1994).

59. Elizabeth Hutchinson, "Progressive Primitivism: Race, Gender, and Turn-of-the-Century American Concerns" (PhD diss., Stanford University, 1999).

60. The Ghost Dance was a ritual dance widely practiced among various Native American groups in the late nineteenth century. Although the dance's performance varied in different locales, in general it was a religious dance meant to connect tribe members with an animistic spirit world and the spirits of dead ancestors. Ghost Dances had a political implication, because they were performed when tribal leaders wished to inculcate an ethos of clean, natural living among tribe members. Such clean living was often conceived of as being in opposition to the newly imposed ways of life brought on by colonial contact with white populations. Ghost Dances were therefore deemed hostile by Bureau of Indian Affairs officials. For more about Ghost Dances and their relation to the Sioux Outbreak of 1890, see James Mooney, *The Ghost-Dance Religion and the Sioux Outbreak of 1890* (Washington, D.C.: GPO, 1896).

61. For more on American Pictorialism and Day in particular, see Rosenblum, *World History of Photography*, 320–24.

62. Edward Steichen, "Ye Fakers," *Camera Work* 1 (1903): 107.

63. For more on Stieglitz and Photo-Secession, see Rosenblum, *World History of Photography*, 325–37.

64. Gertrude Käsebier to Frances Benjamin Johnston, 7 November 1892, Johnston Papers.

65. Alfred Stieglitz to Frances Benjamin Johnston, 1 June 1898, Johnston Papers.

66. Rosenblum, *World History of Photography*, 334.

67. For more on the emergent imagery of the New Woman in Gilded Age American culture, see Holly Pyne Connor, ed., *Off the Pedestal: New Women in the Art of Homer, Chase, and Sargent* (Piscataway, N.J.: Rutgers University Press, 2006).

68. I based the number of surviving cyanotypes on the catalog entry for this portion of Johnston's collection at the Library of Congress website.

69. Richard Henry Pratt to Frances Benjamin Johnston, 7 July 1901, Johnston Papers.

70. Elizabeth Hutchinson, "When the 'Sioux Chief's Party Calls': Käsebier's Indian Portraits and the Gendering of the Artist's Studio," *American Art* 16, no. 2 (2002): 47–51.

71. Richard Henry Pratt, *United States Industrial School, Carlisle, Pennsylvania* (Carlisle, Pa.: Carlisle Indian Industrial School, 1895), 14, 15, 35.

72. *The Indian Helper* 9, no. 37 (1 June 1894).

73. Ibid.; *The Indian Helper* 10, no. 46 (16 August 1895).

74. *The Indian Helper* 10, no. 41 (12 July 1895).

75. *The Indian Helper* 11, no. 42 (24 July 1896).

76. Richard L. Tritt, "Notes on the Indian School Photographs and Photographers," in *The Indian Industrial School, Carlisle, Pennsylvania, 1879–1918*, ed. Linda Witmer (Carlisle, Pa.: Cumberland County Historical Society, 2002), 116–17.

77. I've attributed the images noted in this album to Leslie rather than Choate based on information I attained at the Cumberland County Historical Society. The album is attributed to Leslie in the society's catalog, and Richard Tritt, the society's current photography curator, has stated that the images are indeed by Leslie rather than his mentor Choate.

78. Pratt, "Physical Culture," excerpt from 1902 illustrated catalog (Carlisle, Pa.: Carlisle Indian Industrial School, 1902).

79. For more on the significance of football at Carlisle, see David Wallace Adams, "More Than A Game: The Carlisle Indians Take to the Gridiron," *Western Historical Quarterly* 32 (2001): 25–53.

80. Witmer, *Indian Industrial School*, 46.

81. Pratt quoted in Adams, "More Than a Game," 26.

82. Roosevelt, *The Strenuous Life*, 128.

83. Lears, *No Place of Grace*, 98–102.

84. Stephen Crane, "Red Men Put Up a Gallant Fight—Were Beaten by a Score of Four to Nothing," *New York Journal*, 12 November 1896.

85. Adams, "More Than a Game," 27.

86. Ibid., 34.

87. Robert W. Wheeler, *Jim Thorpe: World's Greatest Athlete* (Norman: University of Oklahoma Press, 1981).

88. "Carlisle's Olympic Heroes," *The Red Man* 5, no. 1 (1912): 27–28.

89. For a discussion of the prominence of eugenic science in the United States

in the early twentieth century, see Nancy Ordover, *American Eugenics: Race, Queer Anatomy, and the Science of Nationalism* (Minneapolis: University of Minnesota Press, 2003).

90. Franz Boas to Richard Henry Pratt, 8 June 1891, Pratt Papers.

Conclusion

1. Richard Henry Pratt to Theodore Roosevelt, 11 October 1901, Pratt Papers.

2. Elizabeth Hutchinson, "Progressive Primitivism," 1–12.

3. Marshall McLuhan, *Understanding Media: The Extensions of Man* (New York: Signet Books, 1964), 170–71.

4. Allison Eckardt Ledes, "A Late Nineteenth Century Collaboration: Anthropologist Frank Cushing and Artist Thomas Eakins—Current and Coming," *The Magazine Antiques* 146, no. 1 (January 1995).

5. Ibid.

6. Hutchinson, "Progressive Primitivism," 1–12.

Bibliography

Archival Sources

Baird, Spencer F., Papers. Smithsonian Institution Archives, Washington, D.C. RU 26, vol. 180.

Carlisle Indian and Industrial School Archives. Cumberland County Historical Society, Carlisle, Pa.

Johnston, Francis Benjamin, Papers. Manuscript Division, Library of Congress. Washington, D.C.

National Archives and Records Administration, Washington, D.C. Records of the Department of the Interior and Bureau of Indian Affairs. RG 75, file 1327.

National Museum of Natural History, Washington, D.C. Records of the Anthropology Department.

Pratt, Richard Henry, Papers. Yale Collection of Western Americana, Beinecke Rare Book and Manuscript Library, Yale University.

Books, Articles, Dissertations, Online Sources, and Periodicals

Adams, David Wallace. *Education for Extinction: American Indians and the Boarding School Experience, 1875–1928.* Lawrence: University of Kansas Press, 1996.

———. "More Than a Game: The Carlisle Indians Take the Gridiron." *Western Historical Quarterly* 32 (2001): 25–53.

American Philosophical Society. "Samuel G. Morton Papers." http://www.amphilsoc.org/mole/view?docId=ead/Mss.B.M843-ead.xml;query=;brand=default.

Antliff, Mark. "Fascism, Modernism, and Modernity." *Art Bulletin* 84, no. 1 (2002): 148–69.

Archives.gov, Teaching with Documents. "Maps of Indian Territory, the Dawes Act, and Will Rogers' Enrollment Case File." The National Archives, http://www.archives.gov/education/lessons/fed-indian-policy.

Armstrong, Carol. *Scenes in a Library: Reading the Photograph in the Book, 1843–1875*. Cambridge, Mass.: MIT Press, 1998.

Arnason, H. H. *The Sculptures of Houdon*. New York: Oxford University Press, 1975.

Barthes, Roland. *Camera Lucida*. Translated by Richard Howell. New York: Hill and Wang, 1981.

Belous, Russell. *Will Soule, the Indian Photographer at Fort Sill, Oklahoma, 1869–74*. Los Angeles: Ward Ritchie Press, 1969.

Berch, Bettina. *The Woman Behind the Lens*. Charlottesville: University of Virginia Press, 2000.

Berlo, Janet, ed. *Plains Indian Drawings 1865–1918: Pages from a Visual History*. New York: Harry N. Abrams, 1996.

Bhabha, Homi K. *The Location of Culture*. London: Routledge, 1994.

Bird, Allison. *Heart of the Dragonfly: Historical Developments of the Cross Necklaces of the Pueblo and Navajo Peoples*. Albuquerque, N.M.: Avanyu Publishing, 1992.

Blume, Anna. "In Place of Writing." In Berlo, *Plains Indian Drawings*, 40–44.

Boime, Albert. *The Art of Exclusion: Representing Blacks in the Nineteenth Century*. Washington, D.C.: Smithsonian Institution Press, 1990.

———. *The Magisterial Gaze: Manifest Destiny and American Landscape Painting, c. 1830–1865*. Washington, D.C.: Smithsonian Institution Press, 1991.

Bol, Marsha. "Defining Lakota Tourist Art." In Phillips and Steiner, *Unpacking Culture*, 214–42.

Boyd, Ann. "Cheyenne." In Malinowski and Sheets, *Gale Encyclopedia*, 221–27.

Burns, Sarah. *Inventing the Modern Artist: Art and Culture in Gilded Age America*. New Haven, Conn.: Yale University Press, 1996.

———. *Pastoral Inventions*. Philadelphia: Temple University Press, 1989.

Caldwell, Charles. "Phrenology Vindicated." *Christian Examiner*, 1834.

"Carlisle's Olympic Heroes." *The Red Man* 5, no. 1 (1912): 27–28.

Catlin, George. *Souvenir of the North American Indians*. 1849. A facsimile of the first edition. Tulsa, Okla.: Gilcrease Museum, 2003.

Childers, Joseph and Gary Hentzi, eds. *The Columbia Dictionary of Modern Literary and Cultural Criticism.* New York: Columbia University Press, 1995.

Chinard, Gilbert, ed. *Houdon in America.* Baltimore: Johns Hopkins Press, 1930.

Churchill, Ward. *Kill the Indian and Save the Man: The Genocidal Impact of Indian Residential Schools.* San Francisco: City Lights Books, 2004.

Colbert, Charles. "Clark Mills and the Phrenologist." *Art Bulletin* 70, no. 1 (1988): 134–37.

———. *A Measure of Perfection: Phrenology and the Fine Arts in America.* Chapel Hill: University of North Carolina Press, 1997.

Combe, George. *The Constitution of Man.* Hartford, Conn.: S. Andrus and Sons, 1842.

———. *Phrenology Applied to Painting and Sculpture.* London: Simpkin, Marshall, 1855.

Comte, Auguste. "The Nature and Importance of the Positive Philosophy." In *The Positive Philosophy of Auguste Comte.* Edited and translated by Harriet Martineau. 2 vols. London: John Chapman, 1853. Quoted in Harrison, Wood, and Gaiger, *Art in Theory,* 151–55.

Connor, Holly Pyne, ed. *Off the Pedestal: New Women in the Art of Homer, Chase, and Sargent.* Piscataway, N.J.: Rutgers University Press, 2006.

Cooter, Roger. *The Cultural Meaning of Popular Science: Phrenology and the Organization of Consent in Nineteenth-Century Britain.* Cambridge: Cambridge University Press, 1984.

Crane, Stephen. "Red Men Put Up a Gallant Fight—Were Beaten by a Score of Four to Nothing." *New York Journal,* 12 November 1896.

Craven, Wayne. *Colonial American Portraiture: The Economic, Religious, Social, Cultural, Philosophical, Scientific, and Aesthetic Foundations.* Cambridge: Cambridge University Press, 1986.

Dall, William Healy. *Spencer Fullerton Baird, a Biography.* Philadelphia: J. B. Lippincott, 1915.

Daniel, Pete and Raymond Smock. *A Talent for Detail: The Photographs of Miss Frances Benjamin Johnston, 1899–1910.* New York: Harmony Books, 1974.

Davidov, Judith Fryer. *Women's Camera Work.* Durham, N.C.: Duke University Press, 1998.

Davies, John. *Phrenology: Fad & Science: A 19th Century American Crusade.* New Haven, Conn.: Yale University Press, 1955.

Department of Anthropology. "Anthropology Conservation Laboratory: Focus on Leadership." National Museum of Natural History, http://anthropology.si.edu/conservation/focus_on_leadership1.htm.

Dinnerstein, Leonard. *Natives and Strangers: A Multicultural History of Americans.* New York: Oxford University Press, 2003.

Douglas, Stephen A. "Oration of the Hon. Stephen A. Douglas on the Inauguration of the Jackson Statue, January 8, 1853." In *The Inauguration of Mills's Equestrian Statue,* 3.

Duncan, Carol. *Civilizing Rituals: Inside Public Art Museums.* New York: Routledge, 1995.

Dunlap, William. *History of the Rise and Progress of the Arts of Design in the United States.* New York: George P. Scott, 1834.

Earenfight, Phillip, ed. *Visualizing a Mission: Artifacts and Images of the Carlisle Indian School, 1879–1918.* Carlisle, Pa.: The Trout Gallery and Dickinson College, 2004. An exhibition catalog.

Emerson, Ralph Waldo. "Nature." In Perkins and Perkins, *American Tradition in Literature,* 344–70.

Engs, Robert Francis. *Educating the Disenfranchised and Disinherited: Samuel Chapman Armstrong and the Hampton Institute, 1839–93.* Knoxville: University of Tennessee Press, 1999.

Erdoes, Richard and Alfonso Ortiz, eds. *American Indian Myths and Legends.* New York: Pantheon, 1984.

Faragher, John Mack, ed. *Rereading Frederick Jackson Turner.* New Haven, Conn.: Yale University Press, 1998.

Faris, James. *Navajo and Photography: A Critical History of the Representation of an American People.* Albuquerque: University of New Mexico Press, 1996.

Farmer, J. David. "Overcoming All Obstacles: The Women of the Académie Julian, An Exhibition Organized by the Dahesh Museum." *The California Art Club Newsletter,* April/May 2000. http://www.californiaartclub.org/newsletter/articles/article_julian1.shtml.

Foresta, Merry A. "Photos for All Time." *Smithsonian.com,* April 2004. http://www.smithsonianmag.com/arts-culture/photos-for-all-time.html.

Foucault, Michel. *Discipline and Punish: The Birth of the Prison.* Translated by Alan Sheridan. New York: Vintage Books, 1977.

———. *The Order of Things.* Edited and translated by R. D. Laing. Rev. ed. New York: Vintage Books, 1973.

Fowler, Orson S. *The Practical Phrenologist.* Boston: O. S. Fowler, 1869.

Fox Talbot, William Henry. "Some Account of the Art of Photogenic Drawing, or, The Process by Which Natural Objects May Be Made to Delineate Themselves without the Aid of the Artist's Pencil." In Harrison, Wood, and Gaiger, *Art in Theory,* 249–55.

Fusco, Coco. "Racial Signs, Racial Marks, Racial Metaphors." In Fusco and Wallace, *Only Skin Deep*, 12–49.

Fusco, Coco and Brian Wallis. *Only Skin Deep: Changing Visions of the American Self.* New York: Harry N. Abrams, 2003. An exhibition catalog.

Gall, Franz Joseph and Johann Gaspar Spurzheim. *Recherches sur le Système Nerveux en Général, en sur celui du Cerveau en Particulier.* Paris: F. Schoell and H. Nicole, 1809.

Galton, Francis. *Inquiries Into Human Faculty and Its Development.* London: Macmillan, 1883.

Goffman, Erving. *The Goffman Reader.* Edited by Charles Lemert and Ann Branaman. Oxford: Blackwell Publishers, 1997.

Gramsci, Antonio. *Selections from the Prison Notebooks.* Translated by Quintin Hoare and Geoffrey Nowell Smith. New York: International Publishers, 1971.

Griffin, Randall C. "Thomas Anshutz's *The Ironworker's Noontime:* Remythologizing the Industrial Worker." *Smithsonian Studies in American Art* 4, nos. 3–4 (1990): 129–43.

Haas, Robert. *Muybridge: Man in Motion.* Berkeley: University of California Press, 1976.

Hall, Loretta. "Navajo." In Malinowski and Sheets, *The Gale Encyclopedia*, 217–26.

Hardorff, Richard G., ed. *Cheyenne Memories of the Custer Fight: A Sourcebook.* Spokane, Wash.: Arthur H. Clark, 1995.

Harrison, Charles, Paul Wood, and Jason Gaiger, eds. *Art in Theory, 1815–1900: An Anthology of Changing Ideas.* Oxford: Blackwell Publishers, 1998.

Heck, J. G. *Iconographic Encyclopedia of Science, Literature, and Art.* Edited and translated by Spencer F. Baird. Vols. 2–3. New York: Rudolph Garrigue, 1851.

Hegel, G. W. F. "Lectures on Aesthetics." In *Introductory Lectures on Aesthetics.* Edited and translated by Bernard Bosenquet. London: Kegan Paul, 1886. Quoted in Harrison, Wood, and Gaiger, *Art in Theory*, 58–69.

Henson, Pamela M. "Spencer F. Baird's Vision for a National Museum." Smithsonian Institution Archives, Institutional History Division, http://siarchives.si.edu/history/exhibits/baird/bairdhm.htm.

Holmes, Oliver Wendell. *Pages from an Old Volume of Life.* Cambridge, Mass.: H. O. Houghton, 1883.

———. "The Stereoscope and the Stereograph." In Harrison, Wood, and Gaiger, *Art in Theory*, 668–72.

Honour, Hugh. *The Image of the Black in Western Art*. 4 vols. New York: Morrow, 1976.

Hutchinson, Elizabeth. "Progressive Primitivism: Race, Gender, and Turn-of-the-Century American Concerns." PhD diss., Stanford University, 1999.

———. "When the 'Sioux Chief's Party Calls': Käsebier's Indian Portraits and the Gendering of the Studio." *American Art* 16, no. 2 (2002): 40–65.

Hutton, Paul A. *The Custer Reader*. Lincoln: University of Nebraska Press, 1992.

The Inauguration of Mills's Equestrian Statue of Andrew Jackson, at Washington, January 8, 1853. Washington, D.C.: GPO, 1853.

Janson, H. W. and John McCoubrey, eds. *Sources and Documents in the History of Art Series: American Art, 1700–1960*. Englewood Cliffs, N.J.: Prentice Hall, 1965.

Jefferson, Thomas. *The Life and Selected Writings of Thomas Jefferson*. Edited by Adrienne Koch and William Peden. New York: The Modern Library, 1998.

Johnson, Tim. *Spirit Capture: Photographs from the National Museum of the American Indian*. Washington, D.C.: Smithsonian Institution Press, 1998.

Kant, Immanuel. *Critique of Pure Reason*. Edited and translated by J. M. D. Meiklejohn. London: G. Bell, 1887.

Latrobe, Benjamin Henry. *The Journals of Benjamin Henry Latrobe, 1799–1820: From Philadelphia to New Orleans*. Edited by Edward Carter III, John Van Horne, and Lee Formwalt. New Haven, Conn.: Yale University Press, 1980.

Lears, T. J. Jackson. *No Place of Grace*. New York: Pantheon, 1981.

Ledes, Allison Eckardt. "A Late Nineteenth Century Collaboration: Anthropologist Frank Cushing and Artist Thomas Eakins—Current and Coming." *The Magazine Antiques* 146, no. 1 (1995).

Leupp, Francis E. *Annual Report of the Commissioner of Indian Affairs*. Washington, D.C.: GPO, 1905. Quoted in Adams, *Education for Extinction*, 2.

Locke, John. *An Essay Concerning Human Understanding, in Four Books*. London: E. Holt and T. Basset, 1690.

Malinowski, Sharon and Anna Sheets, eds. *The Gale Encyclopedia of Native American Tribes*. Vol. 2. Detroit, Mich.: Gale, 1998.

Malmsheimer, Lonna. "'Imitation White men': Images of Transformation at the Carlisle Indian School." *Studies in Visual Communication* 11, no. 4 (1985): 54–75.

Marien, Mary Warner. *Photography: A Cultural History.* New York: Harry N. Abrams, 2002.

Mauro, Hayes P. "Johann Caspar Lavater." In Murray, *Encyclopedia of the Romantic Era 1*: 657–59.

McClintock, Anne. *Imperial Leather: Race, Gender, and Sexuality in the Colonial Conquest.* New York: Routledge, 1995.

McLuhan, Marshall. *Understanding Media: The Extensions of Man.* New York: Signet Books, 1964.

Meijer, Miriam Claude. *Race and Aesthetics in the Anthropology of Petrus Camper (1722–1789).* Amsterdam: Rodopi, 1999.

Mooney, James. *The Ghost-Dance Religion and the Sioux Outbreak of 1890.* Washington, D.C.: GPO, 1896.

Morgan, Lewis Henry. *Ancient Society, Or, Researches in the Lines of Human Progress from Savagery through Barbarism to Civilization.* London: Macmillan, 1877; Marxist Internet Archive Reference Archive, 2004. http://www.marxists.org/reference/archive/morgan=lewis/ancient=society/index.htm.

Morton, Samuel G. *Crania Americana, or a Comparative View of the Skulls of Various Aboriginal Nations of North and South America.* Philadelphia: J. Dobson, 1839.

Moses, L. G. *Wild West Shows and the Images of Native Americans, 1883–1933.* Albuquerque: University of New Mexico Press, 1996.

Murray, Christopher John, ed. *The Encyclopedia of the Romantic Era, 1760–1850.* New York: Fitzroy Dearborn, 2004.

National Museum of Natural History. *Proceedings of the National Museum.* Vol. 1. Washington, D.C.: GPO, 1878.

National Portrait Gallery. "One Life: The Mask of Lincoln." Smithsonian National Portrait Gallery, http://www.npg.si.edu/exhibit/lincoln/pop-ups/02-14.html.

"None Can Compare with It." *New York Times*, 19 June 1893.

Ordover, Nancy. *American Eugenics: Race, Queer Anatomy, and the Science of Nationalism.* Minneapolis: University of Minnesota Press, 2003.

Perkins, George and Barbara Perkins. *The American Tradition in Literature.* 8th ed. New York: McGraw Hill, 1994.

Pfister, Joel. *Individuality Incorporated: Indians and the Multicultural Modern.* Durham, N.C.: Duke University Press, 2004.

Phillips, Ruth, and Christopher Steiner, eds. *Unpacking Culture: Art and Commodity in Colonial and Postcolonial Worlds.* Berkeley: University of California Press, 1999.

Phillips, Sandra. "Identifying the Criminal." In Phillips, Haworth-Booth, and Squires, *Police Pictures*, 11–31.

Phillips, Sandra, Mark Haworth-Booth, and Carol Squires, eds. *Police Pictures: The Photograph as Evidence.* San Francisco: Chronicle Books, 1997.

Pohl, Frances K. *Framing America: A Social History of American Art.* New York: Thames and Hudson, 2002.

Poolaw, Linda. "Spirit Capture: Observations of an Encounter." In Johnson, *Spirit Capture,* 166–88.

Pratt, Richard Henry. "The Advantages of Mingling Indians with Whites." *Proceedings and Addresses of the National Education Association, 1895.* Washington, D.C.: National Education Association, 1895.

———. *Battlefield and Classroom: Four Decades with the American Indian, 1867–1904.* New Haven, Conn.: Yale University Press, 1964.

———. "The Carlisle Idea." Excerpt from illustrated catalog. Carlisle, Pa.: Carlisle Indian Industrial School, 1902.

———. "Physical Culture." Excerpt from illustrated catalog. Carlisle, Pa.: Carlisle Indian Industrial School, 1902.

———. "Twenty-Fourth Annual Report." *Red Man and Helper* 19, no. 3 (1903): 1.

———. *United States Industrial School, Carlisle, Pennsylvania.* Carlisle, PA: Carlisle Indian Industrial School, 1895.

Przyblyski, Jeannene. "American Visions at the Paris Exposition, 1900: Another Look at Frances Benjamin Johnston's Hampton Photographs." *Art Journal* 57, no. 3 (1998): 60–68.

Pyne, Kathleen. *Art and the Higher Life: Painting and Evolutionary Thought in Late Nineteenth-Century America.* Austin: University of Texas Press, 1996.

Rennie, Ysabel. *The Search for Criminal Man: A Conceptual History of the Dangerous Offender.* Lexington, Mass.: Lexington Books, 1978.

Riis, Jacob. *How the Other Half Lives.* New York: Dover Publications, 1971.

Ringlero, Aleta. "Prairie Pinups: Reconsidering Historic Portraits of American Indian Women." In Fusco and Wallis, *Only Skin Deep,* 183–91.

Roessel, Robert A. *Dinétak.* Rough Rock, Ariz.: Navajo Curriculum Center, 1982.

Roosevelt, Theodore. *The Strenuous Life.* New York: Review of Reviews, 1910.

Rosenblum, Naomi. *A World History of Photography.* New York: Abbeville Press, 1997.

Rydell, Robert. *All the World's a Fair.* Chicago: University of Chicago Press, 1984.

Said, Edward. *Orientalism*. New York: Vintage Books, 1978.

Scherer, Joanna Cohen. "You Can't Believe Your Eyes: Inaccuracies in Photographs of North American Indians." *Exposure* 16, no. 4 (1978): 6–19.

Shohat, Ella. *Unthinking Eurocentrism: Multiculturalism and the Media*. New York: Routledge, 1994.

Smith, Shawn Michelle. *American Archives: Gender, Race, and Class in Visual Culture*. Princeton, N.J.: Princeton University Press, 1999.

Solomon-Godeau, Abigail. *Photography at the Dock: Essays on Photographic History, Institutions, and Practices*. Minneapolis: University of Minnesota Press, 1991.

Spurzheim, Johann Gaspar. *Outlines of Phrenology*. London: Treuttel, Wurtz, and Richter, 1829.

Standing Bear, Luther. *My People, The Sioux*. Edited by E. A. Brininstool. Boston: Houghton Mifflin, 1928.

Steichen, Edward. "Ye Fakers." *Camera Work* 1 (1903): 107.

Stoksad, Marilyn, and Michael Cothren. *Art: A Brief History*. 4th ed. New York: Prentice Hall, 2009.

Stowe, Harriet Beecher. "The Indians at S. Augustine." *The Christian Union* (April 1877).

Szarkowski, John. *The Hampton Album*. New York: Doubleday Books, 1966.

Tagg, John. *The Burden of Representation*. Minneapolis: University of Minnesota Press, 1993.

Taylor, Frederick W. *The Principles of Scientific Management*. New York: Harper and Brothers, 1911.

Tomlinson, Stephen. *Head Masters*. Tuscaloosa: University of Alabama Press, 2005.

Trachtenberg, Alan. *The Incorporation of America*. New York: Hill and Wang, 1990.

———. *Shades of Hiawatha: Staging Indians, Making Americans, 1880–1930*. New York: Hill and Wang, 2004.

Tritt, Richard. "John Nicholas Choate: A Cumberland County Photographer." *Cumberland County History* 13, no. 2 (1996): 77–90.

———. "Notes on the Indian School Photographs and Photographers." In Witmer, *Indian Industrial School*, 116–17.

Truettner, William. "Vanishing With a Trace: Art and Indian Life in the Gilcrease Souvenir Album." In Catlin, *Souvenir*, ix–xxvii.

Truettner, William, ed. *The West as America: Reinterpreting Images of the Frontier, 1820–1920*. Washington, D.C.: National Museum of American Art and Smithsonian Institution Press, 1991.

Tuckerman, Henry T. *Book of the Artists*. New York: G. P. Putnam and Sons, 1867.

Turner, Frederick Jackson. "The Significance of the Frontier in American History." In Faragher, *Rereading Frederick Jackson Turner*, 31–60.

Turner, Laura. "John Nicholas Choate and the Production of Photography at the Carlisle Indian School." In Earenfight, *Visualizing a Mission*, 14–19.

Untitled obituary. *The Art Amateur* 8, no. 3 (1883): 56–57.

Valdes-Depena, Antonia. "Marketing the Exotic: Creating the Image of the 'Real' Indian." In Earenfight, *Visualizing a Mission*, 35–41.

Wallis, Brian. "Black Bodies, White Science: Louis Agassiz's Slave Daguerreotypes." *American Art* 9 (1995): 38–61.

Weber, Max. *The Protestant Ethic and the Spirit of Capitalism*. Translated by Talcott Parsons. New York: Scribner and Sons, 1958.

Wheeler, Robert W. *Jim Thorpe: World's Greatest Athlete*. Norman: University of Oklahoma Press, 1981.

Witmer, Linda, ed. *The Indian Industrial School, Carlisle, Pennsylvania, 1879–1918*. Carlisle, Pa.: Cumberland County Historical Society, 2002.

Wölfflin, Heinrich. *Renaissance and Baroque*. Edited and translated by Kathrin Simon. London: Fontana, 1964.

Wood, Peter, and Karen Dalton. *Winslow Homer's Images of Blacks*. Austin: University of Texas Press, 1988.

Illustrations

Figure I.1. John N. Choate, "Wounded Yellow Robe, Henry Standing Bear, Timber Yellow Robe; Upon their Arrival in Carlisle," n.d. Albumen mounted on card. Courtesy of Archives and Special Collections, Dickinson College.

Figure I.2. John Choate, "Wounded Yellow Robe, Henry Standing Bear, Timber Yellow Robe; 6 months After Entrance to School," n.d. Albumen mounted on card. Courtesy of Archives and Special Collections, Dickinson College.

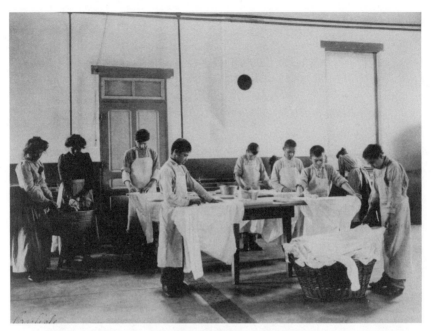

Figure I.3. Frances Benjamin Johnston, "Laundry Class," 1901. Albumen. Library of Congress, Prints and Photographs Division, LC-USZ62-26788.

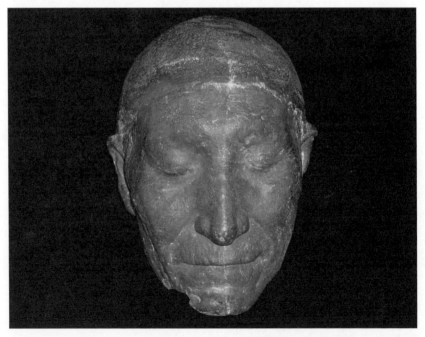

Figure I.4. Joseph Palmer, modeler, from life mask by Clark Mills, *Lone Wolf (Kiowa)*, circa 1877. Plaster, lifesize. National Museum of Natural History, Smithsonian Institution.

Figure I.5. Frances Benjamin Johnston, "Art Class, Carlisle," 1901. Gelatin silver print. Library of Congress, Prints and Photographs Division, LC-USZ62-115831.

Figure I.6. John Leslie, "The School Kitchen," 1895. Gelatin silver print. Photo courtesy of the Cumberland County Historical Society.

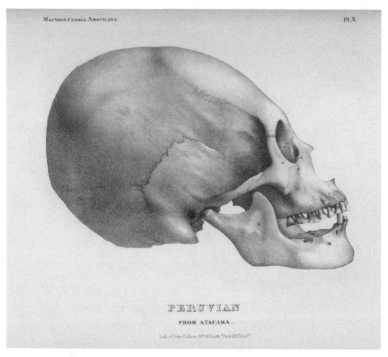

PERUVIAN

FROM ATACAMA.

Lith. of John Collins, No 1 S. side Third St Phila.

Figure 1.1. John Collins, untitled (Peruvian skull), 1839. Lithographic illustration. From Samuel G. Morton, *Crania Americana*. Courtesy of New York Public Library.

Figure 1.2. Benjamin Latrobe, *Market Folks*, 1819. Pencil and watercolor. Courtesy of Maryland Historical Society.

Figure 1.3. George
Catlin, *See-non-ty-a,
an Iowa Medicine
Man*, 1844–1845.
Oil on canvas. Paul
Mellon Collection.
Image courtesy of
Board of Trustees,
National Gallery of
Art, Washington,
D.C.

below:
Figure 1.4. George
Catlin, *Comanche
Indians Chasing
Buffalo*, 1846/8. Oil
on canvas. Paul
Mellon Collection.
Image courtesy of
the National Gallery
of Art, Washington,
D.C.

Figure 1.5. Johann Caspar Lavater, *Silhouettes*, 1790. Ink on paper. From
Plate XXVIII, Johann Caspar Lavater, *Essays on Physiognomy*, trans. Thomas
Holcroft, 4th ed. (London: Tegg, 1844). Collection of New-York Historical
Society.

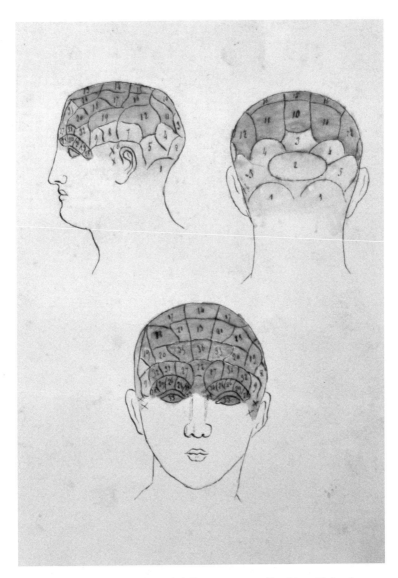

Figure 1.6. Franz Joseph Gall, untitled illustration, 1809. Graphite with hand coloring. Frontispiece of Gall and Spurzheim, *Recherches sur le Système Nerveux en Général*. Courtesy of New York Public Library.

Figure 1.7. John Wesley Jarvis, *Portrait of Capt. Samuel C. Reid*, 1815. Oil on canvas. The William Hood Dunwoody Fund, Minneapolis Institute of Arts.

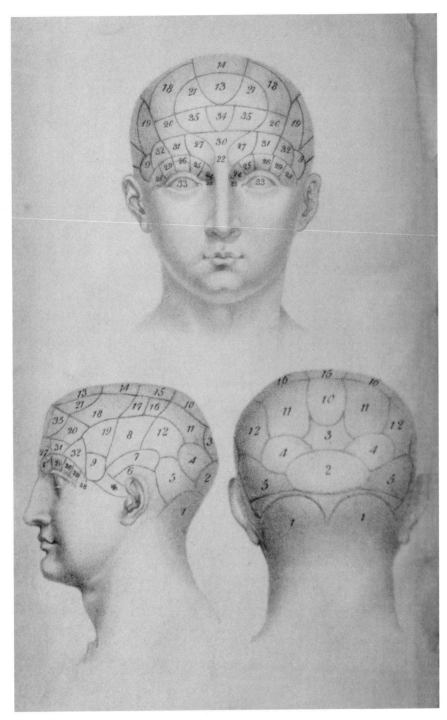

Figure 1.8. Johann Gaspar Spurzheim, untitled illustration, 1829. Lithographic print. Frontispiece from Spurzheim, *Outlines of Phrenology*. Courtesy New York Public Library.

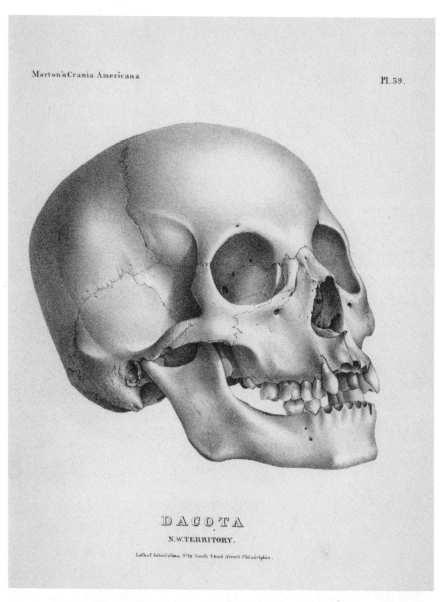

DACOTA

N.W.TERRITORY.

Lith.of John Collins, N°19 South Third Street Philadelphia.

Figure 1.9. John Collins, untitled illustration (Dacota [*sic*] skull), 1839. Lithographic reproduction. Illustration from Samuel G. Morton, *Crania Americana*. Courtesy of New York Public Library.

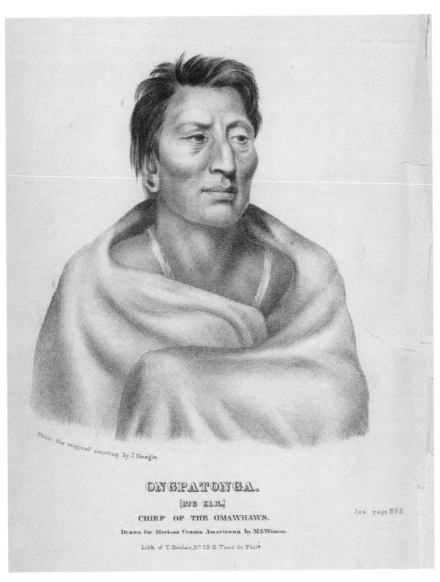

From the original painting by J. Neagle.

ONGPATONGA.

[BIG ELK.]

CHIEF OF THE OMAWHAWS.

See page 292

Drawn for Mortons Crania Americana by M.S.Weaver.

Lith. of T. Sinclair, Nº 79 S. Third St. Phila

Figure 1.10. T. Sinclair, from drawing by M. S. Weaver, from painting by John Neagle, *Ongpatonga (Chief Big Elk)*, 1839. Lithographic reproduction. Illustration from Samuel G. Morton, *Crania Americana*. Courtesy of New York Public Library.

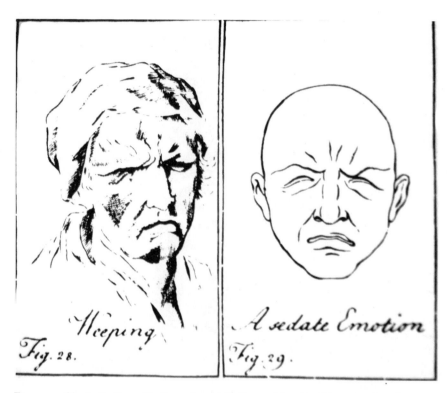

Figure 1.11. Charles Le Brun, *The Expressions,* 1698. Charcoal drawing. Illustration from Le Brun, *Méthode pour apprendre à dessiner les passions* (Paris, 1698). Courtesy of New York Public Library.

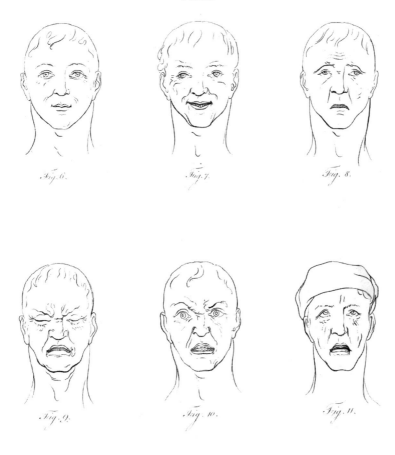

Figure 1.12. Petrus Camper, untitled illustration, n.d. Graphite drawing. Illustration from Camper, *The Works of the Late Professor Camper* (London: J. Hearne, 1821). Courtesy of New York Public Library.

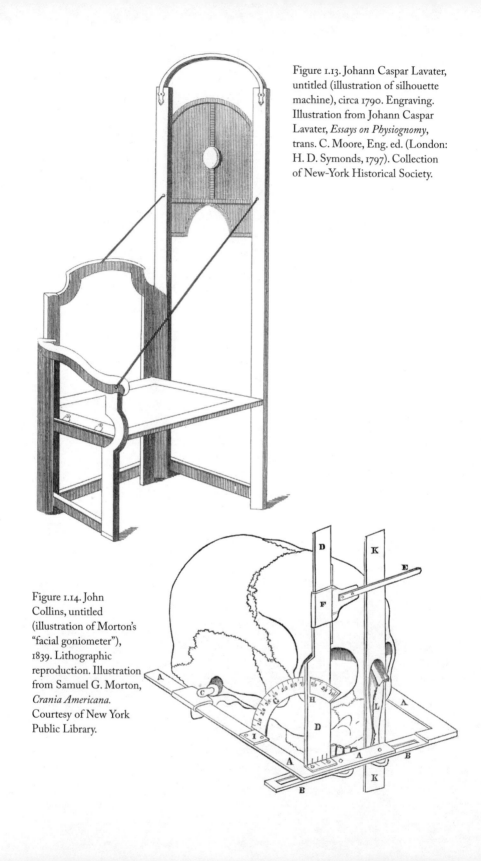

Figure 1.13. Johann Caspar Lavater, untitled (illustration of silhouette machine), circa 1790. Engraving. Illustration from Johann Caspar Lavater, *Essays on Physiognomy*, trans. C. Moore, Eng. ed. (London: H. D. Symonds, 1797). Collection of New-York Historical Society.

Figure 1.14. John Collins, untitled (illustration of Morton's "facial goniometer"), 1839. Lithographic reproduction. Illustration from Samuel G. Morton, *Crania Americana*. Courtesy of New York Public Library.

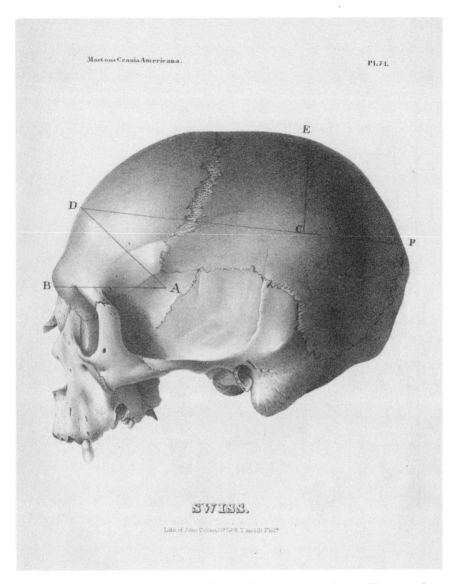

E

D

C

B

A

F

SWISS.

Lith. of John Collins, No 70 S. T. and St. Phil.

Figure 1.15. John Collins, untitled (Swiss skull), 1839. Lithographic reproduction. Illustration from Samuel G. Morton, *Crania Americana*. Courtesy of New York Public Library.

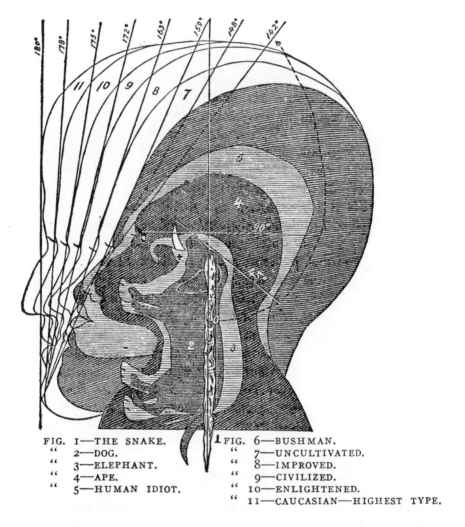

FIG. 1—THE SNAKE.   FIG. 6—BUSHMAN.
" 2—DOG.   " 7—UNCULTIVATED.
" 3—ELEPHANT.   " 8—IMPROVED.
" 4—APE.   " 9—CIVILIZED.
" 5—HUMAN IDIOT.   " 10—ENLIGHTENED.
    " 11—CAUCASIAN—HIGHEST TYPE.

Figure 2.1. Anonymous, untitled (illustration of phrenological facial angle), n.d. Frontispiece from John Davies, *Phrenology*. Collection of the New-York Historical Society.

Figure 2.2. Clark Mills, *Andrew Jackson*, 1853. Bronze. Lafayette Square, Washington, D.C. Photograph by author.

Figure 2.3. Anonymous, "Indian Prisoners at Ft. Marion, St. Augustine, Florida, shortly after their arrival in 1875," 1875. Albumen. Courtesy of Cumberland County Historical Society.

Figure 2.4. Anonymous, "Captain Pratt and Indian Prisoners In the Courtyard at Ft. Marion," circa 1875. Albumen. Courtesy National Park Service, Castillo de San Marcos National Monument, St. Augustine, Florida, and New York Public Library.

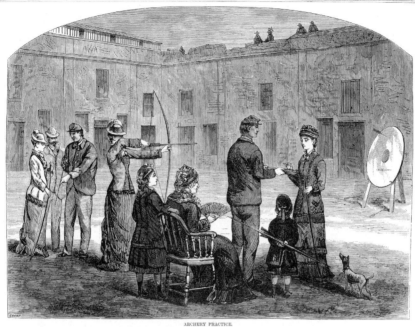

ARCHERY PRACTICE.

Figure 2.5. Anonymous, "Indian Prisoners Teaching Archery Lessons," 1878. Etching. Illustration in *Harper's Weekly*, 11 May 1878. Collection of New-York Historical Society.

Figure 2.6. Anonymous, "Indian Prisoners Formed into a Military Company at Ft. Marion," circa 1875. Albumen. Richard Henry Pratt Papers, Yale University.

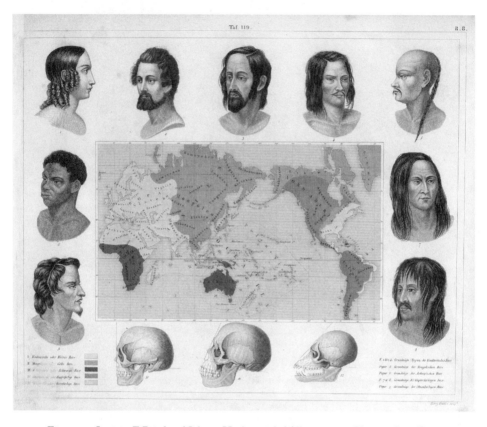

Figure 2.7. Spencer F. Baird and Johann Heck, untitled (illustrations of "races of man"), 1851. Engraving. Illustration from Heck, *Iconographic Encyclopedia of Science.* Collection of New-York Historical Society.

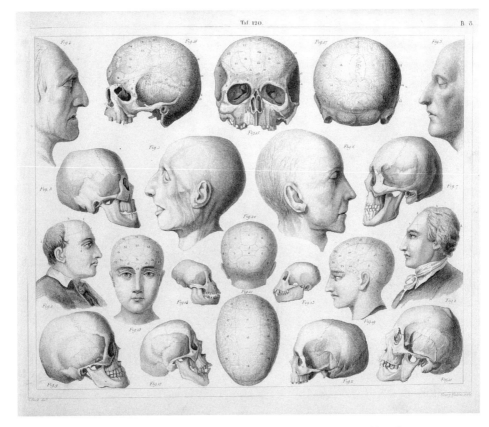

Figure 2.8. Spencer F. Baird and Johann Heck, untitled (illustration of sections of brain), 1851. Engraving. Illustration from Heck, *Iconographic Encyclopedia of Science*. Collection of New-York Historical Society.

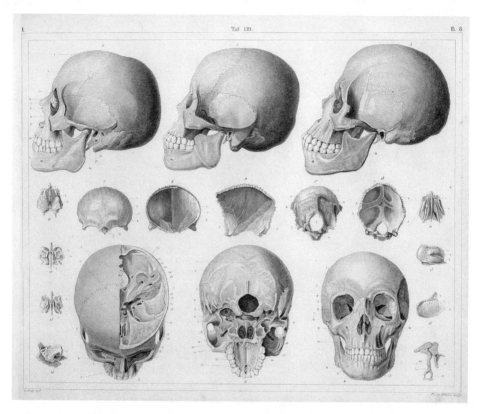

Figure 2.9. Spencer F. Baird and Johann Heck, untitled (illustration of sections of skull), 1851. Engraving. Illustration from Heck, *Iconographic Encyclopedia of Science*. Collection of New-York Historical Society.

Figure 2.10. Jean-Antoine Houdon, *Portrait of George Washington*, 1788. Marble. State House, Richmond, Virginia. Courtesy Library of Virginia.

Figure 2.11. Hiram Powers, *Portrait Bust of George Washington*, 1853. Marble. Minneapolis Institute of Art. Gift of the Minneapolis Tower Company.

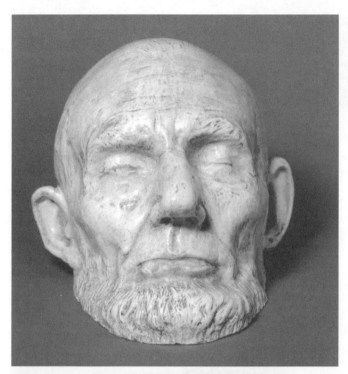

Figure 2.12.
Clark Mills, *Life
Mask of Abraham
Lincoln*, 1865.
Plaster. National
Portrait Gallery,
Smithsonian
Institution.

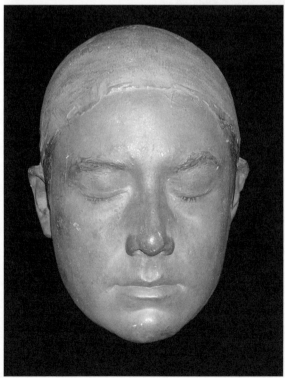

Figure 2.13. Joseph Palmer,
modeler, from life mask by
Clark Mills, *Lezedo Rencountre
(Brulé Sioux)*, circa 1877.
Plaster. National Museum of
Natural History, Smithsonian
Institution.

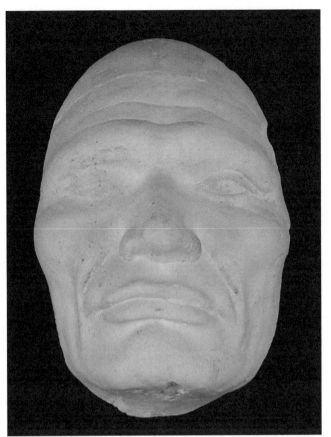

Figure 2.14. Unknown modeler, from life mask by Clark Mills, *Bad Boy (Red Lake Chippewa)*, circa 1877. Plaster. National Museum of Natural History, Smithsonian Institution.

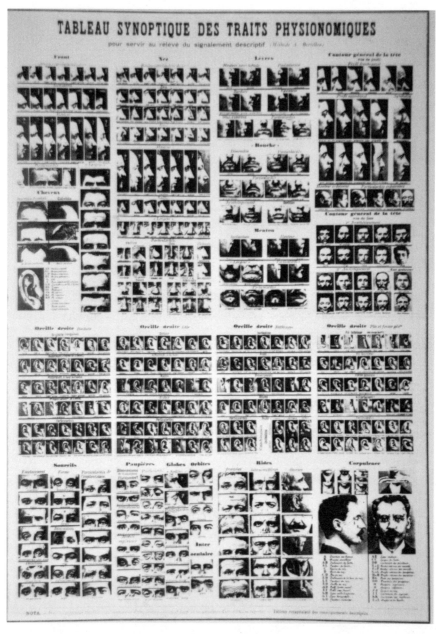

Figure 2.15. Alphonse Bertillon, "Synoptic Table," circa 1893. Photomontage. Historical Archives and Museum of the Prefecture of Police, Paris. All rights reserved.

Figure 2.16. Edward S. Curtis, "The Vanishing Race," circa 1904. Platinum print. Library of Congress, Prints and Photographs Division, LC-USZ62-37340.

Figure 3.1. John Choate, "First students at Carlisle, Dakota Indian boys from Rosebud and Pine Ridge Agencies, the first party to arrive at the Indian Industrial School, Carlisle, Pa., Oct. 5, 1879," 1879. Albumen. Photo courtesy of Cumberland County Historical Society.

Figure 3.2. John Choate, "First students, Sioux Indian boys on arrival at Carlisle Indian School October 5, 1879," 1879. Albumen. Photo courtesy of Cumberland County Historical Society.

Figure 3.3. John Choate, "Group of Dakota Sioux girls from the Rosebud and Pine Ridge Sioux Agencies as they arrived in native dress at the Carlisle Indian School, October 5, 1879," 1879. Albumen. Photo courtesy of Cumberland County Historical Society.

Figure 3.4a. John Choate, "Tom Torlino, A Navajo, as he arrived and three years after," 1882–1885. Albumen. Photo courtesy of Cumberland County Historical Society.

Figure 3.4b. John Choate, "Tom Torlino, A Navajo, as he arrived and three years after," 1882–1885. Albumen. Photo courtesy of Cumberland County Historical Society.

Fig. 3.5. John Choate, untitled (traveling studio), circa 1880. Albumen. Photo courtesy of Cumberland County Historical Society.

Figure 3.6. John Choate, verso of personalized stereo card, circa 1898–1902. Courtesy of Cumberland County Historical Society.

Figure 3.7. Will Soule, "Portrait of a Young Wichita Woman," circa 1867. National Anthropological Archives, Smithsonian Institution, inventory number 01162402.

below:
Figure 3.8. Andrew A. Line, "Carlisle Indian Girls under the Outing System in Pennsylvania Homes," circa 1910. Albumen prints on postcard. Courtesy of Cumberland County Historical Society.

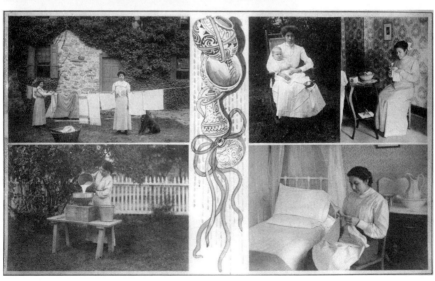

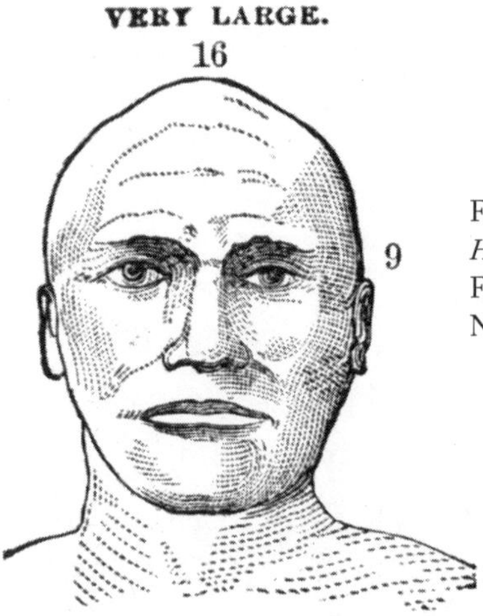

VERY LARGE.
16

9

Figure 3.9. Orson S. Fowler, *Indian Chief/Black Hawk*, 1869. Engraving. Illustration from Orson S. Fowler, *The Practical Phrenologist*. Courtesy of New York Public Library.

Figure 3.10. Jacob Riis, "Bandit's Roost 59 ½ Mulberry Street," circa 1890. Gelatin silver print. Museum of the City of New York, Jacob A. Riis Collection.

116

MARY HOEY,
ALIAS MOLLY HOLLBROOK,
PICKPOCKET.   P

Figure 3.11. Thomas Byrnes, 1886. Albumen. From Thomas Byrnes, *Professional Criminals of America* (New York: Cassell, 1886). Collection of New-York Historical Society.

below:
Figure 3.12. A. J. McDonald, "Geronimo, Chiricahua Apache in front of train taking Chiricahua Apache group from Fort Sam Houston, Texas to Fort Marion, Florida," 1886. Albumen. Courtesy of National Museum of the American Indian, Washington, D.C., NMAI photo number P07009.

Figure 4.1. Raja Lal Deen Dayal, "Before and After," 1899–1900. Gelatin silver prints. Private collection, England. Courtesy of New York Public Library.

Figure 4.2. George Catlin, *Pigeon's Egg Head Going to and Returning from Washington*, 1837–1839. Oil on canvas. Smithsonian American Art Museum, Smithsonian Institution, accession number 1985.66.474.

Figure 4.3. John Choate, "Group of Visiting Chiefs," n.d. Albumen. Archives and Special Collections, Dickinson College.

Figure 4.4. Nicholas Brown, "Two Young Navajo with Bow & Arrow," 1868. Albumen. National Anthropological Archives, Smithsonian Institution, inventory number GN 02442.

Figure 4.5. Anonymous. "Navajo Hogan," circa 1926. Gelatin silver print. Courtesy of the Palace of the Governors Photo Archives (NMHM/DCA), negative number 104650.

Figure 4.6. John Choate, "White Buffalo, Cheyenne, Nature Dress," 1881. Albumen. Photo courtesy of Cumberland County Historical Society.

Figure 4.7. John Choate, "White Buffalo, Cheyenne," 1884. Albumen. Photo courtesy of Cumberland County Historical Society.

Figure 4.8. John Choate, "Our Boys and Girls at the Indian Training School," 1881. Albumen/montage. Photo courtesy of Cumberland County Historical Society.

Figure 5.1. Frances Benjamin Johnston, "Boys Picking Potatoes in Field," 1901. Gelatin silver print. Library of Congress, Prints and Photographs Division, LC-USZ62-55420.

Figure 5.2. Probably Frances Benjamin Johnston, untitled (Carlisle pavilion at 1893 World's Fair), 1893. Albumen. Photo courtesy of Cumberland County Historical Society.

Figure 5.3. Anonymous, "Court of Honor and Grand Basin," 1893. Albumen. Library of Congress, Prints and Photographs Division, LC-USZ62-102149.

Figure 5.4. Anonymous, "Wild West Show's Residential Encampment at 1893 World's Fair," 1893. Albumen. Vincent Mercaldo Collection, Buffalo Bill Historical Center, Cody, Wyoming, P.71.1368.

Sioux Warriors taken prisoners at Pine Ridge and brought to Fort Sheridan, Illinois, in charge of Captain John B. Kerr, 6th Cavalry, U. S. A.

1. Crow Kane, 2. Medicine Horse, 3. Call Her Name, 4. Kicking Bear—Chief, 5. Short Bull, 6. Come and Grunt, 7. High Eagle, 8. Horn Eagle, 9. Sorrell Horse, 10. Scatter, 11. Standing Bear, 12. Lone Bull, 13. Standing Bear, 14. Close to House, 15. One Star, 16. Know His Voice, 17. Own The White Horse, 18. Take the Shield Away, 19. Brave.

115

ELLEN CLEGG,

ALIAS ELLEN LEE,

SHOP LIFTER AND PICKPOCKET.

above:

Figure 5.5. Anonymous, "19 Fort Sheridan Sioux Prisoners," 1890. Albumen. Copyright, Colorado Historical Society, scan # 10028432.

Figure. 5.6. Thomas Byrnes, from *Professional Criminals of America*, 1886. Albumen. Collection of the New-York Historical Society.

Figure 5.7. Frances Benjamin Johnston, "A Class in American History," 1899. Platinum. Library of Congress, Prints and Photographs Division, LC-USZ62-38149.

Figure. 5.8. Thomas William Smillie, "Cheyenne River Delegation," 1888. Albumen. National Anthropological Archives, Smithsonian Institution, inventory number GN si 5737.

Figure 5.9. Frances Benjamin Johnston, "Women operating machinery at the Bureau of Printing and Engraving, Washington, D.C.," 1889. Albumen. Library of Congress, Prints and Photographs Division, LC-USZ62-115743.

Figure. 5.10. Frances Benjamin Johnston, "Students at work on a house built largely by them," from the Hampton series, 1899. Platinum. Library of Congress, Prints and Photographs Division, LC-USZ62-66946.

Figure 5.11. Frances Benjamin Johnston, "Old Time Cabin," from the Hampton series, 1899. Platinum. Library of Congress, Prints and Photographs Division, LC-USZ62-68312.

Figure 5.12. Frances Benjamin Johnston, "A Graduate's Home," from the Hampton series, 1899. Platinum. Library of Congress, Prints and Photographs Division, LC-USZ62-62378.

Figure 5.13. Frances Benjamin Johnston, "Old Folks at Home," from the Hampton series, 1899. Platinum. Prints and Photographs Division, Library of Congress, LC-USZ62-61017.

Figure 5.14. Frances Benjamin Johnston, "A Hampton Graduate at Home," from the Hampton series, 1899. Platinum. Library of Congress, Prints and Photographs Division, LC-USZ62-38150.

Figure 5.15. Frances Benjamin Johnston, "Girls on Climbing Apparatus, Western H.S., Washington D.C.," 1899. Cyanotype. Library of Congress, Prints and Photographs Division, LC-USZ62-2047.

Figure 5.16. Frances Benjamin Johnston, "Croquet," 1901. Albumen. Photo courtesy of Cumberland County Historical Society.

Figure 5.17. Recent view of former Carlisle Indian School quadrangle (today U.S. Army War College). Photograph by author.

Figure 5.18. Frances Benjamin Johnston, "Band," 1901. Albumen. Photo courtesy of Cumberland County Historical Society.

Figure 5.19. Frances Benjamin Johnston, "Boy's Wand Drill," 1901. Albumen. Photo courtesy of Cumberland County Historical Society.

Figure 5.20. Frances Benjamin Johnston, "Boiler House," 1901. Albumen. Photo courtesy of Cumberland County Historical Society.

Figure 5.21. Frances Benjamin Johnston, "Coping Stone Fences," 1901. Albumen. Photo courtesy of Cumberland County Historical Society.

Figure 5.22. Frances Benjamin Johnston, "Farm Scene," 1901. Albumen. Photo courtesy of Cumberland County Historical Society.

HAYING-TIME.   THE FIRST LOAD.

Figure 5.23. Frances Palmer, *American Farm Scene: Spring*, 1853. Lithograph. Published by Currier & Ives, New York. Library of Congress, Prints and Photographs Division, LC-DIG-pga-00771.

Figure 5.24. Frances Benjamin Johnston, "Nature Lesson," 1901. Albumen. Photo courtesy of Cumberland County Historical Society.

Figure 5.25. George Inness, *Morning, Catskill Valley*, 1894. Oil on canvas. Santa Barbara Museum of Art.

Figure 5.26. Frances Benjamin Johnston, "Reading class," 1901. Albumen. Library of Congress, Prints and Photographs Division, LC-USZ62-26797.

Figure 5.27. F. Holland Day, "Crucifixion," 1898. Platinum. Library of Congress, Prints and Photographs Division, LC-USZ62-52924.

Figure 5.28. W. Mills Thompson, untitled, 1895. Ink illustration. Library of Congress, Prints and Photographs Division, LC-USZ6-1450.

Figure 5.29. Frances Benjamin Johnston, untitled (photograph of W. Mills Thompson illustration), 1896. Cyanotype. Library of Congress, Prints and Photographs Division, LC-DIG-ppmsc-04898.

Figure 5.30. Frances Benjamin Johnston, untitled, 1901. Albumen. Library of Congress, Prints and Photographs Division, LC-DIG-ppmsca-18641.

Figure 5.31. Frances Benjamin Johnston, "Self Portrait," circa 1896. Albumen. Library of Congress, Prints and Photographs Division, LC-USZ62-64301.

Figure 5.32. Frances Benjamin Johnston, "Individual Lesson in Instrumental Music," 1901. Albumen. Photo courtesy of the Cumberland County Historical Society.

Figure 5.33. John Leslie, "View of the Campus," 1895. Albumen. Photo courtesy of Cumberland County Historical Society.

Figure 5.34. John Choate, "Dress Parade," circa 1890. Albumen. Photo courtesy of the Cumberland County Historical Society.

Figure 5.35. Anonymous, untitled, circa 1908. Gelatin silver print. Photo courtesy of Cumberland County Historical Society.

Figure 5.36 a and b. Anonymous, untitled,
1896. Printed drawings after photographs.
Courtesy of Cumberland County Historical
Society.

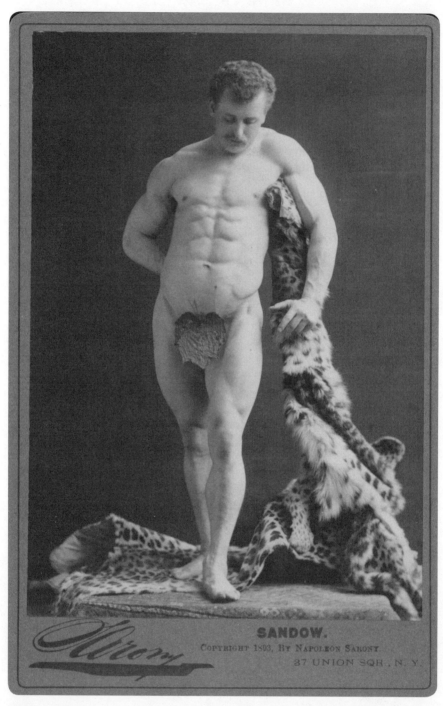

SANDOW.
COPYRIGHT 1893, BY NAPOLEON SARONY.
37 UNION SQR., N.Y.

Figure 5.37. Napoleon Sarony, "Eugene Sandow Posing as Farnese Hercules," 1893. Cabinet photograph. Harvard Theatre Collection, Houghton Library, Harvard University.

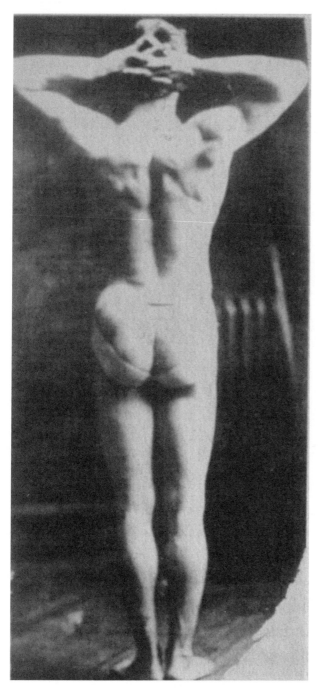

Figure 5.38. Anonymous, untitled (anthropometric photograph of Jim Thorpe), circa 1912. Gelatin silver print. Jim Thorpe House, Yale, Oklahoma.

Figure C.1. Thomas Eakins, *Frank Hamilton Cushing*, 1895. Oil on canvas. Gilcrease Museum, Tulsa, Oklahoma.

Index